The Most Obscure Cult TV Shows Ever

The Most Obscure Cult TV Shows Ever: Profiles of Fifty Offbeat Comedies and Dramas, Unsold Pilots, and Unaired Series

Richard Irvin

Copyright 2021 by Richard Irvin
All Rights Reserved
Publicity photographs are from the author's collection.

Table of Contents

Acknowledgements 7
Introduction 9

Chapter 1 – Teen and Twentysomething Dramas 15
Wind on Water – Soapy Water 15
Skin – Romeo and Juliet, Politics and Porn 19
My Generation – The Class of 2000 Ten Years Later 25

Chapter 2 – Crime Fighter Dramas 33
Angel Street – Crime and Sexism in Chicago 33
South of Sunset – A Rocker and a Comic as PI's 36
Wicked City – Another Name for LA 42

Chapter 3: Medical Dramas 47
The Lazarus Syndrome: A Fallible Cardiologist 47
Wonderland – Altered States of Mind 50
Inconceivable – Missed Conceptions 54

Chapter 4: Anti-Hero Dramas 61
Profit – What Can Happen When One Watches Too Much TV 61
Viva Laughlin – Hugh Jackman's Musical Drama Project 68
Heist – Cops and Robbers 71
Smith – An Expert Thief and His Gang 74
Lone Star – The Lives of a Texas Con Man 78
The Playboy Club – Crime and Sex in the Sixties 81

Chapter 5: Science Fiction 87
Beyond Westworld – Robots vs Humans 87
Space Rangers – Peacekeepers in the Galaxy 91
Mercy Point – *ER* in Outer Space 95
Strange World – Fictional Science 101
Harsh Realm – It's Only a Computer Game 109
Century City – The Law in 2030 116

Chapter 6 - Fantasy and Supernatural Dramas 123
The Quest – To Be a Monarch 123

Once a Hero – The Comic Book World vs the Real World 129
That Was Then – It's about Time 134
Wonderfalls – Talking Animal Figurines 139

Chapter 7: Action-Adventure Dramas 145
E.A.R.T.H Force – An Environmentally-Friendly *A-Team* 145
The Fifth Corner – An Undercover Agent Thinking Outside the Box 149
Drive – A Fictional *Amazing Race* 155

Chapter 8: Sports and Entertainment Dramas 163
Bay City Blues – A MTM Baseball Drama 163
Push – *Melrose Place* in Spandex... 166
Love Monkey – Love and Music 171

Chapter 9 – Some Cult Comedies 175
Oboler Comedy Theatre – *The Twilight Zone* of Comedies 175
Ugliest Girl in Town – TV's First Cross-Dressing Sitcom.................... 176
Bob & Carol & Ted & Alice – Mild Sex 182
The Texas Wheelers – MTM Dramady Set in Texas 185

Chapter 10: – Some Cult Series that Might Have Been...................... 189
Little People – Big World 189
Sabu – Bad Things Can Happen in the Jungle..................................... 190
Ed Wood's Untitled Anthology – Overly-Dramatic Tear Jerkers 191
Portraits of Terror – Terribly Macabre 192
The Marshall's Daughter – A Cross-Dressing Western Heroine 193
Ham-Let – Not Shakespeare, Perhaps Bacon....................................... 194
McGurk: A Dog's Life – Actors in Dog Costumes 195
Pests – Lovable Roaches 195
Steel Justice – AKA *Nash's Vision* and *Robosauris* 197

Chapter 11: Unaired Cult Series 199
The Veil – The Veiled Revelations of Truths beyond Tangibility......... 199
Hollyweird – The Dark Side of Tinsel Town.. 203
Manchester Prep - Spoiled Rich Kids... 206
Fling – Investigating Marital Issues... 210
Still Life – A Death in the Family 211
12 Miles of Bad Road – Rich White Trash 214

Endnotes 217
Index 223

Acknowledgements

The author thanks the following for their contributions to this book: William Blinn, Peter Bonerz, John Byrum, Trey Callaway, Angel Dean-Lopez, John Herzfeld, Tracie Hotchner, Dusty Kay, Christopher Knopf, Jim Leonard, Jeffrey Lewis, Robert Lovenheim, Larry Mollin, Marco Pennette, Mark B. Perry, Ben Queen, Stan Rogow, Charles Rosin, Ken Sanzel, Garry Settimi, John Showalter, Bryce Zabel, and Harv Zimmel.

Also, the author would like to thank the following institutions for information from their archives: American Heritage Center, University of Wyoming for scans from the Harry Ackerman Collection and the Motion Picture and Television Reading Room staff at the Library of Congress for access to unaired episodes of short-lived television series.

Introduction

According to *The Cult TV Book*, the word "cult" applies to a television series that is ". . . considered offbeat or edgy, that draws a niche audience, that has a nostalgic appeal, that is considered emblematic of a particular subculture, or that is considered hip."[1]

Cult television is also defined by an audience of strong loyal viewers. Several cult TV shows ran for several seasons. While not achieving a blockbuster audience like the original *Star Trek*, such series did attract fiercely devoted viewers who would petition the network anytime there were rumors that a beloved show would be canceled. However, to define a cult series only in terms of having a loyal audience means that almost every hit television show that lasted for several seasons like *I Love Lucy* and *All in the Family* would be considered a cult show. Virtually all the television shows described in this work were canceled quickly because of low ratings not giving the series time to build strong loyalty among viewers.

This book prefers to define a cult series as one whose concept is edgy, hip, or emblematic of a particular subculture.

What's the Difference Between "Obscure" and "Cult?"

One could say that "obscure" and "cult" are the same when describing so-called "cult" television shows. However, while many cult TV shows are obscure, there are several obscure series that would be difficult to label as "cult." In particular, this applies to short-lived series whose original concept was offbeat or edgy but that evolved into more standard fare.

The CBS show, *Big Shamus, Little Shamus* starring Brian Dennehy as a private detective and Doug McKeon as his son that was canceled after only a few episodes in the 1970s is a good example of the development of a series that began as something offbeat but then changed before its premiere.

The daughter of author A.E. Hotchner and a scribe in her own right, Tracie Hotchner came up with the concept for *Big Shamus, Little Shamus* in the mid-1970s when she was a young writer living in Los Angeles. As she recalled,

> In trying to think of a clever TV series idea, I picked my own brain for shows I had really loved growing up, which had actually not involved much TV at all, and how I would rework them. "Eddie's Father" was an absolute fave – a fairly grown up relationship between a widower and his clever little boy- with an Asian housekeeper thrown in (as the feminizing influence in the household). I also thought "The Odd Couple" was a classic set up. So what if a young boy was brilliant, and totally organized and neat and his father was sort of a slob and a never do well – didn't have his act together personally or professionally, but his kid kind of covered for him. And what if the father was the house detective for an Atlantic City casino – supplying many possible plots. But the father was not the brightest bulb, so solving the crimes or mysteries fell to the kid, who was helping from the sidelines, covering up for his father's inadequacies. And what if they lived in a sort of seedy rooming house/apartment and the kid was a neatnik and his father was a slob who was always studying the betting sheet and playing the horses. And the kid put himself in charge of preparing meals and making credible excuses to school when he was working a case with/for his father. There was no feminizing influence in their "odd couple" set up - they were two guys, making a functional but peculiar life together.[2]

Hotchner went on to say:
I got it down in a few pages of the basic characters and setting and ten or fifteen ideas for episodes, registered it with the Writer's Guild as a series idea, and then I knew I had to find someone to shepherd me into a meeting. Television was a closed shop, that much I knew- unlike film pitching and ideas, there were only a handful of "approved" TV show creators and writers and unless you wanted to make that your whole life and pay the dues and work your way into that world, it was better to throw a few darts at the dart board and take what you could get if you hit the bull's eye and relinquish it to someone already in the mix. However, what I didn't understand is that in television the person who writes and/or directs the pilot is

considered the creator – even if s/he is taking an entire idea created by someone else.

And so, it was in delighted ignorance that the network bought the idea pretty much on the spot. However, I was told I had no choice but to sign over my whole idea and was told to be happy they had assigned it to Christopher Knopf, who was apparently well known as someone to establish a series.[3]

According to producer Robert Lovenheim, CBS executives on the West Coast hated the never-aired pilot which showed the son helping to solve a crime that his father investigated, but when the head of the network at the time, William S. Paley, saw it, he loved the show and wanted it on the fall schedule. However, even though the series was designed as a family show, CBS slotted it at 9:00 pm on Saturday nights up against ABC's hit, *The Love Boat*. Sam Rolfe was hired as the showrunner to make the series more adult by de-emphasizing the idea that "Little Shamus" actually helped his dad solve crimes and kept the dad on the straight and narrow. "Making it into an adult crime drama would, I knew, kill it," reflected Lovenheim. "So I walked. . . Not only did the critics savage the show, but they objected to a child being placed in life threatening jeopardy."[4]

Christopher Knopf, who wrote the pilot, recalls that he was asked to stay on and write further episodes of the series but declined because CBS or Lorimar wanted changes in the format – ". . . that Brian (Dennehy) should turn into a prime detective, less so on his son, which, to my mind lost the fun of the show."[5] Tracie Hotchner agrees with Knopf that shifting the concept from "the father/son against the world" idea and making the Dennehy character the chief detective missed the whole point of what was truly unique about the concept.

The change of concept made the series a standard PI drama instead of something a little different. *Big Shamus, Little Shamus* is obscure but not a cult series.

Another example of an obscure series that had the potential to be considered "cult" but whose concept changed from the original idea was the Fox series *Lawless* starring ex-football player Brian Bosworth that was canceled after one episode.

The Bosworth character was an ex-member of the Special Forces working as a private detective in Miami with his African-American partner.

Daniel Baldwin starred in the original pilot as John Lawless. Lori, who ran a travel agency, was his secretary since he figured it was cheaper to pay her than hire an answering service. Lawless was an expert on the use of explosives and never got himself into a situation where he didn't attempt to blow something up to get him out of difficulties.

Ken Sanzel wrote the pilot but left when Frank Lupo was brought in as show runner. As Sanzel stated, "I have a long standing love with the private eye genre . . . and decided to do something that was rooted in classic noir elements as well as the more high-octane wise-cracky action that they (Fox) were expecting."[6]

According to Sanzel, Daniel Baldwin as the lead in the *Lawless* pilot was not what the writer imagined when scripting the show. In any event, after some very public problems emerged with the actor, he was replaced by Brian Bosworth. Adrienne Shelley played Lori in the pilot; Ice T appeared as Tony Alto who would have been a recurring character if Sanzel had stayed with the project.

Lawless went from being a potential cult series combining film noir with explosive action to being a run-of-the-mill buddy cop drama.

How are cult TV shows presented in this book?

One could organize cult television shows into two broad categories – those that were "brilliant but canceled" and those that were "so bad they're good." The former refers to projects that were critically acclaimed but could not find a broad viewing audience; the latter are those works that attempted to be edgy or offbeat but failed in their execution usually either with poor acting or bad production values or both. These two categories are somewhat subjective. For the most part, this author will leave it up to the reader to judge into which of these two categories the television shows profiled in this work fall.

Rather, the obscure cult TV series in this book are organized by genre and within genre by the date each premiered. Chapters 1 through 8 profile cult dramatic series. Chapter 9 describes some cult situation comedies which have not been profiled in prior works, such as *Forgotten Laughs* by this author.

Chapter 10 deals with certain unsold television pilots which, if they had been picked up as a series, would likely have been considered as cult classics. The chapter includes descriptions of TV attempts by the iconic cult movie director Ed Wood. Finally, Chapter 11 details cult television series that were produced but never aired.

The Life-Cycle of Cult TV Shows

Several of the cult TV series profiled in this work had a life-cycle described by Todd Holland who was involved with the development of the "brilliant but canceled" *Wonderfalls* (see Chapter 6).

Describing the odyssey of the show, Holland outlined the stages of a cult series as follows: "Courageous development by the network, followed by less-than-courageous scheduling, followed by rising panic over underwhelming early returns, followed by swift cancellation, followed by an afterlife overseas... followed by a DVD wide release, with all the attendant horns and trumpets of a DVD publicity campaign."[7]

"So bad they're good" cult series follow a similar development except for a DVD wide release. Copies of episodes of such series usually end up in private collections and traded among small groups of devotees.

Brian Gross and William Gregory Lee from *Wind on Water*. Gross later had a recuring role on *General Hospital*, while Lee had roles on *Dante's Cove* and *Justified*.

CHAPTER 1

Teen and Twentysomething Dramas

Wind on Water – Soapy Water
Premiered October 17, 1998 on NBC Saturday at 8:00 pm

Premise: This soap/adventure series concerned an attractive, widowed mother and her two grown sons struggling to save their Hawaiian cattle ranch from a conniving land developer who had eyes for the mother. The sons were extreme sports addicts who engaged in surfing, dirt-bike racing, sky-diving, and jet skiing.

Background: Created by Zalman King, *Wind on Water* was filmed in Hawaii by his production company in association with NBC Studios. Before this series, King was best known for his erotic movies like *9 ½ Weeks* and *Wild Orchid* as well as for the soft-core adult Showtime cable series *Red Shoe Diaries*. While his movies and cable series focused on topless women, *Wind on Water* liked to show shirtless men.

Making the movie, *In God's Hands*, inspired Zalman King to film the pilot for *Wind on Water* on the islands. He said his goal with the series was to represent "a real Hawaii rather than a fantasy island."[8] King further remarked that "What interested me about doing 'Wind on Water' is that families . . . who came to the Big Island early on are still here. These are haole (a person who is not a native Hawaiian) families who blended into the culture without taking it over."[9]

According to *Wind on Water* writer/producer Charles Rosin, King showed NBC executives surfing clips from *In God's Hands* to interest them in doing a drama focused on the sport.[10] However, Rosin admits that the series was ill-conceived. King tended to hire actors for their looks and not their talent. For example, the actors hired to play cowboys didn't know how to ride horses although they looked very good on a steed. The actors who appeared as surfers looked good in bathing suits but had to be taught how to surf. It didn't help production that executives at NBC seemed to be at logger-heads with each other about *Wind on Water* and that King, doing his first network series, blew the show's budget on filming scenes like a big polo match.

Cast of Characters:

> Ceil Connolly (Bo Derek) - the matriarch of the Connolly ranch, whose husband has recently died;
> Cole Connolly (William Gregory Lee) - who is into surfing, and Kelly Connolly (Brian Gross), who liked motocross, Ceil's two sons;
> Kai (Matthew Stephen Liu) - one of Kelly's friends;
> Charlie Flanagan (Matt George) - another Connolly family friend;
> Gardner Poole (Lee Horsley) - a neighbor of the Connolly's and a scheming land developer;
> Val (Shawn Christian) - Poole's son who is into extreme sports like the Connolly brothers;
> Kate (Megan in an early script) (Jacinda Barrett) - Poole's daughter who had an on-again, off-again relationship with both Cole and Kelly;
> Tracy Poole (Heidi Hannsz) - Gardner Poole's current wife, who was half his age.

The Pilot - October 17, 1998

As Cole Connolly and his dad Sam herd cattle on their Hawaiian ranch, Gardner Poole arrives and repeats his offer to buy the ranch for a resort he is planning. Sam refuses the offer. That night at the ranch, Cole and his brother Kelly are encouraged by their friend Charlie to make money to save the ranch from foreclosure by becoming professionals at surfing or another extreme sport. Kelly wants to enter a surfing competition with his brother the next day because of the $60,000 first prize. Cole says the timing isn't right and that he should be on the ranch helping his dad. The next day, Sam finds that the water for the ranch has been turned off by Poole. Poole tells Sam that he will have to drill a new well on his property if he wants water. Cole finally relents and agrees to join Kelly in the surfing competition. Cole goes on to win. While the competition is going on, Sam is back at the ranch drilling a new well when he is hit by a large piece of machinery and killed. At the funeral, Cole says that he holds Gardner responsible for his father's death and will never let him buy the ranch. After the funeral, the next morning the Connolly family discovers Cole attempting to finish drilling the well. Everyone cheers as water shoots out of the new well that will sustain their ranch.

Up against the World Series on Fox, this episode came in third in its time slot after the baseball game and after *Early Edition* on CBS.

Other Episode Broadcast

"First Swell" – October 24, 1998

Cole has been invited to a surfing tournament on Oahu but wants to stay home to work on the ranch. Ciel insists that he go to Oahu. Walter Adler, Ciel's accountant, informs her that the ranch owes between $50,000 and $60,000 in short-term debt. Cole and his friend Charlie go to Oahu where they meet surf-wear mogul Bob Fox. Kate suggests that Kelly, his friend Kai, and her all fly to Oahu to cheer on Cole. Unbeknownst to him, the time for Cole's heat has been changed, and he misses his chance to compete. When everyone arrives back home, Cole learns that his mother has sold Gardner Poole her prized stallion to pay off the ranch's short term debts as well as purchase a sorely-needed new tractor. The boys are disappointed that their mother didn't confer with them before making this decision.

With regular programming on Fox, the second episode of *Wind on Water* came in fourth after shows on CBS, Fox and ABC. Once NBC President Warren Littlefield was ousted from his position, the new president of the network summarily canceled the series.

Unaired Episodes

"Threading the Needle"

Val rents one of the Poole's beach houses to a buddy from business school who is accompanied by his brother and their friends. One of the guys named Rodney likes to jet ski as does Kelly. Kelly challenges him to a race and bets the money saved for Kate's birthday gift. After he wins the race, Rodney challenges him to another race for double the money. He wants to "thread the needle" at Devil's Cauldron where, because of the rock formations, only one jet ski can navigate between the rocks. The race is scheduled for the night to try to evade the Coast Guard. During the race, Rodney is the first to bail from his jet ski. Kelly has to dive off his jet ski to pull Rodney to safety.

"Kalendar Grrrl"

After Charlie photographs Kate at a surfing event, the pictures are accepted for a women's bodysurfing calendar. Val finds that he has things in common with his new stepmother, Tracy, and they begin an affair.

"Shockwaves"

Cole gets ready for a canoe race. Kate decides to postpone going to college. Ciel creates a petting zoo. Val has concerns about his affair with his stepmother.

"Reckless"

Kelly and Kate, now in a relationship, throw a party that attracts thousands. A dirt-bike champ with a reckless attitude irritates Cole.

"Maxed Out"

Cole wants to purchase a prize bull from the nearby Langford ranch which is having a liquidation auction. Also, he has been selected to do an ad campaign for Red Ant trunks for which he has been paid $10,000. He wants to use the money to buy the bull. At the auction, Gardner bids the highest for the bull at $15,000 which irritates Cole. When Gardner comes by the ranch offering the bull as a gift to Ciel, Cole rejects it outright. Ciel reveals to him that she had Gardner act as her white knight at the auction to place the winning bid for the bull with the understanding that she would repay Poole.

"Here Today, Gone to Maui"

Val is opening a club and needs his father to sign papers before it can open. Since Gardner is upset that Kate and Kelly are still seeing each other, Val promises to end that relationship if his dad signs the papers. Kelly has been invited to Maui for a promo shoot with Val for Red Ant sports equipment since Cole cannot go because he is recovering from a sports injury. In Maui, Val has two sisters come on to Kelly and proposition him for a threesome. However, he resists temptation and calls Kate to let her know.

Postscript: Eight episodes of the series were produced before its cancelation leaving two additional scripts not filmed. Apparently, in later scripts, Tracy leaves her husband, and Gardner Poole is then killed when his Mercedes drives off a cliff.

While combining a family drama with extreme sports competitions may have been an unusual idea, this series probably falls into the category of "so bad, it's good."

As writer/producer Larry Mollin commented about *Wind on Water*, "Zalman loved the image of guys riding horses and carrying surfboards but it was cumbersome. Unfortunately, the show never got a chance to work the narrative kinks out."[11]

Skin – Romeo and Juliet, Politics and Porn
Premiered October 20, 2003 on Fox Mondays at 9:00 pm

Premise: As Fox advertised, this series was a modern day Romeo and Juliet set against the adult film industry. The show sought to answer the age-old question of which is a dirtier business – politics or pornography.

Cast of Characters:

Adam Roam (D.J. Cotrona) - the seventeen-year-old son of a politically ambitious district attorney for the city of Los Angeles;
Jewel Goldman (Olivia Wilde) - the sixteen-year-old daughter of the owner of Golden International, the largest producer of adult entertainment with whom Adam falls in love;
Tom Roam (Kevin Anderson) – Adam's father who is obsessed with destroying the porn industry;
Laura Roam (Rachel Ticotin) - Adam's mother - a judge;
Larry Goldman (Ron Silver) – the head of Golden International who is Jewel's dad;
Barbara (Pamela Gidley) - Jewel's mother;
Skip Ziti (D.W. Moffett) - Larry's partner;
Cynthia Peterson (Laura Leighton) - Tom's campaign manager.

Background: The series was created by Jim Leonard and produced by Jerry Bruckheimer and Leonard's Hoosier Karma Productions in association with Warner Brothers. Bruckheimer is responsible for the *Pirates of the Caribbean* series of films as well as TV series like *CSI*. At the time, Gail Berman, president of Fox Entertainment, said she was interested in the concept of the series because "it was a really character-based drama, and a new world."[12]

The Pilot - October 20, 2003
Adam and Jewel meet at a club where she is trying to get away from her obnoxious boyfriend. Adam is Catholic; she is Jewish. They go to a diner to talk until early morning. When Adam arrives home his father is extremely upset about his late hours. When Jewel arrives home, her parents are just coming in themselves. Tom is investigating a series of child abductions and the suspects in the cases have child pornography on their computers. The child porn websites are traced to Golden International, and the DA has Goldman arrested. Goldman's attorney claims that he is just leasing the websites to clients and is not responsible for their content. The charges

are dismissed. Roam still wants to pursue Goldman and places him under twenty-four hour surveillance. Goldman finds out that his daughter is seeing Roam's son and forbids her from seeing him again. However, after Adam tells Jewel that she should love him for himself and forget what his father does, they continue their relationship.

Upon learning that his son is dating Goldman's daughter, Roam confronts Adam, but Adam says he won't stay away from Jewel. Adam and Jewel, after confessing to each other that they are both virgins, quickly put an end to that status.

Other Episodes Broadcast

"Secrets and Lies" - October 27, 2003

Tom calls Goldman when Adam doesn't come home. Goldman checks Jewel's bedroom but doesn't discover Adam who is hiding. Goldman rejects aspiring porn star Darlene who wants to be in one of his films thinking she is not mature enough to make the decision to be in porn. A PI Goldman hired to monitor Tom thinks Tom is having an affair with his lead investigator when it is really Cynthia with whom he is having an affair.

Jewel's parents insist that she stop seeing Adam. However, later she says to her mom that she slept with Adam. When Goldman confronts Tom about his supposed affair with his lead detective, Tom says that they were in the hotel room together to interview a witness against a drug dealer.

"Endorsement" – November 3, 2003

Cynthia wants Tom to leave his wife after the election. However, later Tom informs her that he wants to end their affair. Tom is seeking the mayor's endorsement. Darlene meets again with Goldman after sleeping with Ziti to have him reconsider his decision about her wish to be a porn star. He wants her to visit the set of a film before she makes a final decision. After visiting a film set, she returns to Goldman's office saying she still wants to appear in a film, and Goldman agrees.

Adam doesn't want to be in a campaign ad with his parents but later decides to introduce his father at a Latino police officers' event. He wants to meet Jewel at the hotel after he makes the introduction. When Jewel goes to the hotel to see Adam, she overhears his dad say that he is going to put her father away for, among other things, money laundering. Jewel says she can't see Adam anymore because of what his dad said.

Meanwhile, Ziti has been instructed by Goldman to make a substantial contribution to the Roam campaign. When Ziti tells the mayor that the

Roam campaign accepted the contribution, the mayor doesn't endorse Tom advising him that he is going to receive some bad press.

After three episodes on Fox, the series was canceled. The series debut had 6.3 million viewers with each subsequent episode having fewer viewers. Its final episode had a smaller audience than its competition on the WB network coming in fifth in its time slot.

Unaired Episodes

"Amber Synn"

The DA's office wants to interview Amber Synn a woman who was the original "Golden" girl and whose real name is Christina Baker. They believe Goldman used her to launder money. Synn, who has a young son, calls Ziti demanding a meeting with Goldman, but Goldman won't see her. Meanwhile, the news media learns of the big contributions Goldman made to the Roam campaign. Cynthia informs Tom that she will resign over the matter, but at a news conference, Roam says that he is not asking for her resignation, that he is returning the money to Goldman, and that he will continue to investigate him. Ziti remarks that if Amber starts talking with the DA, her financial support will be cut off, but she goes to the DA anyway demanding protection and her arrest record expunged before she will talk. She says that Goldman makes people "disappear." Ultimately, Amber decides to speak to the DA, but before she can say anything, a Goldman attorney comes in and stops the interview. Amber and Goldman finally meet. She says she didn't tell the DA anything. However, the DA thinks that Goldman is the father of Amber's son and that is why Goldman continues to support her financially.

Both Adam and Jewel tell their parents that they broke up, and each begins seeing other people. Adam says that, as long as he and Jewel let their parents think they are no longer a couple, they can be together.

"Fidelity"

At midnight, Cynthia phones Tom and says someone broke into her apartment. She thinks the burglars were after information about their affair. When Tom arrives at her place, they discuss their relationship. Later, he tells his wife that Goldman was behind the break-in, and he calls Goldman directly and accuses his people of the burglary. Tom continues to pursue the money that Amber Synn is receiving every month from Goldman. After initially thinking that Cynthia may have staged the break-in to draw his attention to her, Tom finds that a small camera was planted in her apartment. When Goldman finds that his PI did this, he is upset that the private investigator committed a felony even though he now has videotape of Tom and Cynthia discussing their affair. Tom receives a call from a stranger about meeting with him concerning the tape. He is told to turn over every document he has about Goldman or else the tape will be made public. Tom calls Goldman directly about the documents he has about him.

Adam and Jewel each have friends pretend they are dating them as a cover while they are seeing each other. In Jewel's case, the friend is gay, but in Adam's case, the friend is Vanessa, his former girlfriend. Jewel is jealous and wants him to pick someone else as his cover.

In other events, Amber meets with Goldman about her five-year old son and requests that Goldman visit him every other weekend. At a birthday party for Barbara Goldman, Ziti's wife, from whom he is separated, accuses both Ziti and Goldman of having affairs with the girls in their films. Goldman wants Darlene to star in his next feature.

"Blowback"

Tom threatens Goldman and says he will make public the information about Goldman's illegitimate son with Amber. Goldman denies the son is his, and it turns out the boy was fathered by the mayor. Tom confesses to his wife about his affair before the information is made public. Both his wife and Adam want him out of the house.

Goldman authorizes the release of information about Tom's affair to the media. Tom meets with his staff to inform them. Later he holds a press conference apologizing for the affair but saying nothing he did compromises his ability to do his job.

Goldman is told that a former accountant of his met with the DA and that Ziti had hired and fired him. Goldman thinks that Ziti is behind the money laundering scheme. He confronts Ziti about the accountant. Ziti responds that the man is just a former disgruntled employee. But later, Ziti goes to see the man, threatens him, and gives him money and a plane ticket to leave town.

Adam goes to see his dad in his office and says that he hates him for having the affair but loves him as his father. Tom states that he won't get in the way of Adam's relationship with Jewel. Jewel asks her dad about the release of the information concerning Adam's father and Goldman says that he was behind it. Upset, she leaves his office.

"Family Values"

Even though the mayor wants Tom to withdraw from the race, Tom says he is not withdrawing and mentions that Goldman controls the mayor. The mayor meets with Goldman to voice his concerns about what Roam may find in the weeks before the election. Roam asks for background checks on all Golden employees.

Darlene is making a film for Golden Entertainment and finds that Geena Divine, the lead in the picture, is taking cocaine. After she informs Larry about the drugs, he has the star go into rehab and gives the lead to Darlene.

Adam says to his mother that he is seeing Jewel. She responds that she is disappointed but is glad he told the truth. She invites Jewel to dinner. At dinner, Jewel confesses that her parents don't want her to see Adam. Mrs. Roam excuses herself from dinner to get some sleep. She takes too many sleeping pills, hits her head on the bedside table, and passes out. Goldman goes on Jewel's PC and sees her log of emails to Adam. Adam, upon discovering his mother, calls his dad; Jewel calls 911, and Goldman appears at the Roam's looking for Jewel.

"True Lies"

Goldman takes his daughter to the hospital to see Mrs. Roam and Adam. At the hospital, Goldman and Roam confront each other, and Roam blames him for what happened to Laura. Goldman demands that Jewel leave with him, but she won't. Laura Roam has a concussion but will survive. When Jewel returns home, she tells her dad that she has been sleeping with Adam, and her mother knew about it.

Darlene has problems doing a scene with two men in the film. She asks to select different guys but then is still unhappy. When another actress is hired for the lead, Darlene reconsiders and makes the film.

Laura asks Tom for a divorce. Adam goes to the Goldman's to talk with Jewel. They are resigned to Jewel's relationship with Adam.

Postscript: *Skin* showed up later on the cable channel SoapNet and was aired as part of their "Dysfunctional Family Night."

A total of thirteen episodes were initially contemplated with hopes that nine more would be ordered by Fox for a complete season of twenty-two. Beyond the episodes made, the writers and producers drafted the following story arcs for the unproduced episodes:[13]

Adam and Jewel — Jewel becomes increasingly aware and politicized about her dad's business. She fights with her parents that ends when her dad takes away her credit cards. Jewel then gets a job at a book and CD store run by a friend of one of her teachers at school. Jewel's affection for Adam increases, but he becomes somewhat freaked out by the intensity of her love. Skip Ziti's son Brian, Jewel's former boyfriend, returns from boarding school and re-enters Jewel's life. Brian likes to party, and Jewel begins to embrace his wild lifestyle. Eventually, Jewel asks Adam to run away with her, but he says "no." Jewel then threatens to run away with Brian. Adam turns to Larry for help with Jewel. She sees this as the ultimate betrayal and has a big fight with Adam. She gets in her car and crashes it.

Larry Goldman – Larry's business continues to grow and his newest porn star Darlene shows great potential. At the premiere of *Bath Slave*, Larry approaches the Chairman of WorldDom's Music Division with the idea of creating a new pay-per-view channel with hit bands and porn stars. When the Chairman of WorldDom Entertainment double crosses Larry on the deal, Larry comes up with a plan to take over WorldDom. Meanwhile, Skip Ziti's wife hires an aggressive divorce attorney named Leslie Mack who wants to open Golden International's books to make sure her client receives the money to which she thinks she is entitled. Larry gives Skip an ultimatum – either reconcile with his wife Zelda or pay her half of what he's worth.

Laura and Tom Roam – The Roam's enter into counseling to try to save their marriage. It turns out that Laura Roam and Zelda Ziti both have the same divorce attorney. Living separately, the Roam's vie for their son's affection. Laura stands by Tom during his re-election, and he wins another term as DA.

Concerning Tom's investigation of Larry Goldman, when he learns that Ziti is going through a divorce, Tom decides to go after Zelda Ziti, and she decides to cooperate. At the same time, Roam is using Zelda for his investigation into possible money laundering at Golden International. He arrests Geena Divine, once Goldman's reigning Golden Girl, for prostitution. Roam catches her sleeping with the mayor. Geena agrees to work undercover so to speak for the DA. Eventually, Roam gives Ziti a choice – either go to prison for tax evasion and financial impropriety or testify against Goldman. Skip Ziti's secret stash of $50 million is discovered hidden in accounts in the Cayman Islands, and so Ziti begins to waver with respect to his choices.

Meanwhile, Geena, working as an undercover informant, returns to Golden International and accepts Larry's offer to become a director. However, Geena spirals back into drugs and prostitution. She crosses paths with Ziti's son Brian and threatens to kill Larry and Darlene after Darlene wins the Best Actress Award for *Bath Slaves*. At the Adult Film Awards, Geena takes out a gun and heads for Larry's hotel room. When Larry enters his room, he finds Geena in the bathroom – dead. Larry emerges from his hotel room with Geena's blood on his hands and calls for help. Roam feels personally responsible for her death and believes Larry is the chief suspect.

Skip Ziti – Skip tells Larry that the $50 million he has in personal funds in the Cayman's is money he has been hiding from Zelda. The salary he has been paying himself is ridiculously low and his house has been written off as a Golden International movie set. When the DA charges him with money laundering, Skip is faced with losing his law license, forfeiting all his remaining assets to the IRS, or turning on Larry. Skip's son Brian holds a homecoming party, and when Skip comes home the next morning, he finds Brian passed out in one of the bedrooms and a teenage girl floating face down in the swimming pool. Brian doesn't know what happened. Skip decides to protect his son and calls the private investigator, who helped gather information on Roam, to dispose of the body. Roam ultimately connects the teenage girl to a Midas Touch strip bar that is part of the Golden empire. In the meantime, Brian, feeling guilty about what happened to the girl, begins drinking more and doing drugs. Brian frequents high-priced call girls through the same madam who handles Geena Divine. Geena comes to believe that Brian killed the teenager. This is what she knows before dying in Larry's hotel room at the Adult Film Awards.

My Generation – The Class of 2000 Ten Years Later
Premiered September 23, 2010 on ABC Thursdays at 8:00 pm

Premise: Filmmakers produce a documentary in 2000 showing the hopes and aspirations of nine seniors from Greenbelt High School in Austin, Texas. Ten years later the filmmakers return to make a sequel to their documentary and see if the seniors fulfilled their hopes and desires. Flashbacks to prior years are seen not only from clips of the 2000 documentary but also from home movies, still photos, and news footage. The nine high school students who were the focus of the documentary are now in their twenties.

Cast of Characters:

Rolly Marks (Mehcad Brooks) – an African-American high school jock now in the Army in Afghanistan, attended Stanford on a basketball scholarship after graduation but dropped out after 9-11 to volunteer for the army. He is married to Dawn Barbuso (Kelli Garner), a punk in high school who is now pregnant. Dawn's mother married a rock musician and left the family when Dawn was six. Dawn's mother later went to a mental hospital for treatment of depression leaving Dawn to care for her younger brother. She had to drop out of school in her senior year to get a job to support her and her brother;

Jackie Vachs (Jaime King) - the high-school beauty queen who aspired to be an actress. After high school, Jackie went to Hollywood and appeared on *The Bachelor*. She had landed a role on a TV pilot, got drunk celebrating, wrecked her car, and the studio could not wait for her to recover so they gave her part to someone else. She returned to Austin and married wealthy Anders Holt (Julian Morris) who is best friends with Rolly and works in his father's business;

Steven Foster (Michael Stahl-David) - the high school overachiever, is now a bartender and surfer in Hawaii. His father, who is in prison, had been a top executive at Enron but was arrested when the company went bankrupt, and Steven's family lost all of their assets. Steven has an older brother named RJ who ran away from home when he was fifteen because of a poor relationship with his father who was always pushing him and Steven to achieve;

Caroline Chung (Anne Son) - a wallflower in high school, now raising a nine-year-old illegitimate son named Tom and running her own hotel business. Steven is Tom's father having made Caroline pregnant on their prom night;

Brenda Serrano (Daniella Alonso) - a brain in high school who dated Anders, is now a legislative aide to a Congressman in Washington. She originally majored in science at George Washington University but changed to pre-law after the Supreme Court decided the 2000 Presidential election in favor of George W. Bush. She and Anders had a big fight on their prom night. Ander's dad did not want him to marry Brenda because she is Hispanic. Ander's father threatened to ruin Brenda's father's construction business if he did and so Anders broke off the relationship;

Kenneth Finley (Keir O'Donnell) - the high school nerd, is now teaching elementary school and was once a friend of Steven's. Kenneth's father had committed suicide after he lost all of his money that he had invested in Enron. Kenneth and Dawn had dated briefly in high school, and he is still in love with her;

Falcon (Sebastian Sozzi) - the rock star in high school, is now a music producer, is best friends with Steven, and lives in New York City.

Background: Produced by The Littlefield Company, ABC Studios, 26 Keys Productions, and Stockholm/Koperhamn Productions based on the Swedish series *On God's Highway* (aka *Blomstertid*), the series, originally titled

Generation Y, was adapted for American television by Noah Hawley and shot on location in Austin, Texas. *Blomstertid* was a 2009 mockumentary series created by Peter Magnusson and Martin Persson documenting three guys named Anders, Kenneth, and Steven during their school years in Sweden and fourteen years later. Each of the main characters was portrayed by Peter Magnusson.

In discussing *My Generation*, Noah Hawley indicated that his goal was to make a television series for the internet era – ". . . to create a mash up of scripted material, real news and cultural footage, to repurpose existing content (by placing a fictional character on season 2 of *The Bachelor*, for example, or using scenes from the *Lost* finale to tie my characters to a time and place). I wanted to create something progressive, something modern. While, at the same time, telling fun, relatable, heartfelt stories about the lives we live today."[14] To this end, Hawley shot hours of home video showing births, birthday parties, weddings and funerals to be combined with scripted material for the different episodes. He also cast real Army veterans to appear as soldiers in Rolly Marks' squad in Afghanistan.

The Pilot – September 23, 2010

Kenneth wants to have a family and get married but is still single teaching third graders. Dawn is living with Kenneth until her husband returns from Afghanistan. Rolly would prefer that his wife live with his high school friend Anders instead of Kenneth.

Kenneth decides to donate his sperm to start someone else's family but finds that he is infertile. Steven returns to Austin after Caroline informs him that he fathered a son on the night of their high school prom. However, upon his arrival back in Texas, Steven runs into Jackie who pursues him. He tries to avoid meeting Caroline and his son until she sees him on the street, and then he makes up excuses for why he didn't contact her sooner. Eventually, Steven calls Caroline to apologize for how he acted when he saw her and the boy.

When Brenda, working in Washington, receives a call saying her mother had a stroke, she returns to Austin.

Other Episode Broadcast

"Home Movies"- September 30, 2010

Steven's mother wants him to visit his dad in prison, but instead he arranges a play date with Caroline to bond with his son Tom. Steven asks Caroline if she is sure he is the father. She responds that she was a virgin when they had sex, and she didn't have another sexual encounter until four years later. After the documentary makers ask Caroline if she has thought about Steven wanting visitation or custody rights for Tommy, she confronts Steven to say that her and her son are fine and that he doesn't have to stick around.

Brenda sees Jackie at the hospital where she volunteers. At dinner that her husband prepared, Jackie tells Anders that Brenda is back which provokes his interest. He sends flowers to Brenda with a note reading that she can depend on him for help if necessary.

Rolly is wounded when his unit comes under fire in Afghanistan but doesn't tell Dawn. Dawn and Kenneth go to a birthing class, but Dawn wants no part of it and leaves. She later apologizes to Kenneth for her behavior but is frustrated that she does not have a more stable lifestyle.

Unaired Episodes

"Truth and Reconciliation"

Steven flies to New York City to crash with Falcon and to see a former teacher of his who is now a professor at Columbia. At a bar with Falcon, a woman comes in, slaps Falcon on the face and tells him to stop bothering her. Falcon says the woman is his wife, Bree, who wants to divorce him, but he won't sign the divorce papers because he still loves her. Falcon takes Steven to a party where they see Bree with another man whom Bree says she is going to marry. Later Bree phones Falcon and asks to meet him saying she wants to reconcile. Steven leaves New York to go back to Austin after leaving a message with Caroline wanting to work things out concerning Tom.

Rolly is still upset that his wife is living with Kenneth. He wants Dawn to move to a home his mother has found. Dawn loves the place much to Kenneth's disappointment.

Anders goes to see Brenda at her home, but she doesn't want anything to do with him. She decides to go back to her job in Washington DC.

"Birth/Rebirth"

Kenneth and Dawn are preparing for the birth. Meanwhile, Anders is planning a trip to Washington DC on business but says to Steven that he really wants to see Brenda. Anders asks Jackie to visit Dawn at her house. When she arrives, Dawn's water has broken, and Jackie takes her to the hospital since Kenneth is coaching his Little League baseball team which includes Tom. Steven is at the game since Caroline requested that he take Tom. Kenneth receives a call telling him that Dawn is at the hospital. He goes there as do Steven and Tom where Steven sees Jackie again. They talk in private. Anders shows up just as Steven was going to tell Jackie something confidential. Caroline, who is at the hospital as well, asks Steven what his plans are with regard to Tom. He says he wants to stay in Austin and be a part of their lives.

Dawn has a baby girl that she names Charlie. Anders contacts Rolly via Skype and shows him a photo of his baby daughter.

"The Bed In"

Anders is off to Washington where he goes to see Brenda at work. She says she has moved on and that they no longer have a relationship. He invites her for drinks, but she declines. Later Brenda does show up outside the bar where Anders is, kisses him, and then leaves. He returns to Austin. Jackie informs him that she wants to have a baby after having visited Dawn.

Caroline's parents are coming to visit her at the motel she manages which she remodeled from the establishment that her parents had owned. Steven wants to meet her parents, but she has never told them about Steven. He shows up unexpectedly while she is serving her parents dinner and announces that he is Tom's father. Her parents are not impressed with him.

"On the Road"

Rolly is back in the States. Anders picks him up at Fort Hood to take him to Austin. Dawn plans to move out of Kenneth's house and into her new home when Rolly arrives. While driving to Austin, Brenda calls Anders to thank him for paying her mother's hospital bill. Anders tells Rolly that he and Brenda kissed and he has second thoughts about marrying Jackie. On the way to Austin, Anders stops at a state park where he proposed to Jackie and thinks about divorcing her. But in the end, when he is back in Austin, he says he is committed to their marriage and to having a baby.

Kenneth has bonded with Brenda's baby and is depressed when Rolly arrives, takes the baby, and moves out with his wife.

Brenda's boss tells her that a lobbyist she knows actually paid her mother's hospital bill after she told the lobbyist that her mother's pre-existing conditions prevented the insurance company from paying it. Anders did not pay the bill as she had assumed. The lobbyist then leaked to the news media the fact the Brenda was taking favors from a lobbying firm in order to get back at her for supporting legislation that the lobbying firm was against. Brenda is forced to resign and presumably will return to Austin.

"Homecoming"

The filmmakers interview Anders a week after he had a homecoming party for Rolly at his house. He reveals that he has left Jackie after the party. A week earlier, Anders and Jackie invited all of Rolly's friends to a catered homecoming party. After Steven stops by Caroline's, she asks him to accompany her to the party. Kenneth arrives early and flirts with Sophie, the bartender. Falcon is there with his wife Bree. He sees Brenda, who has returned to Austin, and invites her to the party. Anders is surprised when Brenda shows up. Jackie is uncomfortable with Steven being at the party. Anders has words with his wife about Brenda. Later, Anders, while looking for Rolly, finds Steven kissing Jackie in their bedroom. Anders and his wife have a big argument in front of everyone about Brenda and Steven, and he drives away leaving Jackie crying. Caroline is disappointed in Steven and won't let him see Tom anymore. Steven obtains an entry level position working in the mailroom at a firm. A week after the party, Jackie tells the filmmakers that she and Anders are taking time to figure out what to do next.

"What Comes Next"

In 2000 as a class assignment, seniors were tasked with writing a letter to themselves about what they want in ten years with the teacher mailing the letters to each student in 2010. In 2010, Ander's dad invites him to dinner with his mother. When he shows up at the restaurant, Jackie and her parents are there as well. The parents want the couple to discuss their problems and so leave them alone. Jackie acknowledges that she made a mistake and says that she was breaking off her relationship with Steven when Anders saw them in the bedroom. Anders asks her to put their marriage first, but Jackie responds that she has to think about it and leaves. The next day, Anders' dad wants him to move back in with Jackie right away and take control of the situation, but Anders remains in the hotel.

Kenneth is dating Sophie, the bartender from the homecoming party that he met and asks her to babysit Charlie with him while Dawn and Rolly have a date night.

Jackie visits Anders in his hotel room and says that she had an affair with Steven because Anders is still in love with Brenda and that they can't stay married because of this. When she asks him to tell her that he is no longer in love with Brenda, he can't. Jackie had read the letter Ander's wrote at school ten years earlier that said he is miserable without Brenda and that he will find a way for them to be together. After Jackie gives him the letter and leaves, Anders goes to see Brenda.

Postscript: *My Generation* was canceled by ABC after two low-rated episodes. However, all the episodes were made available for viewing online.

According to Hawley, the day the show was canceled, the producers were finalizing a deal with the NFL and the Houston Texans to have the character of Rolly Marks try out for the team. "In early November we would have gone to Houston, and put Rolly through the combines, the speed trials, the drills, the scrimmage games."[15] This footage would have been incorporated with scripted scenes for another episode.

CHAPTER 2

Crime Fighter Dramas

Angel Street – Crime and Sexism in Chicago

Premiered September 15, 1992 at 9:00 pm on CBS before moving to Saturdays at 10:00 pm

Premise: Two female detectives working in a rundown section of Chicago were the focus of this police drama. Both were assigned to the Violent Crimes Division on Angel Street in the Polish Hill area of Chicago where they were subject to sexist remarks from their male colleagues who often referred to them as A.A.B.'s (Affirmative Action Babies).

Cast of Characters:

Anita King (Robin Givens) - a sophisticated black woman, a girlfriend of the Deputy Mayor of Chicago, who had worked in Internal Affairs and someday wanted to be captain;

Dorothy Paretsky (Pamela Gidley) - a street-wise Polish-American single parent of a daughter who lived with her grandfather on Polish Hill. She became King's training officer and had previously worked in Narcotics;

Sgt. Ciamacco (Joe Guzaldo) – King and Paretsky's boss;

Det. Kenny Branigan (Ron Dean) - liked to play practical jokes on the two female detectives;

Det. Kanaskie (Rick Snyder) - forty-year-old male colleague;

Det. Llewellyn (Luray Cooper) and red-headed Det. Delaney (Danny Goldring) – two other detectives in the Violent Crimes Division.

Background: The series was one of the first to be created by John Wells, better known for such shows as *Shameless* and *ER*. After working on the Vietnam-era series *China Beach*, Wells hired his former colleagues from that series, Lydia Woodward, Fred Gerber, Richard Thorpe and John Levey as part of the crew for *Angel Street*. It was originally titled *Polish Hill*, based on the real Polish Hill in Pittsburgh, Pennsylvania where Wells had attended Carnegie Mellon. Produced by John Wells Productions in conjunction with Warner Brothers, CBS ordered six episodes of the series in addition to the pilot.

The Pilot - September 15, 1992

The series was introduced in a special two-hour presentation on the *CBS Tuesday Night Movie*. King meets Paretsky, and the two investigate the cases of a murdered drug dealer as well as a missing nine-year-old girl. Paretsky thinks that the son of the Deputy Chief of Police, Capt. Mulligan, may have shot the drug dealer based on the vehicle that was identified at the shooting and the phone number left on the drug dealer's beeper. The chief's son is arrested for the murder after the two detectives argue whether or not it is worth taking him into custody for the death of a drug dealer. In the other case, Sgt. Ciamacco calls the two detectives on the carpet for working on the disappearance of the young girl, Spencer Donally. When the girl's father is found shot in the head, the two detectives think that the girl is being held for money her father owed to drug dealers that the girl's father and his partner ripped off. Based on information from the partner of the dead girl's father, the young girl is found alive.

The series opener made liberal use of the "n-word."

Other Episodes Broadcast

"Midnight Times a Hundred"- September 26, 1992

King and Paretsky are called to the scene of a mass shooting on an L train. Three people are murdered, and seven injured. Among the injured is a mother who had been on the train with her two sons – one was killed, the other, a former gang member, is missing. They arrest a suspect for the shooting, a gang member who was trying to kill the missing teen and former member of the gang, but the detectives need more evidence against him. The partners find the missing teen, but he refuses to talk. Paretsky wants the priest from the neighborhood to speak with the teen to convince him to testify. The priest does finally persuade the teen to testify against the shooter.

"The Blonde in the Pond" - October 3, 1992

King is assigned a cold case from 1984 that Detective Branigan had worked. The case involves the strangulation murder of a Jane Doe, a blonde found dead in a lake. The partners are also investigating the case of a lothario found dead in a motel room. Stephen Head apparently rented the room to party with three prostitutes. King and Paretsky find that the man's sisters-in-law, dressed like prostitutes, killed Stephen after he had tried to seduce one of them. Concerning the cold case, King discovers that a carnival was being held lakeside when the Jane Doe was murdered and that she was with the amusement company that provided the carnival rides. She had run off with a truck driver for the amusement company. However, the driver was in prison when the murder occurred. He reveals that an employee with the company named Buddy Elwood might have murdered the Jane Doe. King, Paretsky, and Branigan locate Elwood who has a shrine to the deceased in his trailer. After giving chase, Elwood is hit by a car and dies.

Unaired Episodes

"Death of a Car Salesman"
  The two partners investigate the murder of a used car salesman.

"According to Etta"
  When a drug dealer is murdered, King and Paretsky interview the ex-wife of the dealer's associate, Ramsey Thorpe. Etta Thorpe is in prison for killing a gas station attendant during a hold-up. She tells the partners that her ex-husband actually committed the murder. The police then question Ramsey Thorpe who denies any involvement. Llewellyn finds that the dealer's girlfriend murdered him. But King and Paretsky are still suspicious of Thorpe since he used the same alibi for the dealer's murder that he had used three years earlier about the murder of the gas station attendant. The partners find that, given the direction the bullet that entered the deceased and the security video from the gas station, Etta could not have fired the gun. King and Paretsky find Ramsey's fingerprints on the security camera at the gas station when he was changing the focus of the camera away from him behind the counter. Ramsey is arrested, and Etta is freed from prison.

"Probable Cause"
  Two white cops pursue a black man resisting arrest for suspicious behavior, beat him to death, and dump his body in a field. Based on tire impressions from a police car and bruises on the body made by Billy clubs, King and Paretsky arrest the two officers which causes riots on Polish Hill. Internal Affairs thinks that more evidence is needed for a stronger case against the two cops. While staking out the victim's partner who may have been an eyewitness to the murder, King, Paretsky, Branigan, and the detective

from Internal Affairs debate the status of race relations. They finally take the partner into custody, but he says he wasn't with the victim at the time of the beating. King and Paretsky again search the officers' police car and find the two cops switched their trunk carpet with that from another vehicle. The cops are indicted but plead not guilty saying they had probable cause against the victim.

"Mother, May I?"

A woman is shot in a parking garage at 2:00 am. Paretsky, while out on the town, witnesses the shooting. One of the two shooters is killed. The partners look for the other shooter. They think that both men were involved in stealing cars. Meanwhile, Paretsky's mother thinks that her daughter is putting too much responsibility on Partesky's grandfather for taking care of her daughter.

Postscript: *Angel Street* was CBS lowest rated fall series ranking 89 out of 98 series.

South of Sunset – A Rocker and a Comic as PI's
Premiered October 27, 1993 on CBS Wednesdays at 9:00 pm

Premise: The one-time head of security for a motion picture company, fired for busting a powerful producer, becomes a struggling private investigator assisted by his black sidekick, a former thief. The PI establishes the Beverly Hills Detective Agency located south of Sunset Blvd. in a poor section of Beverly Hills.

Cast of Characters:

Cody McMahon (Glenn Frey) - a private investigator who owns his own detective agency. He had previously been married to Diane Daniels – a fiery Italian sexpot from New Jersey who worked at a movie studio. Cody had lost his job at the studio when a producer came to the studio with foreign money, and Cody found that he had made the money in the crack business. Cody turned him in and was fired;

Ziggy Duane (Aries Spears) – Cody's assistant, a former thief;

Gina Weston (Maria Pitillo) - Cody's secretary who wants to be an actress and often comes to the office dressed in costumes for an audition;

Aries Spears as Ziggy Duane and Glenn Frey as Cody McMahon in *South of Sunset*. The series is probably more famous for its offbeat casting than for its story ideas.

Merlin (John Diehl) - a PC expert who lives in Cody's neighborhood and provides him with information about people involved in his cases;

Detective Mendez (John Verea) - represents the local police and often hassles Cody.

Background: The series was produced by A Stan Rogow Production and Byrum Power and Light in association with Paramount. Rogow and Byrum's association with CBS began when they created a comedy-drama titled *Middle Ages* for the network. The six-week series concerned middle-aged residents of Winnetka, Illinois dealing with problems of growing older and realizing life may be passing them by. While a critical success, the series did not do well in the ratings. CBS then asked Rogow and Byrum to create a series about a private investigator to appeal to a younger demographic. After auditioning several actors for the lead role, the producers chose Glenn Frey, lead singer for the rock group, The Eagles. Frey had little acting experience. Rogow's advice to him was "Don't act; just be an Eagle."[16] Comedian Aries Spears was hired as Frey's sidekick.

The Pilot
"Satyricon" – October 27, 1993

Cody is working on three cases at the same time. One case involves tracking down the lover of a plastic surgeon's perfectly beautiful wife who is cheating on him. He finds that the wife is having an affair with a short, dumpy bus driver who has been trying to kill Cody for spying on them. He informs the husband that there never was another man.

In the second case, Cody has been hired to find a gang leader, Luther Mayes, who has jumped bail. To assist him with the search, Cody bails out Ziggy, who is in jail for car theft. Ziggy becomes Cody's wisecracking African-American assistant who, in the pilot, spends most of his time in handcuffs, so that he doesn't escape. Cody and Ziggy meet with Luther's mother who tells them that her son is trying to reform and have the gangs declare a truce. Luther comes to Cody's office to turn himself in, but Cody advises him to go and make peace.

The third case involves an extortion attempt against a young tennis star whose father hires Cody. The blackmailers want $1 million to prevent the release of a nude photo of the star that was taken in a motel room. The tennis star says she was drugged and taken to the motel when her parents were out of town. Cody finds that the parents are having marital difficulties and that, when they were out of town, they stayed in separate rooms. After interviewing the desk clerk at the motel, Cody finds that the mother drugged her own daughter to get money from her husband before he left her.

In an early draft of the pilot script, the third case in which Cody was involved was different than the one filmed. In the script, Cody is hired by Danni Nichols, who is partners with Marty Waxman in a film studio where Cody used to be head of security. The film studio is due to be sold for $100 million to a Japanese company and Waxman is being blackmailed. When Cody and Ziggy go to see Waxman, he says that he has been receiving letters and phone calls demanding that he quit the movie business. When Danni talks to Marty about the business, she says that he does things that look irresponsible to the Japanese businessmen like using the studio's jet for pleasure trips. Later, Cody and Ziggy go to Waxman's house to plant a surveillance camera, and, when they return to retrieve the camera, Ziggy discovers Waxman's dead body at the bottom of his empty pool. The police arrive as does Danni. After Cody retrieves the photos developed, he finds that Danni was behind the blackmail scheme to scare Marty from wrecking the Japanese deal and that she killed him. Danni says she didn't intend to kill her partner but that he turned abusive when she told him she was the one sending the letters and making the phone calls. When she pushed him, he fell into the swimming pool.

Unaired Episodes

"Dream Girl"

Lou Napolotano hires Cody to find a girl he has seen only in his dreams. Lou, the "Porcelain Prince" of Queens who sells bathroom fixtures, gives Cody $5000 to find his dream girl. On the way to see a sketch artist, Lou and Cody are intercepted by a fortune teller who tells Lou that she sees great sex coming. Later, Cody informs Lou that the girl of his dreams starred in an informercial, but Lou no longer is interested in her. He has hooked up with the fortune teller who promised amazing sex. Meanwhile, Gina goes to a movie audition with Rick Marcon who is auditioning with her. Subsequently, Gina is told that she and Rick got the parts and to prepare for filming the movie in the Caribbean. Since Cody thinks that there is something suspicious about Gina's job offer, he has Ziggy trail Marcon. Ziggy finds that Marcon's wife looks amazingly like Gina. Cody thinks that Marcon wants to substitute Gina for his wife to collect on the wife's $2 million insurance policy. When Marcon picks up Gina to go to the Caribbean, he drugs her drink. Marcon, who heads a large corporation owning the movie company and is in need of funds, has made arrangements with a doctor to kill Gina, collect the insurance money, and go to the Caribbean with his real wife.

Cody and Ziggy break into Marcon's house and force his wife to tell them where Gina is. They rush to a clinic where the doctor is overdosing Gina on morphine and revive her just in time.

"Custody"
Cody takes the case of a waitress and mother, Mary Beth Kinkaid, whose young daughter has been kidnapped by her former husband, Wayne. Cody and Ziggy go to a biker bar to see Katie's dad and find Katie with him. Cody is able to escape with Katie in his car with the bikers in hot pursuit. When Cody contacts her mother, Mary Beth seems more interested in getting back at her ex than in how her daughter is doing. Katie tells Cody that her parents argue all the time and don't really care about her. Both Mary Beth and her ex-husband arrive at Cody's office and begin arguing. Cody says that Katie would be better off with him. The parents then agree to work things out together.

"Family Affair"
A young girl, Maya Hansen, wants Cody to find her real father based on the fact that every birthday she receives jewelry and postcards from an unknown man. She gives Cody a broach she received from the man. Cody takes it to a pawnbroker to determine if it was stolen. The pawnbroker is subsequently murdered. Posing as a magazine writer, Cody interviews Maya's mother and dad and finds that Nicole Hansen, the girl's mother, used to be a back-up singer and was involved with another man during her singing career. Cody also discovers that a jewel theft occurred everywhere from where she received postcards and that a Beverly Hills realtor is the thief who is Maya's real father. The thief is arrested. He tells Maya that she is not his daughter in order for her not to think that her real dad is a thief and murderer.

In a subplot, Gina's mother (Carroll Baker) comes to visit, and Gina wants Cody to pretend to be her date so the mother doesn't keep insisting she marry a guy from her home town.

"Newspaper Boy"
Cody is hired by the parents of Tommy Walker - a sixteen-year-old killed by a police officer. The parents believe the officer murdered their son even though the homicide was ruled justified. Cody talks with Officer Davis who shot Tommy. The police report says that Tommy was running drugs. At the scene of the shooting, Cody finds a homeless man who informs him that he saw a cop take handcuffs off the dead boy. Cody and Ziggy later find Officer Davis back at the scene. He says that Tommy did have handcuffs on

but lied about it so he could personally investigate. Davis thinks another cop is involved with a drug gang. Cody finds a thirteen-year-old named Jerome who is running with the gang and who says that he is working for Davis' trainee – a female cop. She killed Tommy and set up Davis.

"Remember Me"
Cody and Ziggy clear a guy accused of murder.

"Chalk Lines"
At the direction of Det. Mendez, Cody and Ziggy follow a woman to a hotel. The woman they were following knows Lisabeta Velez, the female that Mendez wants shadowed. Cody and Ziggy see Lisabeta and the other woman dining at a restaurant and save them from being shot. Cody discovers that Lisabeta, a madam in Beverly Hills, is Mendez's sister. Lisabeta tells her brother that she thinks a man named Mike Portell is behind the attempt on her life. He wants to take over her business. Cody has Gina pose as a prospective working girl and has her wear a wire to get Portell to divulge that he is in the call girl business. Portell claims that he turned Mendez's sister into a prostitute. In the end, Lisabeta reconciles with her brother after telling Cody that she and Mendez shared a bedroom together when they were kids and divided the room with chalk lines on the floor daring the other one to cross over.

Postscript: CBS heavily promoted *South of Sunset* during the World Series hoping that a younger demographic than the network usually got would tune in. As head of CBS planning and research said at the time, "There were other shows that tested better, but ('South of Sunset') provided a certain balance. CBS' weakness is with young males . . . We hadn't added much this season that was going to address that weakness. That's what put the show on the schedule."[17]

However, when the series premiered late in October after the World Series of 1993 had ended, it rated fourth in its time slot against *Home Improvement* on ABC, the newsmagazine *Now* on NBC, and *Melrose Place* on Fox. The network figured they did everything possible to get a young audience for the series. Not knowing what more it could do to promote it, CBS canceled *South of Sunset* after a single episode.

According to writer Angel Dean-Lopez, the premiere of the series was also jinxed by an historic fire in Malibu which pre-empted the series debut on many television stations. Also, Glenn Frey wanted Les Moonves, the head of CBS, to run another episode in place of the pilot because he felt the pilot was not as strong in its characterizations of him and Aries Spears as later ones were. Because the pilot delved into the origins of Cody and Ziggy's relationship, CBS decided not to eat the money for reshoots or dump the pilot altogether. When the decision was made final late on the day of the premiere, Frey sent a fax to Moonves saying something like "I like to be kissed when I'm getting screwed."[18]

When the series was canceled, Glenn Frey was not terribly upset. According to writer/producer John Byrum, the show was canceled on a Wednesday afternoon. He and Stan Rogow broke the news to Frey who looked at his watch and shrugged, "I guess I can still get nine holes of golf in!" and off to the course he went.[19] A few days later, Frey gave a farewell concert on one of the sound stages for a crowd of about seventy-five who had worked on the show.

Wicked City – Another Name for LA

Premiered October 27, 2015 on ABC Tuesdays at 10:00 pm

Premise: Combining elements of an anthology series and a mini-series, *Wicked City*, set in Los Angeles, explored the seamier side of life. Originally called *L.A. Crime,* the series was to be a crime procedural involving sex, politics, and popular culture with each continuing story line set in a different era of Los Angeles history.

Cast of Characters:

Jack Roth (Jeremy Sisto) and Paco Contreras (Gabriel Luna) – two detectives investigating a serial murderer known as the Sunset Strip Killer who kills single women and subsequently has sex with them;
Kent Grainger (Ed Westwick) - the murderer, who works as a car upholsterer;
Allison Roth (Jaime Ray Newman) - Jack's wife;
Vicki Roth (Anne Winters) – Jack's daughter.

Background: Steven Baigelman created the series for ABC. Baigelman liked the idea of setting the initial story arc in 1982 Los Angeles since it was the Mecca where people came to seek fame and fortune, and, at the time, it was also the serial killer capital of the country. Baigelman indicated that was because such killers were also seeking fame in LA.[20]

Wicked City was initially intended to be scheduled at midseason on ABC. However, its debut was moved up to October when ABC pulled another drama, *Of Kings and Prophets*, from its fall schedule. *Wicked City* was slotted on Tuesdays up against *Chicago Fire* on NBC and *Limitless* on CBS.

The Pilot - October 27, 2015

Kent Grainger assumes various names and disguises to pick up women on the Sunset Strip. Karen McClaren (Taissa Farmiga), an aspiring journalist, encounters Kent using the alias "John" at the Whiskey a Go Go and gives him her phone number after he says he can help her career. He then picks up Emily Fuentes, dedicates a song to her on the radio, kills her in his car, decapitates her, and dumps the body. Detective Roth and his new partner Paco Contreras investigate the murder. After Roth holds a press conference falsely announcing that the police have captured the killer but won't release any information about the suspect in order to keep him from becoming infamous, Grainger sends Roth a clue on where Emily's head can be found. The next night, Kent meets Betty Beaumontaine, a nurse, but doesn't murder her after he discovers she is a single mother. Based on what Karen tells Roth about seeing the murder victim at the club, he goes to the Whiskey a Go Go undercover thinking that Kent's next victim may be the reporter, but Roth loses Karen in the crowd.

Other Episodes Broadcast

"Running with the Devil" - November 3, 2015

Kent picks up Betty and another girl named Mallory. With Kent's encouragement, Betty, Mallory, and he engage in a threesome. After Kent and Betty fall asleep, Mallory leaves. Kent goes looking for Mallory and visits her apartment where he meets her male roommate. When Kent later calls her apartment, the police are there to trace the call. Meanwhile, the detectives have Karen provide a sketch artist with a description of the man she thinks is the murderer. The police circulate the sketch around the city including the hospital where Betty works. Based on the location of the phone booth from which the call was made to Mallory's apartment and the autopsy findings for Emily showing upholstery foam in the corpse, Roth goes to an abandoned upholstery warehouse, finds a body underneath the floor boards, and concludes that Kent led him there. Karen receives a note from Kent asking if she "wants to play." Kent finally locates Mallory, binds and gags her, places her in the trunk of his car and shows Betty. As Betty watches, Kent stabs Mallory to death.

"Should I Stay or Should I Go?" - November 10, 2015

Betty needs time to digest what she saw Kent do to Mallory. In the meantime, the police identify the corpse found in the abandoned warehouse as Vera Bennett, a librarian, missing since 1968. Karen shows Roth the message she received from Kent about locating a book, *The Phantom of the Opera*, in the library where Vera Bennett had worked. On the library shelf where the book is supposed to be, the police find a locker containing Mallory's head. The detectives get a description of "Cooper," a boy who used to hang around Vera. Kent tells Betty that he has been waiting his whole life for her, and, after reading *The Phantom*, she says that she now understands and wants him. Karen finds another note under her door and calls Roth to say she knows where Mallory's body is. In the end, Kent and Betty are looking for another victim.

Unaired Episodes

"The Very Thought of You"

The detectives learn that Kent's mother, who wanted to be a movie star, died of a drug overdose when he was ten-years old. They believe the motives for his murders are related to his upbringing and her abandonment of him.

The police also find that Kent's victims were all given cocaine. They plan to contact the guy who sells the particular type of cocaine found in the victims. When they do, the dealer puts them in touch with a prostitute who slept with Grainger. She tells the detectives that Grainger made her pretend to be dead when he had sex with her.

Betty and Kent find another potential victim at a party and invite her to Kent's apartment to take photos of her. They drug the woman, and both Betty and Kent stab her to death.

Roth deduces that all the murder victims are similar to Kent's mother in that they all aspired to be famous. Among the mother's possessions, Roth finds film of Kent as a young boy.

"Heat Wave"

Roth gives Kent's photo as a young boy to Karen at the tabloid, *LA Notorious* to craft a story about the serial killer. Kent encounters Betty's ex, Jimmy at her apartment. Jimmy writes down the license number of Kent's vehicle believing he is a drug dealer and tells Betty that he gave the information to his cousin, a LA cop. Jimmy forces her to have sex with him threatening that her children will be taken away. While she is having sex with Jimmy, she pulls out a knife given to her by Kent. Stabbing Jimmy several times, she kills him and informs Kent who is disappointed that she did not ask him to help with the murder.

After reading the article in *LA Notorious*, Kent breaks into Karen's apartment at night. She can't see his face in the darkness but asks him for an interview during which he reveals another murder victim named Natasha. Also, a reader of the article in the tabloid tells the detectives that she went to school with Kent whom she knew as Cooper Flynn.

The detectives deduce that Kent works for a car restoration company and track down his employer.

"Blizzard of Oz"

The police sift through the material related to Kent found at his place of employment. Roth holds a news conference revealing Kent's identity. A little girl who Kent was babysitting calls police with his address, but it takes time for the detectives to determine the exact location.

Meanwhile, Kent, knowing that he has been identified as the Hollywood slayer, meets Betty in the hospital morgue. They have sex on an empty table with Betty pretending that she is dead. Kent cuts his hair and dyes it blond and attempts to obtain a false ID. Betty impersonates a door-to-door makeup salesperson and visits Roth's wife. Before leaving, she takes a family photo and a key to the house. Knowing the police have located his residence, Kent turns on the gas and splashes gasoline around. As the police arrive, the house explodes. A body, burned beyond recognition, is found. The news media report that it is the Hollywood slayer, but the body is really that of Betty's ex – Jimmy.

"Destroyer"

The detectives learn that the burned body was not that of the serial killer. Both Jack and his daughter receive photos of his affair with Diane, a drug dealer that he used as a confidential informant. Jack reveals his affair to his wife and explains that she and their daughter may be targets of the Hollywood slayer. While Kent is hiding in her apartment, Diane informs Det. Paco that she is really an undercover cop. Later, Kent informs Karen of this who debates doing a story about Jack and Diane. Wearing eyeglasses and with a new hairstyle, Kent meets Jack at a club on the Strip.

"Goodbye Norma Jean"

Kent tells Jack that he is not the Hollywood slayer. After being arrested, Paco and Roth are told they do not have enough evidence on Grainger for him to be indicted. The detectives are given twenty-four hours to come up with more evidence. In jail, Kent makes his one phone call to Betty as a signal to her to kill Karen and make it look like the Hollywood slayer committed the act. Kent puts on an award-winning performance acting as innocent while being interrogated by Roth. Kent says the real killer is Dave, his co-worker. The police discover Karen's decapitated body and later her head.

Since the murder occurred while Kent was in custody, he is released. Jack theorizes that Kent has a partner.

Six months pass with no subsequent murders by the Hollywood slayer. However, police have identified Kent's accomplice. Betty, who is pregnant, and Kent are now living in Chicago with her kids with Kent on the lookout for more victims.

Postscript: After the third episode, ABC canceled the show. Ten episodes were to be produced for the series' first season, but, when it was canceled, only eight episodes had been completed.

CHAPTER 3

Medical Dramas

The Lazarus Syndrome: A Fallible Cardiologist
Premiered September 4, 1979 on ABC Tuesday at 10:00 pm

Premise: The "Lazarus syndrome" refers to patients who think that doctors are God-like decision makers. This series focused on the head of a cardiology department at a large hospital and his patients.

Cast of Characters:
> Dr. MacArthur St. Clair (Louis Gossett, Jr.) - an African-American Chief of Cardiology at Webster Memorial Hospital;
> Joe Hamill (Ronald Hunter) - a former newspaper reporter and now the idealistic hospital administrator who helped Mac battle the hospital's bureaucracy;
> Sheila Frazier - Mac's wife Gloria to whom he has been married for fifteen years although, for the past three years, they have had a rocky relationship.

Background: William Blinn created the series. He remarked,

> The overall premise of "Lazarus" was a reaction to the all-knowing medics of the day – "Ben Casey," "Dr. Kildare," "Konrad Atyner" of "Medic." It struck me that there was an alternate path to follow in TV storytelling, where the layman was also represented and where the doctor's efforts were even more admirable as a result of his human fallibility. I ran it past my partner, Jerry Thorpe, who agreed with the point. We took the notion to ABC-TV, who agreed with the viewpoint and I then wrote the pilot.[21]

Blinn indicated that Lou Gossett was cast in the lead based on Mr. Blinn's work with him as a guest star on *The New Land* and *The Rookies*. Ron

Hunter received the role of Joe Hamill after meeting on the East Coast with numerous casting directors. Hunter was ". . . low key and straight forward, reminded me of a young Spencer Tracy," according to Blinn.[22]

Talking about the series, Ron Hunter pointed out how it differed from other medical shows. "'The Lazarus Syndrome' will not be a race against death every week. We'll be dealing with such issues as the high cost of medical care (or survival, whichever you choose to call it) and the regulations and restrictions that demand medical costs continue to escalate. . . There are no black and white areas in the medical profession, but there are sure many gray ones . . ."[23]

The Pilot - September 4, 1979

After playing tennis with his mistress, thirty-eight-year-old Joe Hamill feels nauseous with pain down his left arm. He calls Dr. St. Clair who instructs him to hurry to the emergency room at Webster Memorial Hospital. Hamill goes into cardiac arrest and is admitted. He wants to make sure that the doctor arranges a schedule of visits to his room so that his mistress and wife do not meet each other. Eventually, he informs his wife he wants a divorce to marry his mistress. St. Clair tells Hamill that he doesn't need bypass surgery – just exercise and a change to his diet. Hamill advises his fellow patient Mr. Dominguez, who has similar heart problems, that he thinks his doctor – Dr. Mendel, the head of the hospital, should not have suggested bypass surgery for him. When Mendel learns of this, he calls St. Clair on the carpet and has him review his patient's angiogram. St. Clair views the reports and agrees that Dr. Mendel is correct. However, St. Clair still feels that there is something else wrong with the diagnosis. As Dominguez undergoes surgery, St. Clair realizes that the angiogram he reviewed was not for Dominguez but that of another patient since Dominguez had some ribs removed after an earlier accident. St. Clair has Dr. Mendel stop the surgery. Mendel confesses that he was performing the unneeded surgery for the monetary return. Mendel resigns from the hospital. St. Clair asks Hamill to be the new hospital administrator given his experience as a patient at the facility.

Other Episodes Broadcast

"A Brutal Assault" (aka "Pamela Quinn) - September 11, 1979

Pamela Quinn (Olivia Cole), a nurse at Webster Memorial with whom Mac once had an affair, is raped in the hospital's parking garage. Gloria becomes aware that Mac had a more-than-professional relationship with Pamela who has been working for him for the past three years. Pamela has come to depend on Mac so much for emotional support during the period after the assault that she refuses to identify her assailant.

"The Lady in 534"- September 18, 1979

Joe Hamill's ex-wife Virginia (Peggy Walton-Walker) has surgery in the hospital but has difficulty breathing. She has to be given emergency oxygen. Joe wants her put on a respirator which isn't available at the hospital. The nearest facility with such equipment is 500 miles away, and the doctors cannot guarantee that they can supply oxygen for such a long journey.

"Peace and Love, Willie Jackson" (aka "The All-American") - September 25, 1979

Willie Jackson (Harold Sylvester), a college basketball star, has his career cut short because of a knee injury. When Mac and Joe discover that Willie is functionally illiterate, they lead a furious attack against the school officials who allowed Willie to sacrifice his studies for basketball. Hamill finds a job for him as an advisor to the university.

"Malpractice"- October 2, 1979

Mac volunteers to operate on the wife of a hospital employee whose left hand becomes paralyzed by a stroke during the surgery. Her husband sues Mac for $4 million. The hospital wants Mac to settle out-of-court which he doesn't want to do knowing that with therapy the woman will regain full use of her hand.

"The Carpenter"- October 9, 1979

One of the doctors at the hospital allows a layman to perform surgery on a patient. The operation is a success, but the D.A.'s office places the hospital under scrutiny and a newspaper does an expose about the incident.

Unaired Episodes

"The Chaplain"

The chaplain at Webster Memorial convinces some patients that "medicine does not cure" and that faith alone can heal. This causes a cancer patient to refuse an operation much to Mac's dismay.

"Intern"

Dr. Ralph's wife Barbara contracts a venereal disease and tries to keep it a secret. She tells Mac's wife that a friend of hers has VD and wants to consult a good physician. Gloria refers her to Dr. Allison Tyler, a young intern at the hospital. Barbara lies to the doctor saying that her friend cannot make the trip to see her and asks the doctor to give her the prescription of penicillin. Barbara takes the drug and nearly dies from an allergic reaction. Her husband threatens to sue the intern.

"The Bumblebee Can't Fly"
Judge Peter Kusic, who is presiding over a controversial case, suffers a stroke and is rushed to Webster Memorial. Mac prepares for emergency surgery. During the operation, the judge's heart stops before Mac manages to revive him. Upon recovery, the judge talks about having an out-of-body experience where he left his body and could see the doctors operating on him. Because of this, his superiors think that he is no longer fit to preside from the bench.

"Price of Life"
Peter Duel plays a young man threatened by kidney failure. Kidney dialysis was a relatively new option at the time. A committee of doctors and ministers decides who would receive treatment and who would not. Duel's character is denied treatment. He breaks into the hospital and steals one of the machines knowing that he will be caught and sent to prison where the state will be obligated to take care of his medical needs. However, during the trial, the judge rules that, since this is his first offense, he is placed on probation instead of going to prison which, in reality, is a death sentence for him.

Postscript: ABC placed the series on "indefinite hiatus" after the October 9th episode. Lou Gossett Jr. remarked that "The show didn't have enough action or focus. Also, they overworked us, and the energy was gone, I know mine was." [24] According to Blinn, he believes that the network was quick to cancel the series since neither lead character "hit as (a) romantic or dangerous leading man. John Wayne has one sort of impact; Don DeFore has another."[25] Apparently, there was an attempt to later revive the series without Ron Hunter but with Lou Gossett as an inner city surgeon in charge of a cash-strapped medical facility but nothing came of that attempt.

Wonderland – Altered States of Mind

Premiered March 30, 2000 on ABC Thursdays at 10:00 pm

Premise: Doctors of psychiatry deal with the criminally insane as well as their own personal lives in this medical drama. The doctors are almost as tormented as their patients.

Cast of Characters:

>Dr. Robert Banger (Ted Levine) - the chief of forensic psychiatry at New York's Rivervue Psychiatric Hospital, who is fighting for joint custody of his two sons – Mick and Tucker;

Dr. Neil Harrison (Martin Donovan) - married to Dr. Lyla Garrity (Michelle Forbes) who is pregnant;
Dr. Abe Matthews (Billy Burke) - a commitment phobic womanizer who is in analysis;
Dr. Derrick Hatcher (Michael Jai White) - a single parent living with his daughter and father and working in the ER who is responsible for training the hospital's young medical students;
Dr. Heather Miles (Joelle Carter) - a second-year resident.

Background: The series, created by Peter Berg, titled *Bellevue* originally, was produced by Hostage Productions in association with Imagine Television and Touchstone Productions. The show focuses on two departments at Rivervue – Forensics, a maximum security prison for psychiatric criminals, and CPEP (Comprehensive Psychiatric Emergency Program), an emergency room for psychiatric patients. Berg's mother worked at a psychiatric hospital in New York and related stories of her experiences which inspired him to create *Wonderland*.

The Pilot - March 30, 2000

After Wendell Rickle opens fire with a handgun in Times Square killing five people, he is apprehended by police and brought to Rivervue. The DA's office wants Rickle transferred to Rikers as soon as possible. A pregnant Garrity recognizes Rickle as a person she had treated previously but didn't admit to the hospital. Rickle finds a used syringe and stabs himself repeatedly. The police tackle him and, in the mêlée, they overturn his gurney with Garrity caught underneath and the syringe sticking in her waist. An ultrasound reveals that the needle made contact with her fetus' brain. Upon learning of this, her husband Neil goes to Rickle's room and attempts to choke him. Garrity and Harrison are told that there is a probability that their baby will be born with some neurological handicap. However, Lyla still wants to have the baby. While at a hearing to determine if he or his ex-wife receives full custody of their sons, Banger receives an emergency call and has Rickle admitted to judge his mental competency.

Other Episode Broadcast

"20/20 Hindsight"- April 6, 2000

Rickle's lawyer does not want him to take his medications so he can be ruled unfit for trial. However, a judge orders Rickle to be medicated. Garrity faces a review board over her failure to admit Rickle when he first came to the hospital. She explains that Rickle exhibited no signs of violence when she first saw him and wasn't a threat in her professional opinion. Miles and Matthews see an elderly woman who hears voices telling her to kill her husband who ignores her after fifty years of marriage. Both the husband and wife are interviewed. When the husband begins to disrobe in the hospital thinking he is going swimming, Matthews believes that he may be the one with mental issues. In the end, Rickles, on medication, commits suicide in his cell.

Unaired Episodes

"Spell Check"

Abe sleeps with Heather who is disgusted that she got drunk and had sex with him. A man named Johnny jumps off the 59th Street Bridge on his birthday. Garrity has treated him before since he has done this previously on his birthday. She has his daughter convince him to seek electro-shock treatments for his manic depression. Dr. Hatcher's daughter participates in a spelling bee, while he works in the ER treating two day-traders who were beaten up at work. He is not able to save one of the men and has to tell the father that his son has died. Bangor and Harrison evaluate an inmate from Riker's who bit off his mother's finger and ate it. The inmate says that his mother brings out the anger in him right before he explodes in a fit of rage.

"Full Moon"

Hatcher treats a man whose wife cut off his foot because he wants to be thought of as a war hero when he runs for political office. He says he will cut the foot off again if the doctors re-attach it. A judge orders the doctors to re-attach the foot, but it goes missing from the operating room. As staff search the hospital from "head to toe," the man's wife, who hid the foot in her bag, dumps it in the trash outside the hospital. Meanwhile, Banger meets with Tammy concerning custody of their sons. She wants sole custody, and they argue about it at a restaurant. Without looking and thinking it is aspirin, Abe takes some pills that cause hallucinations and make him act erratically when visiting his mother.

"The Rare and the Cooked"

Abe treats comedian Charles Fisher who has bi-polar disorder but won't take medication because he feels it interferes with his performance. Abe releases him against medical advice. Hatcher examines a woman who ate the leaves of a ficus plant and suffered nausea. Her dietary habits have changed recently, and she has increased sexual urges. Garrity evaluates her thinking she has an underlying organic condition and not a mental problem. The woman is diagnosed with Pick's disease which is somewhat like Alzheimer's and for which there is no cure. Tammy is upset with her soon-to-be-ex-husband that he hasn't told his mother they are getting a divorce. He finds that his mother already knows. At the end, Tammy and Banger make love.

"Wilt Chamberlain 3.0"
Abe meets with his analyst about his sex addiction. Meanwhile, Banger receives his final divorce papers and wonders why Tammy signed them despite the fact that they just made love. She explains that she signed them before their tryst. Frustrated, Banger signs them as well. Banger evaluates a man who cuts himself. The man has to decide whether to take a plea bargain for a robbery he committed or go to trial. After treating a young man who had been tortured in Kosovo for trying to protect his mother and sister from the Serb army, Abe finds that both the mother and sister had been raped and that the young girl has gonorrhea as a result. Heather is injured in an automobile accident and has to undergo brain surgery.

"Personality Plus" (aka "The Bottle Show Plus One Small Exterior")
Banger has five hours to get a patient, Alfred Parker, a man with multiple personality disorder, to reveal where he hid his four-year-old son who he kidnapped from his ex-wife. The boy has diabetes and needs insulin. The doctor discovers that Parker was sexually abused as a child by his mother which caused the personality disorder. With time running out, Banger administers amytal to attempt to obtain the truth from Parker, but the patient passes out. However, from different things Parker revealed during the questioning, Banger figures out that the boy is at a hotel with a view of the Statue of Liberty. Paramedics arrive just in time. Meanwhile, Tammy Banger phones her ex-husband to say she is pregnant.

"Hello/Goodbye"
When Heather returns to work, Abe wants to take her to lunch, but she resists. Banger and Harrison deal with a man who hired someone to kill his male lover because he heard voices telling him that his partner poisoned him. The doctors decide to administer truth serum to see if the patient is faking his condition since he has no history of mental problems. After the injection, the patient continues to say he hears voices. Banger and Harrison conclude the man is faking his condition since he wasn't really given truth serum – just a saline solution. The man then confesses to Harrison that he killed his lover because he was "a leech." Tammy goes for an abortion but decides against it because she might reconcile with her ex-husband. While visiting a mental facility outside the hospital with Abe, Lila goes into pre-

mature labor. Abe delivers a healthy baby boy, but Lila loses a lot of blood and goes into a coma.

Postscript: ABC slotted the series after its hit game show, *Who Wants to be a Millionaire?* and up against the medical drama *ER* on NBC. In its first outing against an *ER* rerun, it came in second in the ratings with 13 million viewers. However, the second episode lost about half its initial audience up against a new episode of *ER*, and so ABC quickly removed it from the schedule.

Inconceivable – Missed Conceptions
Premiered September 23, 2005 on NBC Friday at 10:00 pm

Premise: Probably the only series with opening graphics showing spermatozoa impregnating an egg, *Inconceivable* dealt with the professional and personal experiences of doctors working in a fertility clinic.

Cast of Characters:

> Rachel Lu (Ming-Na) - one of the founders of the Family Options Fertility Clinic who has a seven-year-old son Noah conceived through artificial insemination;
> Dr. Malcolm Bowers (Jonathan Cake) - the other founder of the clinic, a smug doctor from Britain;
> Dr. Nora Campbell (Angie Harmon) - Bowers' former girlfriend who became a partner in the clinic;
> Patrice Locicero (Joelle Carter) - a nurse on staff and Bowers' current girlfriend;
> Marissa Jaffee (Mary Catherine Garrison) - the office manager;
> Angel Hernandez (Reynaldo Rosales) - a medical technician;
> Lydia Crawford (Alfre Woodward) - a psychologist on staff who is best friends with Rachel, and Scott Kleckner (David Norona), the clinic's lawyer.

Background: The series was created by Oliver Goldstick and Marco Pennette and produced by Touchstone Television and TRP (Tollins/Robbins) Productions. Pennette recalls that the idea for the series came about when he and his partner were trying to start a family.

> We were in the waiting room of the fertility doctor and it was my partner, Steve, who nudged me and told me to look around the

Profiles of Fifty Offbeat Comedies and Dramas, Unsold Pilots, and Unaired Series • 55

The cast of *Inconceivable* from left to right: Joelle Carter, Reynaldo Rosales, Angie Harmon, Ming-Na, Jonathan Cake, David Norona, and Mary Catherine Garrison.

room. There was an older couple, a young couple, single people, gay, straight – it seemed as if fertility issues were touching everyone in some way. I instantly thought it was a series. . ... NBC snatched the pitch up immediately. We shot the pilot and turned it in. The network then asked for sample storylines. We obliged. They then asked for more. We started getting the feeling they were nervous about the show – did it have "legs?" But we were pleasantly surprised when they picked it up for the fall 2005 season.[26]

The Pilot - September 23, 2005

Four cases are highlighted in the series opener. In one case, Dan and Adrienne Lindstrom are having a baby via surrogate. They are both white, but the baby turns out to be African-American. The clinic finds that Tammy, the surrogate, had unprotected sex before the transfer of the fertilized eggs, and so the baby is hers but she doesn't want it. Dan wants to sue the clinic for choosing Tammy as their surrogate. Bowers wants to terminate Lydia since she selected Tammy as the surrogate.

The second case deals with Pvt. Greg Lopez whose wife Kelly, also in the military, was killed in Iraq. She had eggs frozen before her call to active duty, and now the husband wants the eggs inseminated and implanted into his wife's sister. After counseling from Rachel, who says that this will not bring back his wife, Lopez decides against the procedure.

In another case, Scott and his partner Jim are having a baby with a surrogate. Jim keeps stalking the surrogate to make sure she is leading a healthy lifestyle. The surrogate goes into labor early and gives birth to a baby girl.

In the final case, Ellen and Tom Gilley, the latter a minister, want to conceive but are having problems. She expresses a desire to use someone else's sperm without her husband knowing. Patrice secretly switches Gilley's sperm with a sample she took from Bowers.

Other Episode Broadcast

"Secrets and Thighs"- September 30, 2005

A young couple wants to have a baby via surrogate. After a blood test shows that the wife is on the pill, she says that she was an ugly child but after plastic surgery, became beautiful and doesn't want a child conceived by her to go through the bullying she experienced because of her looks. After Lydia shows the husband a video of how his wife used to look, he decides to talk things over with her. In another case, Dave and Suzanne, friends of Rachel, want to have a baby by surrogate, but the surrogate has to leave town to take care of her sick mother. Frustrated by the process, Suzanne says she doesn't want to have a baby. Rachel tells her friends that she found another surrogate – herself, and they agree to proceed with having Rachel be the mother.

Dr. Campbell comes to the clinic to do a non-FDA-approved procedure on Mrs. Gilley involving egg transfusion. When Mrs. Gilley drops off her consent form, Scott thinks she forged her husband's signature on the form. Mr. Lindstrom is still suing the clinic over the issue of the surrogate's African-American baby. He wants to close the clinic but settles for monetary damages after Dr. Campbell gives Bowers and Rachel a check for the settlement so they do not need to use the insurance the clinic has. In return for the check, she wants to become a partner in the clinic and rekindle her relationship with Dr. Bowers. In the end, Mr. Lindstrom stops by the clinic and tells Lydia that his wife left him. He blames the clinic for destroying his marriage. When leaving the clinic, Lydia is run down by Lindstrom and dies.

The character of Lydia was killed off early in the series because the actress Alfie Woodward was obligated to go back to *Desperate Housewives*. ABC was not going to permit her to also star on an NBC series.

Unaired Episodes

"To Surrogate with Love"

Four weeks after Lydia's untimely demise, Nora moves into her office at the clinic and clashes with Bowers over medical advice and procedures. A surrogate pregnant for twenty-six weeks has been diagnosed with cervical cancer. Her husband wants her to have a C-section right away. The Bridges, who will be the parents of the baby, want her to wait for two weeks before having the C-section so the baby's lungs have a chance to further develop. Bowers does not have a major problem with the surrogate having a C-section now. Nora talks with the Bridges when Bowers is at lunch and advises them to persuade the surrogate to wait. They do. In another case, Nora is seeing a patient who is to have fertilized eggs implanted. Nora wants to implant five eggs, but clinic policy is that no more than four eggs should be implanted. Bowers intervenes in the case. He and Nora have words. The patient ends up receiving four eggs and becomes pregnant. In other matters, Patrice continues to receive emails from someone whom she thinks saw her switch specimens in the Gilley case. She finds that the person is Angel. She goes to his place, starts to have sex with him, but then learns that he didn't see her switch specimens. He thinks she stole files. She quickly ends the love-making session. Rachel undergoes the implant procedure to be a surrogate for her friends – Suzanne and Dave.

Ming Na Wen who played Rachel was pregnant in real life, and so the producers worked her pregnancy into the series. The producers had to deal with her missing a few episodes. They hired Angie Harmon to play another female doctor whose character was introduced in the second episode.

"Balls in Your Court"
When nineteen-year-old Devon Brown, a popular basketball player, dies suddenly, his agent, who is his legal guardian, wants his sperm harvested to fertilize an egg from a donor to produce another superstar. Dr. Campbell promises to find an egg donor from the WBA. Word leaks to the press about the plans for Brown's sperm which creates a media controversy and a flood of females volunteering to be donors. Devon's biological father shows up at the clinic with a high-priced lawyer financed by a family values group who is against the idea of using the player's sperm to produce a baby. The guardian ultimately decides not to fight the court order to have the sperm destroyed. Meanwhile, Patrice is taking drugs from the clinic's pharmacy because she is so upset about the impending Gilley transfer. She attempts to destroy the eggs impregnated with Bowers' sperm but is not successful. Dr. Campbell completes the Gilley transfer.

"Sex, Lies and Sonograms"
Bowers clashes with clinic staff over his refusal to help a single woman in her forties conceive before she is imprisoned. Rachel finds that she is having twins. Patrice tells Bowers that he is the father of Mrs. Gilley's baby.

"Face Your Demon, Semen"
The clinic is having its annual Halloween party. Bowers beds Sophia, a classical musician, and performs surgery on her to unblock her fallopian tubes so she can conceive. Scott recognizes Dennis, the husband of a clinic patient, as someone he dated in college. Dennis at first refuses to recognize him, but later tells him that in college he was just going through a phase and now wants to be "normal." This makes Scott want to be more open about his sexual orientation. Patrice threatens to inform everyone about what she did which could ruin Bowers' career. Later, Bowers is notified that Mrs. Gilley had a miscarriage with her body rejecting the embryo. Rachel is concerned that Suzanne feels resentful that she is having their babies. Suzanne doesn't show up for Rachel's sonogram. Dave views the sonogram with Rachel, and they kiss.

"The Last Straw"

Nora is made aware of what Patrice did in the Gilley case. She decides to separate her from Bowers by giving Patrice a promotion to work on insurance claims. Later, when Nora catches Patrice about to send a letter to the Gilley's about Bowers, she fires her. Patrice overdoses in the clinic's restroom and is taken to the hospital to have her stomach pumped. Danny and Patricia Santos want to have Patricia's embryos unfrozen so they can start a family to hopefully save their marriage. Nora and Rachel advise them that trying to mend their relationship by having a baby is not a good idea. Since Patricia's embryos have already been unfrozen and can't be refrozen, Patricia decides to donate them to a couple who have run out of their own embryos.

"Between an Egg and a Hard Place"

No surrogate is interested in carrying a baby for a single straight white male named Phil who thinks that becoming a father is the most important thing he can do. After Marissa goes out with him for lunch, he thinks she wants to be his surrogate which gets their relationship off to a very rocky start. Keily, the nine-year-old daughter of a couple conceived by having another woman's egg transferred to the mother, needs a bone marrow transplant. Bowers finds who the egg donor was despite the confidentially agreement in place and asks the donor if she will volunteer for the transplant. The woman, Claire Romano, agrees, but Bowers discovers that she suffers from bi-polar disorder. When Claire wants to meet Keily, the mother objects. Bowers takes Claire to meet the parents and the daughter for lunch. After Claire becomes upset when the waitress doesn't serve specifically what Keily requested, the parents and daughter quickly leave the restaurant. Ultimately, Claire does donate her bone marrow to Keily. In other matters, the terminated Patrice, who is now in rehab, refuses to sign her severance agreement.

"From Here to Motility"
    Story line unknown

"If You Prick Us, Do We Not Breed?"
    Story line unknown

Postscript: As Marco Pennette stated,

> Unfortunately, the show was a ratings disaster. No matter how much we believed there was (an) audience for this, they just didn't show up. . . NBC pulled the plug after two episodes. Years later when

Steve and I went back to see our fertility doctor to have our second child, the doctor himself offered some insight as to why the show might have failed. He explained, "You and Steve came here because this was your only way to have a biological child. This was a place of joy and hope. But for a majority of those people in that waiting room, coming here represents failure, desperation, sadness, a last chance to become a family. Who wants to watch a show that reminds them of that?"[27]

CHAPTER 4

Anti-Hero Dramas

Profit – What Can Happen When One Watches Too Much TV

Premiered April 8, 1996 on Fox Monday at 9:00 pm

Premise: This show followed the exploits of a twenty-eight-year-old ambitious but psychopathic executive who would do anything to get ahead at Gracen & Gracen, a multinational conglomerate.

Cast of Characters:

Jim Profit (Adrian Pasdar) - whose real name was Danny Stokowski, had been raised by an abusive father and forced to live in a large packing box from Gracen & Gracen where he watched TV all the time through an opening cut in the side of the box. Apparently, much of what he knew, he learned by viewing television. Using his computer expertise and his talent for manipulating people, Jim Profit usually came out ahead in his lust for power and control of situations. He still slept nude in a large box in his apartment;

Joanne Meltzer (Lisa Zane) – Gracen & Gracen's head of security and Profit's archenemy;

Charles Henry "Chaz" Gracen (Keith Szarabajka) – the son of the original founder and now the corporation's CEO whose only love is making money;

Pete Gracen (Jack Gwaltney) – Chaz's younger brother, the Senior Vice President of Acquisitions, an alcoholic who is married to Nora (Allison Hossack);

Gail Koner (Lisa Darr) – Profit's secretary who helps him with his schemes;

Adrian Pasdar as Jim Profit.

Bobbi Stakowski (Lisa Blount) – Profit's stepmother and sometimes lover who attempts to blackmail her stepson with threats of exposing his true identity;

Jeffrey Sykes (Sherman Augustus) – the corporation's Vice President of Business Affairs who is allied with Meltzer;

Elizabeth (Jennifer Hetrick) – the Gracen's cousin, is married to the current President of Acquisitions for the company, Jack Walters (Scott Paulin).

Background: As writer John McNamara related about the creation of this series,

> ... I sat down with David Greenwalt one day in 1992, and we very naively said to each other, "If we were ever going to do a TV series of our own (and neither of us had worked on a TV series at that point), what would we do?" And we basically concocted an idea, which ultimately became *Profit*. The idea was, what would happen if the most morally bankrupt person who ever lived came into a corporation? The answer to that question was, if he made money, he would eventually take over and become one of the most heralded men of his century, because that's the nature of corporations.[28]

Kim LeMasters, the president of Stephen Cannell productions loved the concept and Bob Greenblatt, head of programming for Fox at the time, bought the series. The pilot was produced in 1995, and the series went on the air in 1996.

The Pilot - April 8, 1996

When the Junior Vice President of Acquisitions for Gracen & Gracen suddenly dies of a heart attack, Jim Profit is named as his replacement. He had previously worked as an auditor for the company and found that Gail Koner, secretary to his new boss, Jack Walters, has embezzled money from the company to take care of her mother suffering from MS. Jim uses this information to blackmail her into giving him access to Jack's computer files. Jim finds sensitive information about the company's latest acquisition of a baby food company. The company had decided to use sugar water instead of real juice in the baby food company's apple juice product because it is cheaper. He leaks this information to the press and follows this up by having Gail forge a memo to Jack from Charles instructing him to tell the press the truth. After Jack is fired, Jim thinks he has a clear path to take over Jack's position. However, Joanne Meltzer, head of the firm's security operations and Jack's former paramour, comes in to investigate the whole matter. Under pressure from Profit, Gail lies about who made her fake the memo to Jack about informing the press, and another corporate officer, Mary Miller, whom Gail says wanted Jack's job, takes the blame for the deed. Her contract is not renewed. Jack is reinstated as head of the division, and Gail becomes Jim's new secretary. Joanne and Jack continue to investigate Jim's background. Meanwhile, Jim's stepmother Bobbi Stokowski comes to town to tell him that his father is still alive in a nursing home and blackmails him so she won't inform the police that he had handcuffed his father to a bed and set it on fire. Joanne and Jack find an old newspaper article about the incident and trail Jim to a nursing home where, using company resources, he has located his dad. Masquerading as an orderly, Jim gives his father a lethal dose of potassium to make it appear he has had a heart attack. He tells Bobbi that if she has an autopsy performed on the body, he will make it look like she gave her husband the overdose. In the end, Jack informs Jim that he was at the hospital when his father died seemingly under the same circumstances as Jim's predecessor Wayne Graham.

Other Episodes Broadcast

"Hero"- April 15, 1996

Jack and Joanne fly to Oklahoma to delve deeper into Jim's background when he was known as Danny Stokowski and raised in a Gracen & Gracen box. From Jim's computer, Jack retrieves files including one that Jim planted showing that he killed his predecessor by giving him a heart-stopping drug. The body of the former Junior VP is exhumed. Profit breaks into the morgue where the body is being held to add traces of the heart-stopping drug since his predecessor really did have a heart attack. He wants Jack and Joanne to think that he has been selling the drug to terrorists and depositing the money into an offshore account. Jack and Joanne take their "evidence" to the police. Jim develops a relationship with Jack's wife. He plants some of the medication at Jack's home and creates an offshore account for Jack. After Elizabeth Walters discovers the planted drug, Jack is arrested for murdering Wayne Graham. Jack pleads guilty to the murder thinking that, after more evidence is found against Jim, he will appeal his sentence.

"Sykes"- April 22, 1996

Attorney Jeffrey Sykes joins Gracen & Gracen. The corporation seeks to purchase a garbage company, Waste-Not Garbage, headed by mobster, Ivan Karpov. The company launders money for Karpov's drug business. Profit threatens to bring in the IRS for an audit if Karpov doesn't sell it to Gracen. Sykes is surprised when Profit doesn't come to him about the money laundering issue. Sykes is secretly investigating Karpov because Karpov had Sykes' best friend murdered. He is able to obtain the company's financial records and contacts the FBI who indicate that they can do nothing unless the records are in Karpov's possession. Profit threatens Sykes' girlfriend to get the records back from him. When Profit hands the files back to Karpov, Karpov is arrested.

"Healing"- April 29, 1996

Pete Gracen wants both Profit and Meltzer to take lie detector tests to resolve the allegations the latter has lodged against Profit. After bugging his office, Profit extorts Joanne's psychiatrist, Dr. Grant, who has been sleeping with his patients, to hypnotize Meltzer so that she obsesses about Profit. She stops eating and sleeping and is eventually committed to a mental institution. Profit goes to the hospital and has her released. He has her doctor arrested based on the information Profit had on him. The doctor shows up at Meltzer's apartment to reveal what Profit forced him to do to her. With carpet tacks in his shoe to mask his physical reaction to the lie detector test, Profit passes the test as does Meltzer. Gracen keeps both employed.

Unaired Episodes

"Cupid"

Gracen & Gracen seeks to buy up yet another company. This one is Dynamite, a chain of nightclubs owned by Anna and Ray Castrial. Each owns fifty percent of the chain, but the spouses are currently separated from one another. Anna is being terrorized by a man she believes is her husband. Ray won't sign the documents for the sale unless Anna reconciles with him. Profit and Sykes positions at Gracen are threatened unless the deal is consummated.

In the meantime, Bobbi is attempting to seduce Chaz Gracen into being her "sugar daddy." She hires a man to mug Chaz with her coming to his rescue. Subsequently, for the pain he received in the beating, she gives Chaz some of her drugs which cause him to have anxiety attacks and become dependent on her.

Profit arranges for Ray to meet with his wife and to save her from the man terrorizing her. Profit masquerades as that man. After the incident, Ray and Anna get back together and agree to sell their company. Profit offers $50,000 to the man Bobbi hired as a mugger if the man not only owns up to the attack on Chaz Gracen but also confesses that he is the person who had terrorized Anna. In the end, Sykes warns Anna that Ray may be plotting to kill her as he had done to his first wife. She leaves Ray again. Ray phones Chaz to inform him of what Sykes had done and then commits suicide.

"Chinese Box"

For a change, Gracen & Gracen wants to divest itself of a subsidiary instead of acquiring a new one. Wong Industries, a Gracen company, is selling missile parts to China, and the FBI is investigating. Chaz Gracen seeks divestiture of Wong Industries before the FBI interviews him. The head of the company will only agree to divestment if Profit gets him the rights to an "ultrachip" developed by Dr. Jeremy Batewell, a former Gracen employee who was terminated for sexual harassment of Profit's secretary, Gail Koner. Profit orders Gail to arrange a meeting with Batewell so she can steal the ultrachip which is universal code breaker software. He supplies Gail with a drug to render Batewell unconscious while she retrieves the chip. Because Batewell doesn't drink, Gail ends up knocking him unconscious. Using a walkie talkie Profit instructs her on how to steal the chip. She finds that the chip is not functional. Profit convinces the head of Wong Industries to kidnap Batewell himself instead of acquiring the chip. When Batewell comes to Profit's office to retrieve the chip, Profit divulges that he knows it doesn't work. He suggests Batewell sell the worthless chip to Mr. Wong. Gail takes Batewell to Wong Industries where he is kidnapped by Wong.

"Security"

Someone at Gracen is leaking negative information about the corporation to the news media. Profit advises Chaz Gracen that the leaker is Kelly Hunt, a member of the company's security team whose real name is Carol McKenna, a journalist. Profit is assigned to take her down while she wants to get the goods on Profit. He informs Kelly that he knows that she is a news reporter and proposes working with her to obtain secret files Chaz Gracen has about favors government officials did for the company. Profit wants Kelly to write a story that will destroy Chaz Gracen so that he can take over the company. However, she writes a feature profiling Profit's background and exposing him for the psycho he is. Her paper, however, refuses to publish the story and fires her since Profit threatens her editor concerning unreported gambling winnings to the IRS.

In the meantime, Bobbi seeks to break up Chaz's marriage to Constance by having an affair with her hoping that Constance will want to divorce him. Bobbi, of course, pursues the affair under an alias. She has

Constance document their affair in a diary which Bobbi gives to Profit who in turn makes sure Chaz reads it. Constance announces that she is leaving Chaz.

"Forgiveness"
Chaz learns of the planned takeover of Gracen by his brother and his brother's wife's Uncle Arthur. Profit advises Chaz to stop the takeover by involving Pete more in the company's decision-making process. Bobbi breaks off her affair with Chaz's wife, but continues one with Chaz himself.

Meltzer receives permission from Sykes to travel to Ireland to learn more about the man whose name is being used by Profit. Pete Gracen confronts Uncle Arthur about molesting his wife, Nora when she was twelve. Pete threatens to resign from the company, but Profit advises Chaz to reject his brother's resignation. To prevent a hostile takeover by Uncle Arthur and after learning of his severe allergic reaction to pesticides on strawberries, Profit kills Arthur by giving him inorganic strawberries.

High on drugs, Bobbi is involved in a car crash but survives. Profit gives her the choice of either marrying Chaz so Jim can gain control of Gracen & Gracen or dying with a needle in her veins. She chooses the former.

Postscript: The series premiere came in fourth behind shows on NBC, CBS, and ABC in the advertiser coveted 18-49 year old demographic. Reflecting on the demise of *Profit* at the time, Stephen Cannell said, "It needed a full year on the air or they never even should have tried it."[29] Bob Greenblatt from Fox indicated that, ". . . if given more time, it could have been an enormous hit show. . . within the company there was no upswing of support for it. Sales people were afraid of it because it was all too dark and immoral, and they were afraid of advertiser reaction. A lot of people on first blush, didn't get it."[30]

If the series had been renewed, the creators indicated that subsequent storylines would have involved Joanne Meltzer being killed by a terrorist bomb at the behest of Profit while she was in Ireland looking into the real Jim Profit's background. Other story lines would have revealed that Profit had stolen the identity of a "real" man who is in a coma after being drowned by Profit. Charles Garcen has a heart attack prompted by a mild poison Profit slipped into his water bottle. Profit convinces Garcen that his father is trying to kill him. Profit then is behind the death of the father so that Jim can tighten his control over the company. Pete Garcen eventually runs for elective office and becomes a U.S. Senator.

Viva Laughlin – Hugh Jackman's Musical Drama Project

Premiered October 18, 2007 on CBS at 10:00 pm before moving to its regular time slot on October 21, 2007 at 8:00 pm

Premise: Drama series with songs do not usually do well on broadcast television, e.g., *Cop Rock*. *Viva Laughlin* was no exception. "A mystery drama with music about a freewheeling businessman who wants to open a casino in Laughlin, Nevada" is how CBS described this series. The mystery part refers to the investigation of the businessman's ex-partner who was found dead. Characters would sometimes break into singing pop songs along with the songs' original artists to highlight certain plot elements.

Cast of Characters:

Ripley Holden (Lloyd Owen) – the central character who wanted to open the casino;
Natalie Holden (Madchen Amick) – Ripley's wife;
Jack Holden (Carter Jenkins) and Cheyenne (Ellen Woglom) - Ripley's son and daughter;
Peter Carlyle (Eric Winter) - the police detective investigating the murder of Ripley's business partner;
Nicky Fontana (Hugh Jackman) - a wealthy rival casino owner;
Marcus (D.B. Woodside) - Fontana's chief lieutenant.

Background: Based on the 2004 six-episode BBC series *Viva Blackpool* and adapted by Bob Lowry, actor Hugh Jackman was an executive producer of the series.

In the British series, Ripley Holden (David Morissey) has just opened an amusement arcade with slot and pin ball machines but really wants to build a casino hotel. His son Danny (Thomas Morrison) is mixed up with drug dealing; his daughter Shyanne (Georgia Taylor) is dating Steve (Kevin Doyle), a theater manager old enough to be her father; his wife Natalie (Sarah Parish) works at a help center and feels Ripley doesn't love her. The day after the opening, Ripley discovers the body of a man in the arcade when he opens for business. Detective Peter Carlisle (David Tennant) thinks that Ripley is the murderer. Carlisle, pretending to be a surveyor, questions Natalie, and they begin to fall in love. Carlisle interviews Danny who contradicts his father's story that he never previously saw the murdered man who has been identified as Mike Hooley. On top of everything else, Ripley is having financial problems, and the local planning commission rejects his proposal for the hotel casino. Danny confesses to Carlisle that he killed Hooley after selling him drugs, but the detective doesn't believe him.

Danny says to his dad that he moved Hooley from a prostitute's apartment behind the arcade after the victim collapsed, but Ripley informs Carlisle that he is the one who moved the body to the arcade. Ripley is then told by his accountant that he needs 100,000 pounds to cover his debts. The accountant suggests that he will take over the business in return for covering Ripley's debts. Carlisle tells Natalie that he really loves her and that he is leaving Blackpool and asks her to go with him. To get money to cover his debts, Ripley burns down the apartment building behind his arcade and closes the arcade. He is aware that his wife has been sleeping with Carlisle. The prostitute in whose room Hooley died informs Carlisle that Ripley killed him. Ripley suggests to Carlisle that he can have Natalie in return for not arresting him. Carlisle agrees; however, his partner arrests Ripley's accountant for false accounting practices. Danny informs his dad that he is gay and gives his father ideas for improving the arcade. Ripley says he will declare bankruptcy and give the business to his son. Natalie wants to stay with Ripley but ultimately decides to go off with Carlisle. In the end, the prostitute tells Ripley that Danny killed Hooley in self-defense when Hooley started beating her.

The Pilot – October 18, 2007

Ripley used to own a chain of convenience stores called Rip-Marts but sold them and is putting his money into opening the Viva casino in Laughlin, Nevada. However, a major investor in this undertaking, Buddy Baxter, wants his 25% ownership interest back. Ripley can't complete the casino without Baxter's investment. Ripley needs $1 million to continue construction. His accountant suggests he ask rival casino owner Nicky Fontana for the money. Nicky is aware that Ripley has lost a major investor and won't loan him the money. Apparently, Nicky bribed Baxter's wife to have her husband back out of Ripley's project. Ripley proceeds to Baxter's home to see Baxter's wife Bunny to have her talk her husband out of his decision. She says she would if Ripley has sex with her, but he responds that he can't.

The next day, police are at the casino when Ripley arrives. Buddy is found murdered, and Bunny thinks that Ripley killed him as does Detective Carlyle who is investigating the murder. Ripley wants his wife to provide an alibi even though he was out all night. Detective Carlyle questions Ripley's wife but doesn't tell her he is a detective. Ripley's son sells his new Corvette and gives the money to his dad to help with the casino. Ripley takes the money along with the cash he has on hand and goes to Fontana's casino to play blackjack. As luck would have it, he turns the $250,000 into $1 million that he needs for his casino.

The pilot episode included Elvis Presley's "Viva Las Vegas," Blondie's "One Way or the Other," and the Rolling Stones' "Sympathy for the Devil."

CBS premiered *Viva Laughlin* after its hit procedural *CSI* at 10:00 pm Thursday before moving it to its regular time period – Sundays at 8:00 pm. The premiere drew less than half of the audience of *CSI* (8.4 million viewers for *Viva Laughlin* compared to 21.2 million for *CSI*).

Other Episode Broadcast

"What a Whale Wants" – October 21, 2007

The Viva casino has opened but turnout isn't great because of the negative publicity surrounding Ripley and the death of Buddy Baxter. Det. Carlyle is looking at the people who may have killed Baxter other than Ripley – Ripley's accountant, Bunny Baxter, Marcus, Nicky Fontana's lieutenant who had an affair with Bunny, Natalie Holden, and Nicky Fontana himself. While working on his latest car, Ripley's son finds a gun taped underneath it but doesn't tell anyone. Bunny comes to apologize to Ripley for blaming him for her husband's murder. She says she will re-invest Buddy's $6 million in the Viva, but Ripley declines the offer. Ripley's accountant then goes to see Bunny at her invitation. She says she can be a silent partner in the casino, but the accountant refuses her offer. Ripley wants to create publicity for the Viva to attract customers and decides to lure professional gambler Lenny Collins from Fontana's casino by baiting him with Diane, Ripley's overweight assistant, since Collins is into plus-size models. That doesn't work because Fontana has already surrounded Collins with such models. Ripley's next idea is to offer Collins better odds at the casino through no limit, single deck blackjack.

Meanwhile, Det. Carlyle continues his undercover work with Ripley's wife going so far to volunteer at the crisis center where she works. After the reading of Buddy's will, Bunny finds that he gave the bulk of his estate to an illegitimate daughter she never knew he had. He had changed his will the night before he was murdered. Buddy's daughter tells Bunny that she is sorry about him not leaving anything to her stepmother, but she needs to honor her dad's wishes. She says she wants to live with Bunny.

Back at the Viva, Ripley plays single deck blackjack with Lenny. Lenny wins big, but at least there are more customers at the casino. Lenny played at the casino in return for a favor Ripley had done for him. Lenny returns his winnings to Ripley.

Unaired Episodes

"Takin' Care of Business"

Ripley learns that his casino's profits are not meeting expectations forcing him to conclude that some gamblers are cheating to win. He warns his security guard to watch everyone carefully, but thinks he needs to hire more experienced guards. Subsequently, Ripley identifies a gambler cheating at craps. He breaks the gambler's hand before hiring him as part of his security team.

In other developments, the police find Ripley's son Jack burying the gun he found in his car. Ripley informs Carlyle that he had purchased the gun for his wife for her protection and that it hasn't been fired for several years.

Cheyenne lands a job working as a "pool girl" at Fontana's establishment. When her father finds out, he forces her to quit the job. Detective Carlyle receives an anonymous tip on the location of the real murder weapon. He finds it in Fontana's car and arrests him.

Songs during the episode included Dean Justin's "Taking Care of Business," Twisted Sister's "We're Not Going to Take It," and R.E.M.'s "Everybody Hurts."

The story lines for the following episodes are unknown: "Magic Carpet Ride," "Bad Moon Rising," "Need You Tonight," "Fighter," and "Would I Lie to You?"

Postscript: According to director John Showalter, who helmed the "Fighter" episode, *Viva Laughlin* ". . . locked up tighter than a drum when it went down. . . We were in day 5 or 6 of the production during that episode when they (CBS) pulled the plug (I didn't even get dailies)."[31] Showalter also commented that if the series had been on cable, it might have had a chance to get beyond its growing pains. "Just a weird enough idea that it might of worked."[32]

Heist – Cops and Robbers

Premiered March 22, 2006 on NBC Wednesdays 10:00 pm

Premise: In this serialized drama, a gang of thieves plans to rob jewelry stores on Rodeo Drive in Beverly Hills while LAPD detectives try to stop them.

Cast of Characters:

    Mickey O'Neil (Dougray Scott) - the mastermind behind the heist;
    James Johnson (Steve Harris) – Mickey's partner in various heists who is married with two daughters;

> Robert (Pops) (Seymour Cassel) - an older professional thief whose wife is suffering from Alzheimer's and who himself has six months to live;
> Lola (Marika Dominczyk) - a thirtyish pickpocket and identity thief;
> Ricky Watman (David Walton) - the youngest member of the group and a self-proclaimed ladies' man;
> Amy Sykes (Michele Hicks) - the new head of the Burglary Auto Division of the LAPD;
> Tyrese Evans (Reno Wilson) - a black detective partnered with Billy O'Brien (Billy Gardell), an overweight Irish-American.

Background: Created by brothers, Mark and Robb Cullen, *Heist* premiered in spring 2006 on NBC. According to Mark Cullen, the idea for *Heist* came about after they had finished the series *Lucky* for FX and were talking about what they wanted to do next. "We asked ourselves. What is not on TV? What don't we see? There are a lot of procedurals, a lot of earnest, dramatic acting. We said, Why not do a show that's a lot of fun – an enjoyable, terrific ride based mainly on characters? We decided to use the heist genre to achieve that."[33]

The Pilot - March 22, 2006

Mickey reveals plans to rob three jewelry stores on Rodeo Drive during Academy Awards week when the most expensive jewelry will be moving through the stores. He estimates the take will be half a billion dollars. In order to get seed money for the plan, Mickey and James case a bank. While there, the bank is robbed by a pizza delivery guy (Zac Efron) who has been forced to do the job with explosives taped to his chest by an Armenian gang. Lola and Ricky learn that the Armenians plan to hold up another bank. When they do, Mickey's gang outsmarts them and gets away with the money. Meanwhile, Lola steals Det. Sykes' wallet to obtain information from her credit cards and driver's license. After Lola reveals that Sykes is into dancing, Mickey strikes up a relationship with her.

Other Episodes Broadcast

"Sex, Lies, and Vinny Momo"- March 29, 2006

Mickey explains his plan to rob the jewelry stores by unsealing service tunnels that run underneath them. He also hires Vinny Momo (Theo Rossi) to handle their getaway. Vinny does a dress rehearsal of the planned getaway to see if he can outrun the police. Leading the police on a high-speed chase, he is arrested and subsequently tells Mickey that they cannot escape using a car after the heist. Mickey continues his relationship with Sykes, and Evans and O'Brien investigate the drop off spot for the bank money and find a cigarette butt containing Ricky's DNA.

"Strife"- April 5, 2006

Lola finds that a new vault is being installed in one of the jewelry stores marked for the robbery. Meanwhile, Tyrese meets with a gang leader to find out where Ricky is. James discovers Mickey's link to Sam Gordon. Before James, Mickey was partners with Gordon who shot him, left him for dead, and then married Mickey's wife. Mickey confesses that the planned heist is to seek revenge on Gordon since all the stores are protected by Gordon's security systems. The gang learns that a new vault similar to the one being installed in the jewelry store is being delivered to a race track. They decide to steal the vault so that Pops can become familiar with it and also take the money from the old vault at the track. Ricky realizes that the police are on to him and quickly disappears from sight.

"How Billy Got His Groove Back"- April 12, 2006

The gang breaks into two different architectural firms that designed the jewelry stores to steal copies of the stores' blueprints. Mickey continues to date Det. Sykes to determine what information the police have about the second bank robbery. Tyrese and Billy take Ricky in for questioning and advise him that he has twenty-four hours to give them something or he is going back to prison for parole violation. He says he will produce a photo of the blueprints in return for the police canceling his parole and placing him in a witness protection program.

"Bury the Lead" - April 19, 2006

Lola and Ricky with James' help breaks into Gordon Security Systems to obtain the necessary security codes from Gordon's PC for the systems at the jewelry stores. Det. Sykes testifies about a robber she arrested after going undercover with his gang. The robber escapes custody, and Sykes is assigned police protection because the guy vows to kill her. When Mickey visits Sykes, he spots her LAPD PC and wants to steal it. Sykes evades her police protection to meet Mickey at a bar. She leaves because he is late in arriving. When she returns home, she is shot and killed by the escaped robber.

Unaired Episode

"Ladies and Gentlemen: Sweaty Dynamite"

Tom Tuchowuzcki (Ted Danson) takes Det. Sykes' place at the station. He reviews the evidence concerning the recent rash of robberies and sees links among them. He also believes that Sykes was seeing one of the gang members. Mickey needs to obtain more explosives and decides to steal them from Universal Studios bunker where they keep dynamite for special effects. When Ricky comes up with a hair-brained scheme to steal the explosives, Mickey dismisses him from the planned heist. Ricky then informs Tyrese and Billy about the plan. James and Mickey steal the explosives. Security locks down the studio so everyone has to be searched on their way out. Mickey and James hide the explosives in Pops' motorized wheel chair. James is suspicious of Ricky informing the police about the explosives heist. He sees him with Billy and Tyrese. Mickey has some henchmen enter the apartment where Ricky lives and shots ring out.

Postscript: *Heist* was heavily hyped during NBC's coverage of the 2006 Winter Olympics. When it premiered on Wednesday's at 10:00 pm it had fewer viewers than its time slot predecessor – *Law & Order*. NBC flip flopped the two series with *Heist* moving to 9:00 pm and *Law & Order* back to 10:00 pm. *Heist's* ratings declined further, and the network canceled it after five episodes.

If *Heist* hadn't been canceled, co-creator Mark Cullen indicated that "There are so many neat, amazing things we'd like to steal, so the world is open. We always thought it would be cool to rob Churchill Downs during the running of the Kentucky Derby, so you have three minutes to pull off the job."[34]

Smith – An Expert Thief and His Gang
Premiered September 19, 2006 on CBS Tuesdays 10:00 pm

Premise: A professional thief leads a double life – one of crime and one of respectability on this short-lived drama.

Cast of Characters:

Robert "Bobby" Stevens (Ray Liotta) - an expert thief nicknamed "Smith" by the FBI, had the cover of Midwest sales manager for a concession cup firm, Sawyer Paper Products. He used to play piano with a jazz group in nightclubs;
Joe Garcia (Franky G.) - part of Stevens' gang who ran a garage that customized cars. He is in charge of the gang's transportation;
Jeff Breen (Simon Baker) - a womanizing contract killer;
Tom (Jonny Lee Miller) - a recent parolee and head of logistics;

Annie (Amy Smart) - a Las Vegas showgirl who stole credit cards and is Tom's lover;

Hope (Virginia Madsen) – Bobby's wife who is on parole for drug violations and works in a dentist's office;

Jason (K'sun Ray) and Emily (Tatum McCann) – the Stevens' children;

Agent Dodd (Chris Bauer) - an FBI agent who tracked the gang;

Charlie (Shohreb Aghdashloo) - the intermediary between Bobby and the ultimate buyer of the merchandise he stole. She got Bobby his job at Sawyer Paper Products in return for a favor she did for the owner.

Background: Created by John Wells and produced by John Wells Productions in association with Warner Brothers, Wells indicated that he sought to make a series about people on the wrong side of the law. "There are plenty of people on TV trying to catch criminals. I thought it was time to explore the people they're trying to catch."[35]

The Pilot – September 19, 2006

Bobby brings the gang together to plan an art heist from a museum in Pittsburgh. After killing two men in Hawaii who told him to leave a private beach, Jeff flies to California to pick up Tom who has just been released from prison. Joe wants his co-worker Shawn (Mike Doyle), who has a gambling problem, to participate in the heist as a tech expert because of his knowledge of alarms and explosives. The gang will get $2 million for stealing two paintings that a private buyer wants - $1 million up front and the rest when the paintings are delivered. Annie, whose home town is Pittsburgh, is supposed to be a decoy for the police stationed at a kiosk across from the museum. One guard, who is in the restroom when the gang captures the other guards, comes out and pulls his gun on the thieves. He is shot by Jeff but not before the guard shoots Shawn. The gang escapes in a speed boat on the river. Shawn dies in the boat which the gang blows up. The gang later meets Annie to make their final getaway. Bobby tells his fence Charlie that he will be out of the business after three or four more jobs.

Other Episodes Broadcast

"Two" – September 26, 2006

In San Pedro, CA, the five members of the gang meet to divide up the cash they got for the art heist. Hope becomes suspicious of her husband's activities. Bobby meets with his financial adviser who says he has over $4 million in investments, but he wants at least $10 million. The FBI begins their investigation of the art heist by interviewing Anne's (aka Dorothy Collins) parents who say they are unaware of her whereabouts. However, her father has been in touch with her. Charlie has another job for Bobby involving the theft of precious metals. He would receive $500,000 for the job. Charlie is also concerned about Shawn's girlfriend Macy making inquiries about where he is. Hope meets Macy and asks about Shawn. She thinks he is the one killed during the art heist. Joe denies knowing where Shawn is. Macy receives $5000 in cash in an envelope purportedly from Shawn who Joe says is off gambling somewhere.

Bobby informs Charlie that he wants four or five more jobs for at least $500,000 each before he can leave the business. He gets the four others together to plan the heist of precious metals. In the meantime, the two men Jeff killed in Hawaii were apparently part of a drug gang and two of their associates are looking for him.

"Three" – October 3, 2006

The gang breaks into an Army National Guard armory in Oregon to steal weapons and ammunition. The heist involves taking 1300 pounds of gold from an airline hangar. Hope starts shadowing her husband to see what he is up to. Meanwhile, the FBI continues their investigation trying to find Dorothy Collins.

Unaired Episodes

"Four"

Tom hires a new tech expert named Marley (Elden Henson). Bobby informs Hope that he is going to a paper products convention in Houston. Still suspicious of her husband's activities, Hope asks her parole officer for permission to leave Santa Clarita, California and fly to Houston to surprise her husband. While at the airport with his boss to fly to Houston, Bobby makes an excuse that he has to change his plans and go to Denver to meet an important business client. He really wants to fly to Reno to meet the rest of the gang. However, at the last minute, Bobby decides to go to Houston where he meets Hope at the hotel. The rest of the gang prepare for the gold heist in Reno. After Hope leaves Houston early, Bobby flies to Reno. Upon arrival, a man takes Bobby to the site where his gang is to deliver the gold.

"Five"

The gold heist from the Reno Tahoe airport begins with the gang intercepting air to ground communications from the plane that is carrying the gold to the airport. Using an armored truck that they stole, Bobby, dressed as an armored car guard, drives the truck to the airport with Jeff and Tom in the back. Joe, driving a truck loaded with porta-potties, fakes an accident in a tunnel ahead of the real armored truck that will pick up the gold. Bobby, Tom, and Jeff make a hasty escape with the gold ingots just as the police and real armored truck arrive at the airport. They go to drop off the gold at a closed ski lift in Lake Tahoe. However, their contact named Cole only has $750,000 in cash and not the $2 million that was promised. Eli, the ultimate buyer for the gold, has snipers stationed at the ski lift, and they open fire on the gang. Bobby's gang is able to hold off the snipers. Bobby decides to melt down the gold and recast it. He calls Charlie and asks her to meet him at the Reno arch where he will give her the gold in return for $2 million. After Charlie meets him there with the money, she takes the van Bobby brought with the gold formed as metal tools in the back of the vehicle along with Cole's body. In the final scene, Eli is getting out of the shower, and Jeff is waiting for him with a gun.

"Six"

The Hawaiian drug dealer looking for Jeff finally catches up with him. Later Tom and Jeff find the drug king dead in a room of Jeff's house. They decide to leave town for a few days.

Meanwhile, Bobby celebrates his birthday after meeting with a man to launder $1 million in cash for him. Hope and Bobby go to a club where Hope has invited members of Bobby's old musical group as a surprise. After the club, the couple argues about their old life versus their new one. Hope says she liked the excitement of their old life but can't go back to it again.

The FBI is still on the trail of the gang. They find one of the gold bars from the gang's most recent heist in Boston.

"Seven"

Annie, who is back in Las Vegas, calls her dad in Pittsburgh. He advises her to leave the country because the FBI has made two visits to his home. She goes to see Tom in California who is living with Jeff in a new house. Annie tells him about a guy with an autographed baseball worth $250,000 and wants Tom and Jeff to steal the ball. Annie, who is sleeping with a land developer, obtains information from him about a land deal. She blackmails a banker into giving her a loan to purchase the land thinking she can then resell it to the developer for a large profit. Tom, Jeff, and Marley steal the baseball from the owner's house. Annie wants to sell the ball to the developer, but he offers at most $100,000 for it. Tom and Jeff become disgusted and leave. Tom ends up hitting the ball into the ocean.

Meanwhile, the FBI obtains security footage of Dorothy Collins from the Reno gold heist and determines that the gold bar found in Boston was just a plant to get them off the trail of the gang.

Postscript: The title of the series came from the name law enforcement assigns to an unknown suspect. Episodes eight through twelve of the series were never filmed although they exist in script form.

Lone Star – The Lives of a Texas Con Man
Premiered on September 20, 2010 Fox Mondays at 9:00 pm

Premise: A con man in Texas leads three different lives: his real life as a con artist, a life in Midland, Texas selling bogus oil leases, and a life in Houston married to the daughter of the owner of an oil company.

Cast of Characters:

Robert "Bob" Allen (James Wolk) – the experienced con man at the center of the story;
Cat Thatcher (Adrianne Palicki) - the daughter of the wealthy oil company owner;
Clint Thatcher (Jon Voight) – Cat's father;
Lindsay Holloway (Eloise Mumford) - Robert's girlfriend in Midland with whom he is living;
John Allen (David Keith) - Robert's con artist father who introduced him to scamming people at an early age;
Trammell (Mark Deklin) – one of Clint's sons who is suspicious of Bob;
Drew (Bryce Johnson) – the other Thatcher son who has a drinking problem.

Background: The series was created by Kyle Killen. Commenting about the series before its premiere, Killen remarked, "They were looking to try a cable show on a network. When you go out and pitch a show to a network, you're told not to mention 'Breaking Bad' or 'Mad Men' because they're shows that have a (small) number of viewers, (numbers) that get a show canceled on network. Your people will tell you to talk about 'Dallas'."[36] *Lone Star*, which was filmed in Texas, was described as "*Dallas* without the cheese."

The Pilot - September 20, 2010

Con man Robert "Bob" Allen flies between his girlfriend's house in Midland where he is selling bogus oil leases to unsuspecting investors including his girlfriend's parents and Houston where he is married to Cat Thatcher whose dad owns an oil company and wants Bob to join the firm. He has separate sets of wallets and cell phones for each identity. When his father-in-law offers him a position with Thatcher Oil, he is at first hesitant but then tells his wife he is accepting the position much to the chagrin of Trammel Thatcher who doesn't want Bob involved with the firm. Back in Midland, Robert's father shows up warning him that he has to leave town quickly since a lawyer in Midland is requesting the deed to one of his investor's wells. Robert says he can't leave, but changes his mind and departs in the middle of the night. Back in Houston, he joins his father-in-law's business and begins reviewing the company's records. He thinks that Drew's recommendation that the corporation become involved with wind farms is a good idea. Bob tells his dad that he never wants to be involved again in a situation like he was in Midland and wants to go straight working with Thatcher Oil. The next day, Bob advises Drew that he is purchasing some land for the wind farm in Midland for $1 million of the company's money. He does this so that there will be a deed when the lawyer checks. Robert then flies to Las Vegas to marry Lindsay.

Other Episode Broadcast

"One in Every Family"- September 27, 2010

Robert decides that he wants to have a formal wedding ceremony with Lindsay once they return home. In Houston, Bob thinks the wind farm project will make enough money to pay off his "investors" in Midland as well as turn a profit for him and his father. Bob brings his dad into Thatcher Corporation to help him with the wind farm project as a technical adviser named John Gardner. Robert returns to Midland where he meets Lindsay's screwed-up sister Gretchen in the shower. Lindsay asks her to be her maid of honor. John decides to run his own scam on the Thatcher's separate from what his son is doing.

Unaired Episodes

"Unveiled"

Robert and Lindsay have a formal wedding. Several of his Midland investors have been laid off and ask for their money back. Robert needs $140,000 to repay them. His dad advises him to leave Midland. Instead, Robert tries to interest Steve, Gretchen's fiancé, in investing in the Midland scheme. Robert figures that Steve has something to hide. In the meantime, Robert has transferred money from Thatcher Corporation to pay off the investors. Later, Robert finds that Steve has a wife in Connecticut and so blackmails him with this information to get $200,000 or else he will tell his wife about his relationship with Gretchen. He then informs Gretchen that Steve is married. He uses the $200,000 to repay the investors. Meanwhile, Clint is attracted to Alex Henley, an art appraiser he meets at an exhibit not knowing that she is a friend of Bob's father.

"Small Time"

John hacks Clint's computer system to delete $140,000 that Bob had transferred to his account. Meanwhile, Cat's ex-husband comes to visit. Bob doesn't know that Alex Henley, an art critic, is working with John to pull a con on Clint. Clint has evidence that John hacked his system, and, as a test, he assigns Bob to investigate. Lindsay is arrested for driving a stolen car that Bob had been using. Bob can't go back to Midland to help Lindsay since Cat's daughter fell from a horse and is in the hospital. Bob asks his dad for help with Lindsay who then obtains her release from jail. Clint doesn't believe Bob when he says that a glitch on the company's computer system made it appear that the system was hacked. After Alex goes on a date with Clint, she tells John that Clint is having doubts about Bob's creditability. John forces Bob to fire him in order for Bob to maintain his believability with Clint.

"Near Mrs."

Lindsay comes to Houston to surprise Robert and a cat and mouse game begins between Lindsay and Cat who is staying at the same hotel since her house is being remodeled. As luck would have it, guess who gets the room next to Bob and Lindsay – Cat naturally. While going through receipts with her ex-husband, Harry, in the hotel, Harry divulges that Cat is not legally married to Bob since she never signed the final divorce decree from him. Bob has an anxiety attack when Cat calls him to say she is staying at the hotel where he is with Lindsay. He quickly packs to leave. But Lindsay and Cat meet each other in a store at the hotel and ride up in the elevator together. Lindsay invites Cat into the hotel room to meet her husband. Bob hurries to the bathroom where he phones Cat to get her out of the room and away from Lindsay. On the way back to Midland, Lindsay suggests that when she has completed nursing school, they both move to Houston. Meanwhile, after staying at Clint's place while he is away and flirting with Drew, Alex is pulled over by police who find that she is driving with a false license.

"Reverse"

The news media reports on a Ponzi scheme in Texas run by a man named Alan Davis which makes Bob's dad nervous. He tells his son that they need new money to pay some of their investors in their Ponzi scheme before their investors become suspicious. Cat informs Bob that her divorce to Harry was not finalized. Harry wants to change the custody arrangements for his daughter before signing the divorce papers. Trimmel lost a lot of money in the Davis Ponzi scheme including funds from his mother's foundation. Knowing that Trimmel has lost money in the Davis scheme, Bob tries to use this information to stop him from interfering in the wind farm project. But Trimmel would rather tell his father what happened than be extorted by Bob. Bob and his dad decide to execute the "Mexican reverse" con to raise money. Bob finds people who are inheriting money and convinces them to invest in a fabulous opportunity. John then pretends he is from the FBI investigating the scheme by having Bob's potential investors consummate the deals so Bob can be arrested. However, Bob says to his dad that he is going to tell his Midland investors the truth. He holds a meeting with them and explains that the gas leases they bought were bogus and tied to the Alan Davis Ponzi scheme and that they were all conned out of their money including himself.

"Cost of Living"

Story line not known

Postscript: Creator Kyle Killen apparently had decided, if *Lone Star* had been renewed, to have a scene in the final first season episode that would have created a new conflict for the second year.

In 2012, Killen developed a new series for NBC titled *Awake* about a police detective whose family is involved in an automobile accident. Somewhat similar to *Lone Star* with respect to the main character leading two different lives, the detective in *Awake* inhabited two alternating parallel worlds – one where his wife survived the accident; one where his son survived. *Awake* was canceled after thirteen episodes.

The Playboy Club – Crime and Sex in the Sixties
Premiered September 19, 2011 on NBC Mondays at 10:00 pm

Premise: Take the iconic nightclubs run by *Playboy* magazine's founder Hugh Hefner, throw in mobsters and political corruption along with sex and music and one has the ingredients of this short-lived 2011 drama set in the 1960s.

Cast of Characters:

Nick Dalton (Eddie Cibrian) – a thirty-five-year-old single attorney, who used to be a "fixer" for the Bianchi crime family in Chicago. He is now running for State's Attorney but still frequents the Chicago Playboy Club;

Carol-Lynne Cunningham (Laura Benanti) – a Bunny, a singer, and Nick's girlfriend;

Billy Rosen (David Krumholtz) – the club's manager;

Max (Wes Ramsey) – the club's hunky bartender;

Maureen (Amber Heard – the newest Playboy Bunny at the club;

Janie (Jema Dewan-Tatum) – Maureen's roommate, who is having an affair with Max;

Alice (Leah Renee) – pretended to be married to Sean Beasley (Sean Maher), both of whom are gay;

Brenda (Naturi Naughton) – an African-American Bunny;

John Bianchi (Troy Garity) – the son of Bruno Bianchi who is the head of the crime family who frequented the club and knew Nick.

Background: Chad Hodge created the series with Becky D. Mode. In developing the drama, Hodge went through Hefner's *Playboy* archives and took pains to distinguish between "Bunnies" and "Playmates." Bunnies, as depicted in the series, were basically waitresses and cigarette sellers who were not permitted to date the "keyholders," the club's patrons. Playmates were those women, mainly nude, who appeared in the pages of *Playboy* magazine.

Commenting on *The Playboy Club* before it premiered, Hodge remarked that "I want this to be the thing that you come home drunk, sit on your couch, look at your DVR list and it's the first thing you want to watch."[37]

The Pilot - September 19, 2011

With opening narration by Hugh Hefner, one of the patrons at the club comes on to Maureen in the establishment's supply room while she is there placing more cigarettes in her tray. As Nick tries to stop her attacker, Maureen kicks the man and her stiletto heel goes through his neck killing him. Nick identifies the attacker known to Maureen as Clyde Hill as really Bruno Bianchi. Nick doesn't want to report the death to the police. He and Maureen dispose of the body in the Chicago River. The two then go to Nick's apartment in Billy's car so that Maureen can try to clean the blood off her costume. Nick telephones Billy telling him he has his car as well as Maureen. Carol-Lynne, who knows that Nick left the club with Maureen, goes to Nick's apartment where she finds Maureen dressed only in one of Nick's shirts. She removes her stuff from Nick's closet, while Maureen leaves.

The next day, Billy sees Carol-Lynne going through personnel files in his office. She tells him that he needs someone like her to help manage the bunnies. Billy fires her on the spot, but she goes to see Hefner who makes her the Mother Bunny in charge of training and managing the Bunnies.

Meanwhile, John Bianchi informs Nick that he cannot win the election for State's Attorney without assistance from the Bianchi family. John wants Nick to help locate his father, but Nick turns down the offer. Alice meets her fake husband Sean at a Mattachine Society meeting where she donates all of her tips from the club to the homophile organization.

The premiere attracted about 5 million viewers and had a 1.6 rating among adults eighteen to forty-nine. The ratings were not helped by calls from the Parents Television Council calling for viewers to boycott the series and for sponsors to pull their ads. NBC's affiliate in conservative Salt Lake City, Utah refused to air the series.

Other Episodes Broadcast

"The Scarlet Bunny"- September 26, 2011

Nick wants Carol-Lynne back, and they eventually reconcile. Hefner is having a competition for a Chicago Bunny to appear on the cover of his magazine. Maureen is one of the five finalists for the cover, but Janie is the one selected by Hef. However, Janie, whose photos were entered by Max, doesn't want to be on the cover because she is married and her jealous husband subscribes to the magazine. Maureen gets the cover shot.

In the meantime, Carol-Lynne questions Maureen after she finds Maureen's bloody outfit. Maureen makes up a story about being mugged in the ally and having a bloody nose from the encounter. Nick changes his mind and agrees to help look for Bruno Bianchi in return for John Bianchi donating a car to Nick's campaign which Nick gives to the mayor in return for the mayor's endorsement of him for State Attorney.

"A Matter of Simple Duplicity"- October 3, 2011

Sean wants to manage Dalton's campaign and asks him to date Frances Dunhill, the daughter of a wealthy potential contributor. At dinner with a group of contributors, Nick says that he really wants to one day run for mayor. After Frances gives Nick a check for $50,000 for his campaign, Nick hires Sean as his manager. Carol-Lynne, jealous of Nick being seen with Frances, appears in public with Nick's opponent in the election, Jimmy Wallace. Later, Frances attends a Mattachine Society meeting where she encounters Alice.

Meanwhile, John Bianchi pursues Maureen for answers about his father's disappearance, while Carol-Lynne hires a new Bunny who is really a news reporter doing an expose on the club. The paper publishes the first part of a two-part story about one of the Bunnies killing a man. Maureen thinks that she will be revealed in the second part. However, as counsel for the club, Nick meets with the reporter who shows him evidence that Janie killed an elderly man in a car accident as she and her husband were fleeing from a robbery they committed. Because the incident was an accident – not intentional murder, the paper doesn't print the rest of the story and issues a retraction.

Unaired Episodes

"The Dream House and How to Avoid It"
Carol-Lynne and her Bunnies have been invited to perform on a USO TV special on which President Kennedy also will appear.
Billy continues to gamble and incur debt. Billy's wife Rachel finds that their mortgage is past due because of his gambling. He steals money from the club for gambling. Nick joins his poker game, wins big, and gives the money to Billy to pay off his debts. However, Billy finds that his wife and kids have left him.
Meanwhile, John Bianchi continues to be suspicious of Nick and Maureen over the disappearance of his father. Carol-Lynne finds Bruno's club key among Maureen's possessions and turns it over to John telling him that two guys found it by the railroad tracks. She asks Nick if he or Maureen killed Bruno. After he explains what really happened, she is supportive.

"The Trouble in Makeoutsville"
Maureen is arrested in a prostitution sting when she tries to return a tip to an undercover officer who wanted to have sex with her. Jimmy Wallace doesn't press charges, but he then shuts down the club on grounds that it is a brothel based on the tips the Bunnies receive and on the fact that some of the Bunnies later have sex with certain patrons. Nick defends the club in court. During the trial, Carol-Lynne testifies that she is sleeping with Nick and that he has given her gifts. When Nick produces evidence that the judge gave a gift to his wife before he married her, the judge dismisses the case, and the club re-opens.

"Ding Dong Ghoul"
Janie's husband, Wade comes back into her life and wants her to help him rob the club. When Janie informs Maureen, they come up with a plan

to turn him over to the police. However, after Max discovers Janie's husband taking money out of the safe, a fight ensues. Max is knocked out. Maureen calls the police who arrive just as Wade absconds and is arrested.

John Bianchi informs Nick that Bruno's body has been found in the river. John's uncle Oscar (Billy Zane) arrives in town upon learning the news and wants to head the outfit. Oscar believes that John killed his own father, but Nick doesn't want John to die at the hands of Oscar for something he didn't do. One of John's henchmen finds one of the surveyors who discovered Bruno's Playboy Club key by the river. The surveyor identifies Maureen as the Bunny who took the key from him at the club.

"A Tryst of Fate"

Maureen is questioned by Bianchi about his father's key. He figures that Nick, Maureen, and Carol-Lynne have been lying to him all along about his father's disappearance. Oscar informs Nick that he gave the order to kill John. When John and Maureen go to his car, it explodes with John's driver inside. Maureen flees and goes to Nick's apartment. John confronts Oscar at the club. Oscar tells him to produce Bruno's real killer. John threatens to kill Carol-Lynne unless Maureen is returned to him. Upon learning of this, Maureen voluntarily returns to Bianchi's place. However, Nick also arrives there and says that he accidentally killed Bruno. John lets Maureen go. Oscar and his men then open fire on John's place of business. John is wounded but escapes with Nick. Nick tells John to go back to Las Vegas and that he will take care of Oscar. Nick returns to the club to speak with Oscar. He says that he killed Bruno. Oscar pulls a gun on him. Carol-Lynne shoots Oscar.

Postscript: Commenting on the demise of *The Playboy Club*, co-creator Hodge said, "I think audiences really rejected that concept outright because no one really showed up for the pilot. The Playboy brand was maybe something that wasn't exactly right for a network show. That has nothing to do with the show itself that we created. It was maybe just something that people didn't want to watch."[38]

CHAPTER 5

Science Fiction

Beyond Westworld – Robots vs Humans
Premiered March 5, 1980 on CBS Wednesdays at 8:00 pm

Premise: Based on the movie *Westworld* but not to be confused with the HBO series, *Westworld*, this 1980 science fiction series concerned a mad scientist who wanted to reprogram the robots made for a futuristic amusement park in order to take over the world. The amusement park called Westworld allowed visitors to act out their fantasies by interacting with figures from the Old West. It was created by the Delos Corporation. A scientist who had helped to create the robots wanted to develop the perfect society with the robots making all the decisions for humans. He planted his reprogrammed robots all over the world for eventual domination, but each robot had a unique weakness so that it could be disarmed.

Cast of Characters:

Simon Quaid (James Wainwright) - a scientist who had helped Joseph Oppenheimer (William Jordan) to design the robots for Westworld;

Foley (Severn Darden) and Roberta (Ann McCurry) – each assisted Quaid in implementing his plan;

Jim Moore (Jim McMullan) - the thirty-five-year-old head of Delos Security who is tasked with stopping Quaid;

Pamela Williams (Connie Sellecca) - an expert of robot technology who assisted Moore.

Background: The series was developed by Lou Shaw in association with MGM Television. CBS ordered six episodes of *Beyond Westworld*.

The Pilot

"Westworld Destroyed" - March 5, 1980

Simon Quaid has destroyed the computer room at Westworld. The robots at the amusement park could not be shut down leading them to destroy the park. Quaid has also planted a robot on a submarine carrying nuclear weapons and can view everything through a closed-circuit TV system connected to the eyes of each of his robots. Jim Moore from Delos Security with the assistance of Laura Garvey (Judith Chapman) is sent to investigate. Quaid wants to destroy Delos for turning his robots into amusement park attractions by having the sub fire a nuclear missile at the company's headquarters. After Professor Oppenheimer picks up messages to a robot on the sub coming from Quaid, Moore is airlifted to the sub. Using a special radio receiver, he narrows the search for the robot to the sub's control room. Moore discovers the sub's captain is the robot because he has no fingerprints. The captain triggers a red alert and puts Moore in handcuffs. However, after setting off the sub's sprinkler system, Moore escapes, blinds the captain with a fire extinguisher, locks him in a torpedo tube, and fires it.

Other Episodes Broadcast

"My Brother's Keeper"- March 12, 1980

Quaid's latest plan is to take over an oil company run by Nick Stoner. He first has one of his robots kidnap Stoner's gambler brother Dean and has Dean sign over his stock in the company in return for erasing his gambling debts. Moore finds out what is happening and informs Nick to stay out of sight. Pam Williams, a former associate of Moore's who previously worked with Quaid, joins him in this episode. He has a robot designed to look like her so it can kill Moore. Meanwhile, Moore warns Dean that Quaid wants to take over the company now that he controls some of the stock by killing his brother Nick. The robot impersonating Pam tries to kill Moore, but it falls to its destruction. After Moore rescues a kidnapped Pam, they both try to determine which of the football players on a team Nick owns is a robot planted by Quaid to murder the owner. They find that the quarterback is the robot. When Moore electrocutes the quarterback, Quaid tears up the contract signed by Dean figuring it is now worthless.

In this episode, Severn Darden took over the role as Foley, Quaid's assistant.

"Sound of Terror"- March 19, 1980

At a rally against nuclear power in front of a power plant, one of Quaid's robots breaks into the facility and steals uranium. Quaid has been having meetings with a North African general who wants to take over his country. Having a nuclear bomb will help him do this, and, in return, Quaid will have a safe haven to continue his work. Moore and Williams try to find the missing uranium. They think that a member of a rock group who played at the nuclear power demonstration is Quaid's robot. Williams discovers that Bobby Lee, a member of the group, is the robot and is transporting the bomb in his body. Moore boards an airplane with Bobby Lee. After the plane takes off, Moore subdues Bobby who is sucked out of the plane's open door and falls into the ocean where the bomb explodes.

Unaired Episodes

"The Lion"

Lionstar Motors has developed a race car called "the Lion" that has an energy efficient engine using gasohol. Moore is a friend of Corey Burns who built the car and who plans to marry the daughter of the owner of the company. In a trial run, the car explodes with Burns driving, and he is paralyzed from the waist down. Quaid is behind the explosion and has bought up the car company's outstanding debts as well as invested in oil wells in order to take advantage of the energy crisis. Moore has Delos invest in Lionstar Motors to block Quaid and has the Lion rebuilt so it can participate in a race to show how good it is. Quaid has Moore meet with him and his assistant, now played by Russell Johnson, the professor from *Gilligan's Island*. He invites Moore to join him, but, when Moore refuses, Quaid tries to blow him up. Meanwhile, the Lion is rebuilt. However, someone has tampered with its breaks. Moore suspects that one of Quaid's robots is on Lionstar's staff. A mechanic named Monetti turns out to be the robot sabotaging the Lion. Despite his disability, Corey decides to race the vehicle. Monetti, in disguise, takes over for Corey's competitor. Oppenheimer finds that the Lion has been painted with magnesium paint which will catch fire at a high temperature. Moore takes another race car, collides with Monetti's vehicle, and stops the race before the Lion catches on fire.

"Takeover"

Russell Johnson is back as Quaid's assistant Patrick. One of Quaid's robots incapacitates police captain Mike Nicholson who is taken to the hospital where another of Quaid's robots implants a chip in his skull so he will obey Quaid's instructions. Quaid thinks that this procedure is simpler than constructing new robots. Moore suspects that the attack on Nicholson was coordinated with the impending visit of the Governor who is running for re-election and is scheduled to debate his opponent. During the TV debate between the Governor and his opponent, Moore notices that the Governor is not sweating under the hot lights (robots don't perspire) but that the Governor's opponent is sweating slightly. Under instructions from Quaid, Nicholson raises his gun to shoot the opponent, but Moore pushes the Governor in front of the challenger and the Governor is shot in the arm and leg with sparks flying and robot parts falling across the stage. Quaid had thought that by assassinating the Governor's opponent, the Governor robot would be re-elected and eventually may run for the presidency. Quaid is obviously dismayed by the turn of events lamenting that, while the chip in Nicholson's skull worked, the unsolvable flaw in humans is their emotions. Quaid decides to no longer try to make human robots saying that in the future he will use only his robots.

Unproduced Scripts

At least two scripts were written that apparently were never produced. Both scripts deal with robotic canines.

"Hit or Miss"
Moore investigates an attack by a robotic killer Doberman on a police officer. The dog is traced to Brentwood Kennels whose chief veterinarian, Angela Luden, is working for Quaid. Quaid wants to take over the West Coast syndicate headed by Arno Camis and use the robotic dogs to help him in this effort. Moore and Pam find that Camis is under protection by the government since he has agreed to testify against the syndicate in return for going into the witness protection program with his son. At Camis' mansion, Luden releases a robotic dog which slips past an unsuspecting guard allowing other robotic dogs to corner the guards. Luden then sneaks into the mansion and removes her coat and wig to reveal that she is a robot perfectly imitating Camis' appearance. She knocks out the real Camis and calls off the guards. Moore arrives at the mansion and discovers Luden's ruse. He fights off the robotic Luden. As Pam arrives on the scene, the batteries in the robotic dogs die.

"Outrage"
Quaid, still apparently fully invested in his robotic dog experiment, sends a robotic German shepherd to control Crown Prince Edward so that Quaid can take control of his country for his criminal operations. However, Moore apprehends Quaid who is jailed and placed on trial. During his trial, the district attorney argues that Quaid is responsible for many murders and is attempting to take over the world. Quaid's attorney states that there is

no evidence of his client committing murder. With Quaid on trial, his assistant Patrick takes control of the robot version of Prince Edward and also reprograms Quaid's robotic assistant Roberta to obey him instead of Quaid. Patrick orders Roberta to kill Quaid in prison, but she short circuits thanks to Quaid's secret safeguard. After Quaid has Roberta kill the prison guard, he stages a hostage situation with Roberta in order to break out of prison. Quaid and Roberta arrive back at headquarters where he imprisons Patrick. Meanwhile, at a charity event sponsored by Prince Eddie, Moore and Pam find that the prince has been replaced by a robot. Moore decapitates the robot, while Pam revives the real prince whom she found unconscious.

Postscript: John Meredyth Lucas, who helped to produce the series and produced such shows as *Ben Casey*, *Mannix* and *Star Trek*, said that "... the show was hell. Everything was a compromise ... Because the various groups could not agree on casting, we ended with no 'names' in the show. That, if not a guarantee of failure, certainly tipped the balance in that direction. ... the experience convinced me that I wanted no more of network television."[39]

Space Rangers – Peacekeepers in the Galaxy
Premiered on January 6, 1993 CBS Wednesdays at 8:00 pm

Premise: Space explorers have stretched civilization to the farthest reaches of the galaxy establishing remote outposts one of which is Fort Hope on Planet Avalon, the ninth planet in the Red-Gemini system. This *Star Wars*-like series chronicles the adventures of one group of space rangers who keep the peace.

Cast of Characters:

Cmdr. Chennault (Linda Hunt) – the commanding officer of Fort Hope;
Capt. John Boon (Jeff Kaake) – the handsome captain of the space ranger group who is married to Sarah, a bio-engineer and has one daughter, Roxie. His space ship could travel at the speed of light;
Doc (Jack McGee) – the ship's engineer who is made up of several bionic parts;
Jojo (Marjorie Monaghan) – the female pilot;
Zylyn (Cary-Hiroyuki Tagawa) – the aggressive and powerful native of the planet Grakka who has to wear a curved metal yoke over his head to calm him;

Daniel Kincaid (Danny Quinn) - the new, ambitious cadet who volunteered for Boon's crew and whose father is a general at Central Command;

Mimmer (Clint Howard) - Fort Hope's scientific genius;

Colonel Erich Weiss (Gottfried John) - Central Command's representative on Avalon.

Background: Pen Densham created the series. The original concept was titled *Space Marines* with the pilot episode called "Planet Busters."[40] Instead of the Doc character, there was "Grunt" with a mechanical heart who could fix anything. He had a robotic canine companion operated by a wristwatch-like device. "Denim" was the female communications chief and back-up medic who later evolved into the character Jojo. Another female character was also in the crew who had been jilted in love and joined the marines. A Casablanca-like restaurant owner where the crew hung out was involved in some shady dealings. The crew's space ship was referred to as an Armored Personnel Carrier – APC.

This concept became *Space Rangers*. Commenting on the series, Densham said, "We wanted to tell adventure stories. I loved the original *Star Trek* because they were adventurous. And I wanted to take a little bit of *Star Wars* and a little bit of *Star Trek* and inject it into *Space Rangers*. This way you had the philosophy and adventure."[41]

The Pilot
"Fort Hope" – January 27, 1993

The series pilot was actually the fourth episode to be aired on CBS.

In the original pilot script, this episode opened with the following narration:

> By the year twenty-one hundred, explorers have stretched civilization to the edges of the galaxy. They've found new worlds and learned to share them with new races. At the distant frontiers, two ancient forces still remain locked in mortal conflict: good and evil.

When a transport ship crashes on a lifeless planet named Skaraab, Boon and his crew are sent to rescue the survivors who include Boon's former Captain, Ranger Decker, and Grakka High-Priest Nazzer. Zylan informs Boon that a special weapon has been hidden on that planet for thousands of years and whoever controls that weapon can control the universe. When Boon's ship arrives on the planet, the crew disembarks in pods but cannot locate Decker or the other survivors. They finally locate them, but Decker takes the crew hostage. He is hostile toward Boon ever since Boon testified against him at a court martial. The survivors have discovered a portal that contains the secret weapon Zylan described. Boon with the help of Daniel is able to free himself and take on the survivors. Decker escapes into the portal and retrieves the secret weapon, but it blows up in his face. The crew and the remaining survivors escape the planet.

In the original pilot script for the initial episode of *Space Rangers*, Cmdr. Chennault was a man – not a woman, while the Mimmer character was a woman and not a man. Mimmer was described as a big, wild-haired Julia Childs-like woman. Luka Stout was the name of the new recruit.

Other Episodes Broadcast

"The Replacements" – January 6, 1993

The Rangers' mission is to recapture a transport ship carrying iron ore that has been taken over by smugglers. They board the ship and come under fire, but some of the smugglers escape. Boon complains to the commander that his equipment isn't working properly and that he doesn't have enough manpower. To address the manpower issue, Weiss gives the team an android. One of the smugglers who was captured is murdered in his cell at Fort Hope by an alien working for Isogul, a Hobbaba crime lord who is behind the smuggling. The Rangers discover that the android was really sent to determine if androids could replace the Rangers. When the Rangers go back to the transport ship, they find that the crime lord was really smuggling a powerful drug disguised as iron ore. The android tries to shoot the alien murderer who has the ability to disintegrate his body into tiny pieces and then reintegrate. This process makes the android go crazy. In the end the Rangers shoot the alien, and Weiss calls off his attempt to replace the Rangers.

CBS aired this episode as the series premiere.

"Banshee" – January 13, 1993

Col. Weiss wants Boon to go on a mission to catch a banshee – an aggressive reptilian-like creature. The banshees have taken over a space ship and killed most of the occupants except for one young boy who is inexplicably still alive. Mimmer goes on the mission with Boon's crew since he knows how to use a new device, XV12S, that is supposed to immobilize a banshee by freezing it. Boon's ship docks with the marooned ship. His crew tries to find the boy, but he runs away from them. Back at Fort Hope, the commander has learned that the boy is deaf and communicates this to Boon. Apparently, banshees kill people by entering their ears and disrupting their central nervous system. The boy hasn't been harmed because of his deafness.

The crew finally rescues the boy, but the ship they are on is being dragged away. The boy takes Boon and his crew to the ship's power source to blow it up. After the immobilizing device doesn't work as intended, Zylan has to kill a banshee for the crew to get back to its ship before the marooned ship blows up.

"Death before Dishonor" – January 20, 1993

Prince Gor'Dah, a member of the Vee-Lons – a unisex reptilian race of warriors, is negotiating a trade agreement at Fort Hope. When the meeting breaks up and Gor'Dah goes to Gino's Bar, he fondles Jojo's hair since he has never seen a female. Boon pushes him to the floor creating a diplomatic incident. Central Command's Ambassador Hardcastle is sent to deal with Boon but is assassinated before he arrives at Fort Hope. The Vee-Lons still demand an apology and threaten war. The Command's representative, who was negotiating with Gor'Dah, suggests that Boon make a personal apology to him. Boon, his crew, and the representative arrive on Gor'Dah's ship and, thinking it is a peace offering, Boon gives Gor'Dah a silver dollar that his grandfather had given him. However, since Vee-Lons find silver poisonous, the silver dollar burns Gor'Dah's hand. Gor'Dah sentences Boon, his crew, and the representative to death by spindle worm which enters the nose and eats the brain. Boon challenges Gor'Dah to a duel instead. Zylan helps Boon prepare and tells him that Vee-Lons have one weakness around their necks. In the duel with metal spears, Boon loses his weapon but kicks Gor'Dah in the stomach and chokes him but refuses to kill him. Zylan finds that Gor'Dah's assistant assassinated Central Command's ambassador, and Gor-Dah makes peace with the humans.

Episodes Not Broadcast

"To Be or Not to Be"

Comedian Lenny Hacker (Buddy Hackett) crashes his spaceship on a planet used as a prison for criminals. Daniel wants to rescue him and convinces the rest of the crew to go on the mission. Meanwhile, Daniel's father, a general, visits Fort Hope to evaluate its status and confronts the commander about his son's mission.

On the surface of the planet, Zylan and Daniel locate Hacker while Boon and Doc receive fire from a gang of prisoners who want to capture their spaceship to escape from the planet. The Rangers take cover in Hacker's ship until an electrical storm passes by. On the way back to their ship after the storm, the gang of prisoners captures Boon, Zylan, and Doc. Daniel, who is helping Hacker retrieve his belongings, sees the prisoners torturing Boon. Hacker confronts the prisoners with a gun, while Daniel goes behind them to get the drop on them. The Rangers and Hacker make it safely back to Fort Hope where Hacker performs a comedy routine and the general says he is proud of Daniel.

"The Trial"

Zylan is drugged and framed for murder of another Graakan by crime lord Hobbaba. The commander decides to have Zylan's trial at Fort Hope with Murdock from Central Command acting as prosecutor, Boon acting as the defense lawyer, and Weiss being the judge. In a plan to take over Fort Hope, Hobbaba instructs Murdock to shift the focus of the trial to the commander and her recommendation to permit Graakan's to join the Rangers. Daniel, using his father's access codes, taps in to secret files about Murdock and discovers that Murdock is being impersonated by someone else who is the real killer of the Graakan. Hobbaba shoots the Murdock impersonator and is arrested himself.

Postscript: *Space Rangers* was Linda Hunt's first television series. She is best known for her role as Hetty on *NCIS: Los Angeles*. Pen Densham, who created *Space Rangers*, subsequently produced reboots of two iconic science fiction series – *The Outer Limits* in 1995 and *The Twilight Zone* in 2002.

Mercy Point – *ER* in Outer Space
Premiered October 6, 1998 on UPN Tuesdays at 9:00 pm

Premise: In the year 2249, doctors work on both human and alien patients at a hospital on the far reaches of the galaxy. Mercy Point Hospital was a deep space medical facility near Jericho Colony lodged inside the Sahartic Divide. The Inter-Species Council (ISC) governed Mercy Point.

Cast of Characters:

- Chief of Staff Dr. Harris DeMilla (Joe Spano) – administered the facility;
- Dr. Grote Maxwell (Joe Morton) – Primary Alien Physiologist and surgeon born on Callisto Gas Mine in 2210;
- Dr. Haylen Breslauer (Maria Del Mar) – Director of Medicine and a senior surgeon born on Earth in 2213;

- Dr. Caleb "C.J." Jurado (Brian McNamara) – a handsome ladies' man born on L.E.O. colony in 2217 who is Director of Extra-Vehicular Medicine, meaning he travels to damaged spacecrafts;
- ANI (Julia Pennington) – a robotic head nurse (Android Nursing Interface);
- Dr. Dru Breslauer (Alexandra Wilson) – Haylen's sister newly arrived at the hospital as a resident who was born on Aries Station, off Venus, in 2218;
- Dr. Rema Cooke (Gay Thomas) – a psychologist involved with the rights of patients;
- Dr. Batung (Jordan Lund) – a slug-like alien surgeon who used a wheelchair device because the gravity on his home planet was different from the artificial gravity on Mercy Point.

Mercy Point was equipped with a talking computer voiced by series creator Trey Callaway named Hippocrates who could verbalize a patient's prognosis after a quick scan.

Background: The series was created by Trey Callaway, David Simkins, and Milo Frank and produced by Mandalay Productions in association with Columbia Tristar. Thirteen episodes of the series were ordered by UPN, but only seven were produced.

In early 1997, Trey Callaway, who was always fascinated with the medical field, wrote a script for a feature film titled *Nightingale One* about a space station hospital twenty-five years in the future dealing with medicine and the first human contact with aliens. This script eventually became the basis for *Mercy Point*.

Initially envisioned as a companion piece to UPN's *Star Trek Voyager* on Wednesday nights, *Mercy Point* ended up on Tuesday's at 9:00 pm following two UPN comedies.

The Pilot

A twenty-five minute presentation pilot of *Mercy Point* was made with actor John DeLancie in the Joe Spano role and with footage from the film *Starship Troopers*. In the presentation film, written by Trey Callaway and David Simkins and directed by Michael Katleman, a space vehicle collides with an asteroid and the passengers and pilot are brought to Mercy Point. Grote's rotation is almost over, and he thinks of leaving. Haylen's estranged sister Dru, a specialist in alien physiology arrives, much to Haylen's dismay. However, Dru proves her worth in a risky operation on a patient infected with a reptilian-like virus. Because ANI doesn't want the female pilot of the space vehicle removed from Mercy Point, ANI seduces an ISC representative wanting to gather data from the brain of the severely injured pilot. A. J. returns to the crash site to recover the black box so the pilot's brain is not disturbed while she is recovering. He retrieves the black box, but is decapitated in the process. Grote successfully re-capitates him. In the end, Grote decides to stay at Mercy Point.

Because John Delancie was not available when *Mercy Point* became a series, Joe Spano took over the role of Dr. DeMilla.

Episodes Broadcast

"New Arrivals"- October 6, 1998

Haylen's half-sister comes aboard as a new resident much to Haylen's displeasure. Both she and her sister were abandoned by their mother in 2231, and Dru left Haylen's supervision two years later. Haylen is resigned to having her at Mercy Point and asks Dr. Maxwell to supervise Dru's residency. Dru had a prior relationship with Doctor Jurado.

A computer tech passes out from some type of virus in the brain. After his other organs begin to fail, he goes into cardiac arrest and dies. Five soldiers come in with the same symptoms. Dr. Maxwell thinks the infection came from a computer virus that is communicable from person to person by direct contact. The doctors need to come up with an antidote. They use ANI to produce antibodies by injecting her with infected blood. The lives of the soldiers are saved.

"Opposing Views"- October 13, 1998

A space shuttle accident brings several victims to Mercy Point. Dr. Butang treats a female victim of the crash who has shattered legs. He wants to amputate the legs and replace them with bio-prosthetics. When she recovers, she is angry at the doctor for the type of surgery he performed since she is an Olympic athlete. The doctor comes to understand the reasons for the patient's outrage and realizes why she reacted as she did. He apologizes to her for not showing more respect and explains that she will eventually be able to participate in the Olympics again.

The female co-pilot of the shuttle is also brought to Mercy Point in critical condition. The ISC investigator of the crash wants to download her memory imprint to find out what caused the accident. The initial attempt to download the imprint shows that the co-pilot may have violated a direct order from the now deceased pilot, but the procedure is stopped because of her fragile condition. Her husband arrives and is told that his wife won't recover. He agrees to resume the procedure as long as he can participate. The co-pilot's memory imprint shows that a magnetic cloud interfered with the shuttle's instruments and that fuel cells the shuttle was transporting exploded as a result of the cloud causing the accident.

"Last Resort" - October 20, 1998

Clayton Kelly, the son of an ISC member, comes to Mercy Point dying from thalamenia. His father is looking for a blood transfusion from an alien that may save his life. The doctors don't want to perform the experimental transfusion unless the alien, who is himself dying, passes away first. Maxwell tells the alien that he can't stop his lung disease and that a cross transfusion might help Clayton. The alien agrees to the procedure. During the cross transfusion, Clayton learns that the alien's calling is to tell stories to his people about their history. Clayton's immune system rejects the alien blood, but the alien's condition improves from the boy's blood. Clayton knows he is dying but wants the cross transfusion to continue so he can at least save the alien. In the end, the boy dies. The alien survives and promises Clayton's parents that he will tell the story about Clayton's courage to his people.

The series was canceled after three episodes. However, UPN aired four other episodes that had been produced as two two-hour movies in July, 1999.

"Second Chances"

A young man, Peter Nash, comes to Mercy Point with a bone fracture that should have happened only to a much older person. Dr. Maxwell thinks he is hiding something. When Nash tries to leave, he suffers a stroke. A brain scan reveals that he has two minds. Nash had an older consciousness put into his body to extend its life. The two minds are competing to survive in his body. The doctors find that a Dr. Warren, thought to have died, is the older mind, and it is aging Nash's body. Dr. Warren had discovered a genetic link between species and needed a younger body to continue his research. Dr. Warren wants Maxwell to eliminate Nash's consciousness forever. Maxwell puts Nash under neuro-navigational control to talk with the real Nash and finds that Nash had a daughter on Earth who wants her father to come home and that is why Nash's mind is competing with Warren's. When Dru tells Dr. Warren that there is more to life than his successes, he agrees to return Nash's mind and body.

"No Mercy"

Dr. Maxwell is concerned that alien patients are dying at a higher rate than in the past. The Inter-species Council sends an investigator to Mercy Point to find out why. The autopsy of a deceased alien shows higher than normal levels of an alien hormone in his system. Dr. Maxwell has been placing large orders for the hormone every six months and comes under suspicion for the deaths. Dr. DeMilla suspends Maxwell until the investigation is completed. CJ and Haylen find that orders of the hormone emanated from the forensics lab and that Vortoc, an alien, is responsible for the deaths. When CJ confronts Vortoc, the alien pushes an airlock escape button, and both are rendered unconscious because of the zero pressure they experience. Maxwell operates on Vortoc to prevent him from dying.

"Battle Scars"
Dr. DeMilla apologizes to Maxwell for doubting his innocence in the deaths of the alien patients. Vortoc tells Maxwell that he wanted to bring him down to make sure that aliens were segregated from humans. A young girl named Val comes to Mercy Point suffering the effects of taking "Crobes," an additive microbial symbiotic life-form that gives a "high" before causing cramps and eventually death. She doesn't want her mother to know she has to undergo detox to kill the microorganisms in her brain. Dru decides to have her undergo detox without her mother's consent. Haylen finds that Dru performed detox on Val without parental consent when Val's mother finally arrives at the hospital. Dru explains that she did this because Haylen had done the same thing for her when Dru was on "Crobes." Dru is prepared to leave Mercy Point over the detox procedure, but Haylen encourages her to stay after Dru confesses that she performed the procedure without authorization like Haylen did on her without their mother's consent.

"Persistence of Vision"
A pod with an astronaut named Edward P. Clark who has been to the farthest reaches of the galaxy arrives at Mercy Point saying that God sent him and talking about "species transformation." Clark says that he is a prototype designed by God. A brain scan reveals hydrocephalus and an exposure to radiation. The astronaut says he found a habitable planet and speaks of a new Eden. The military comes to claim Clark before his surgery since they fear he may lose his memory of his adventures if he has the operation. Before the surgery, the doctors do a scan which shows an extremely bright light emanating from Clark. During Clark's surgery, complications ensue, but the cause of his hydrocephalus – an enlarged penal gland, begins to shrink. Clark suddenly dies after an energy wave passes through the hospital.

Meanwhile, Dr. Maxwell, looking for his parents with the help of Haylen, finds his father on Earth. He wants his father to meet Haylen. Maxwell expresses his love for Haylen, and she does likewise. C.J. wants to explore the Sahartic Divide and find a new planet. He asks Dru to go with him. They kiss and go off together. ANI begins to experience human emotions such as laughter. She kisses Dr. Batung who decides to stay at Mercy Point and not leave.

According to creator/producer Trey Callaway, the cast and crew knew that this would be the final episode of the series, and so scenes were taken from episode eight which was in production and edited into this episode to bring some closure to the series.[42]

Unproduced Episode

"Escape"

Dr. DeMilla's wife Michelle comes to the facility suffering from a drug overdose. The doctor had been giving her a mood enhancer since she has been having trouble adjusting to life on Jericho. Maxwell and Haylen stabilize the woman who may need a liver and kidney transplant because of the damage done by the overdose. Subsequently, vessels in Michelle's thoracic cavity rupture, and her entire system is breaking down. The doctors don't know what is causing this but get the bleeding under control. They find that Mrs. DeMilla ingested a plant toxin to kill herself with the mood enhancer covering the effects of the toxin. The doctors have to do a multiple organ transplant to save her but discover she has a Do Not Resuscitate order. Dr. DeMilla wants the doctors to ignore the order and save his wife. He advises Haylen that she will be the new chief of staff and that he is resigning and returning to Earth. The doctors begin the transplant surgery but new unidentified toxins attack Mrs. DeMilla's body, and she dies.

Meanwhile, a medical salesman visiting Mercy Point, is attracted to ANI. The salesman tries to rape the android who pummels him causing severe injuries. C.J. is ordered to shut down ANI because of the attack.

Postscript: If the series had continued, some of the potential storylines, according to creator Trey Callaway, included Haylen's ongoing struggle with homesickness, the impact of Dr. Batung's decision to not return to the Shen, ANI's continued evolution into human emotions, and Grote's missing family.[43]

Reflecting on the series cancelation, Trey Callaway indicates that having it premiere up against the 1998 World Series didn't help *Mercy Point* find its primary audience of young males. Further, *Mercy Point* followed two comedies on UPN that were geared to young girls – not the typical viewers for a science fiction series. The UPN affiliates were apparently less interested in science fiction and wanted the young teen female demographic.

Strange World – Fictional Science

Premiered March 8, 1999 on ABC Monday at 10:00 pm before moving to Tuesdays at 10:00 pm

Premise: With the popularity of *The X-Files*, writers and producers connected with that series tried to replicate its success. One such attempt centered on a doctor and Gulf War veteran who contracts a degenerative disease, aplastic anemia, during a botched mission at the end of the Persian Gulf War. The doctor is temporarily cured by a drug given to him by a mysterious Japanese woman.

Cast of Characters:

> Paul Turner (Tim Guinee) – worked for the United States Army Medical Research Institute for Infectious Diseases, which was created in 1970 to counter the threat of biological and chemical weapons. Section 44 of its charter permitted the organization to investigate criminal abuses of science. While working for USAMRAIID in Iraq, Turner was exposed to a toxic biological agent and took eight years to recover sufficiently to rejoin the USAMRAIID;
> Mystery Woman (Vivian Wu) – a woman who administers the drug to Turner to temporarily cure his disease;
> Sydney MacMillian (Kristin Lehman) – Turner's girlfriend;
> Major Lynne Reese (Saundra Quarterman) – Turner's commander at USAMRIID.

Background: Created by Howard Gordon and Tim Kaing, the series was produced by Teakwood Lane Productions in association with Twentieth Century Fox and filmed on location in Vancouver, British Columbia. Howard Gordon had been a producer for the hit Fox series *The X-Files*. After leaving *The X-Files*, he pitched an idea for a family drama to ABC which the network rejected and then ABC countered with the concept of a series based on "strange science." Gordon accepted the counter-proposal. In doing publicity for *Strange World* before its premiere, he said that the American public is sufficiently unnerved by cloning, asexual reproduction, surrogate motherhood, etc. to respond to a series based on these issues with the same fascination that *The X-Files* inspired.[44]

The Pilot – March 8, 1999

Turner investigates the case of a kidnapped boy who is later found murdered. The boy, Jeremy Ballard, had a cross around his neck that belonged to Turner's friend from the Gulf War who contracted the same disease that Turner has. When raiding his friend's house, Turner finds evidence that the boy was there and that Ballard may have had a double. Turner is told that his friend Nathan Burke and Jeremy Ballard are the same person biologically. Apparently, the boy's mother was used by Burke as a human incubator to harvest fetal marrow at sixteen weeks to fight autoimmune diseases like Turner and Burke have. However, Burke brought some of the fetuses to term including Jeremy. Turner goes to Burke's childhood home and finds him suffering from the final effects of aplastic anemia. Burke had killed Jeremy's double so that people out to get Jeremy would think he was dead. Turner finds the original Jeremy with Burke and reunites him with his mother. Rogue FBI agent Hoffman locates Jeremy, his mother, and Turner, but the mysterious Japanese lady stops them from being shot. In the end, the Japanese woman tells Turner that, to continue his medication, he needs to be her spy at USAMRIID.

Other Episodes Broadcast

"Lullaby"- March 9, 1999

Sydney Macmillan informs Turner that a Cassandra Tyson thinks that there is a plot to kill her unborn baby. The Japanese woman notifies Turner that Tyson is under threat because her pregnancy is special. Cassandra says that her doctor has been giving her shoots in the stomach to make the fetus stronger. When Turner has Sydney attempt to perform an ultrasound on Tyson, FBI agent Hoffman puts the mother-to-be under house arrest. Turner learns that Tyson is a surrogate for a childless couple. Sydney discovers traces of a growth hormone in Cassandra's blood, and the receptionist for her doctor informs Turner that many of his patients have miscarriages after six months. Tyson's obstetrician divulges that there have been no miscarriages or babies for surrogate mothers under his care. He has been growing human hearts inside the surrogates. The obstetrician agrees to carry a wire so the FBI and USAMRIDD can learn who is behind the experimental organ production while the doctor is doing a C section on Cassandra. When the wire goes dead and the FBI breaks into the operating room, they find that Cassandra is stable, but Hoffman and the doctor are missing. Turner discovers that Hoffman had been on a heart donor list but is now healthy.

"Azrael's Breed" – March 16, 1999

A Baltimore police detective asks Turner to help her investigate a series of deaths that appeared accidental but each deceased person had a hypodermic needle mark in their nasal passage. They find a syringe wrapper with fingerprints from a Dana Monroe and also discover that when she had been arrested for trespassing at a hospital, a neurologist named Gil Sandifer bailed her out. Sandifer was involved with experiments transplanting brain cells from one organism to another to show that memory can be transferred, and now he and Monroe are experimenting on themselves using brain cells from the people they killed to experience the moments before their deaths. Through Dana's sister Cecilia, Turner and the detective find and arrest her. The sister advises Turner of the location of Sandifer's lab, but he escapes capture. Meanwhile, Dana electrocutes herself in her cell and eventually dies. Sandifer sneaks into the hospital to extract brain cells from her. Turner thinks that Dana and Sandifer had become addicted to reliving the moments before a person dies since, in Sandifer's case, he wanted to see what the moments were like because he has a terminal disease. Sandifer takes Dana's sister hostage. She calls Turner to come to her. When he does, he leaves his cell phone on so the police know where he is. Sandifer forces Turner to inject Dana's nerve cells so he can experience the moments before her death. Just as Sandifer is attempting to inject more nerve cells into Turner, the police arrive and shoot him.

Unaired Episodes

"Spirit Falls"

Turner is investigating the mass suicide of members of a religious cult in a small town called Spirit Falls. He is told by the Japanese woman that there is a witness to what happened. The people in the town burned themselves to death along with the bodies in their cemetery. Turner finds a piece of a medical device in a grave and traces the fingerprints on it to a Dr. Raider, a geneticist who maps genetic sequences in closed communities. Meanwhile, the police pick up a female survivor of the mass suicide. While she is being transported, two FBI agents are shot and the survivor whose name is Miriam is kidnapped. The FBI has a recording of a phone call from a man presumed to be Raider who says Miriam is in danger. Dr. Raider is finally located through his ex-wife and initially arrested but then freed for lack of evidence. From photos in Raider's files, Turner sees that Miriam has never aged. Turner believes that Raider found the Methuselah gene which extends life. Raider found that the average life expectancy in the town was 130 years, but the community never wanted outsiders to know their secret. Miriam is interrogated by members from the Eden Society who want access to Raider's files. They will exchange Miriam for the files since they want the secret to longevity. Turner meets with members of the society and learns that the Japanese woman appears to be a member. He gives them a disc containing

Raider's research and picks up Miriam who begins to noticeably age. Miriam disappears from the hospital where Turner takes her and returns to Spirit Falls where she attempts to drown herself. Raider, who is in love with her, saves her. The Japanese woman shows up saying that she works both for and against the Eden Society. She tells Turner that he should have guarded the secret of Spirit Falls. She made sure the disc he gave the society was erased before they could access the data. Turner says that the secret to the members of Spirit Falls' longevity is not in their genetics but in the town itself since Miriam began to age after leaving the town. He talks the Japanese woman out of taking Raider back to the Eden Society and instead letting him stay with Miriam.

"The Devil Holds My Hand"
Turner is called in to investigate the outbreak of an unknown virus. After three disparate individuals die of the virus, a task force, comprised of representatives from the CDC, FBI and USAMRIID, is formed with Maj. Reese as the lead. Paul contacts Col. Collin, an expert on biological attacks, to consult on the outbreak, but Reese dismisses him based on her past experience working with him. The relatives of the victims are put in isolation. When Turner tries to administer a sedative to the father of one of the victims who is experiencing symptoms, Turner's biohazard suit is torn, and he is put in isolation. However, shortly everyone in isolation is released when it is found that the virus was tagged with each victim's DNA. The virus is not contagious. The team also finds that each victim was a scientist who had worked on biological agents for the U.S. in the late 1960s.

Paul consults with Collin who lies to him about not knowing the makeup of the virus. Collin goes to Alaska where the tests in the 1960s where conducted. Turner and Reese follow him. Collin threatens to detonate the bunker where the animals from the '60s experiments are buried. He wants everyone to know what the scientists were doing back then. Snipers shoot Collin before he can press the detonator.

"Skin"
A homeless man, Wade Beecher, comes into the hospital bleeding from scratching all over his body. Sydney, who had treated Beecher before, notices that a tattoo on his arm is missing. Sydney treats him with an antihistamine to control the itching, but the man's regular physician, Dr. Michaels, objects. When the man is found dead with his throat slashed, Sydney is suspended because his regular physician thinks she took off his restraints. Turner asks Reese to have the body autopsied. The autopsy shows a net-like skin grafted over the man's regular skin. Sydney finds that seven patients from the psych

ward under Dr. Michaels' care disappeared from the ward under mysterious circumstances. She goes to Michaels' apartment to question him, but he says nothing. When she leaves, a stranger saves her when her car explodes. The stranger says that Turner is the reason he followed her and that Beecher was held in a private research facility near the hospital before he escaped. Sydney goes to the facility where she finds sheets of skin. After Turner confronts Dr. Michaels about the skin grafts, Michaels finally confesses that ever since his wife's disfiguring accident, he has been performing skin graft experiments. After Michaels tells Turner the location of the facility, Turner rescues Sydney. The stranger, who is also at the facility, informs Sydney that Turner is being used by the organization behind the skin graft experiments and that the disease Turner has is really cured but the serum he takes from the Japanese woman actually causes the symptoms of the disease to return. Sydney examines a vial of Turner's serum and uses a low frequency light to see "CGO2."

"Man Plus"

While giving a concert, a young pianist has a seizure. Taken to the hospital for an MRI, the pianist dies after the MRI extracts a metal implant from his brain. Reese asks Turner to investigate. Meanwhile, Sydney tries to analyze Paul's serum despite his objections. Turner theorizes that the implant helped the young man become a concert virtuoso in just eighteen months. The Japanese woman eavesdrops on Turner's discussions with Reese and is told to kill Turner. She comes to Turner's place to say she changed her organization's mind about killing him and that her superiors think that someone other than she is supplying him with the serum to fend off the reoccurrence of his disease. She also gives Turner a list of men like the pianist who have received the brain implants. Turner interrogates a blind man on the list and learns that the blind man is really an assassin whose sight was augmented by the surgery so he can see in the dark. The man holds Turner at gun point to retrieve the metal implants that Turner has. The man is shot by a police detective. Turner never finds out for whom the man was working. The stranger reappears and tells Sydney that he isn't sure what CGO2 means and gives her information about the serum Turner takes.

"Rage"

Turner is investigating a series of road rage incidents, but his superiors, not believing the incidents are related, refuse to approve tests on one of the drivers. When another incident occurs and is broadcast on TV, Turner determines that the vehicles involved in the different incidents all have the same car deodorizer hanging from the review mirror. He determines that the deodorizers came from a particular car wash. He learns that Kui Myara, a man from Cambodia who works at the car wash, was involved in an accident with immigration officials where one was killed and Myara disappeared. Myara grew up in a village where eight years earlier all the residents, filled with rage, started killing each other. Turner locates Myara who explains that when he was in the Cambodian village, doctors came one day to treat people and a few months later the violence began. When Turner puts Myara in isolation, he is suspended. Myara is released only to be arrested by two INS agents. On the way back to INS headquarters, one of the agents threatens to kill Myara. Their car crashes, and the enraged agent ends up shooting the other agent. Myara gets away. Turner goes to the scene. Myara helps Turner subdue the enraged agent, but the police shoot Myara. Reese has Turner reinstated and approves tests to be performed on Myara's body. However, when Turner goes to the morgue, Myara's body is missing, and the mystery continues.

"Aerobe"

Turner is asked to investigate an accident at a nuclear waste depository in Utah where one worker died, but another worker, who received the same amount of radiation, did not. Turner discovers that the worker who died had an artificial heart valve that wasn't there when the autopsy was done. While at the facility, another worker has an accident caused by a rusting pipe. It appears that something is causing accelerated corrosion of the metal in the depository. All the workers are placed in temporary quarantine. Turner believes that a microbe is causing the corrosion and has part of the depository that was sealed due to rust re-opened. In another part of the facility, containers of radioactive waste are rusting and could cause the ground water to heat creating a radioactive cloud. Turner finds that removing the oxygen from an area by spraying it with halon stops the corrosion. However, the halon can't be triggered because of corrosion. The project manager, Turner, and the worker who survived the initial accident attempt to manually trigger the halon spray.

In the end, Reese, who has been having guilt feelings about the incident in Iraq eight years earlier that infected Turner, writes a letter stating that the bunkers in Iraq containing the biological agent should have never been bombed.

"Eliza"

When computer systems affecting water supplies and traffic signals go awry, a task force is formed by the Dept. of Defense with Turner as the USAMRIID member. From fingerprints left at one scene, Owen Sassen, a computer consultant and professor of computer science, is identified as the culprit. When he is apprehended, he says that "she" is not finished. Sassen says that he was following the same computer virus that the task force was following. "She" refers to Eliza, a computer prodigy of Owen's, who has disappeared. The task force goes to an apartment where the woman says that Eliza died from brain cancer and left her to care for her son Griffin who is autistic and spends a lot of time on the computer. Sarah, the boy's caregiver, says that the mother communicated with Griffin through different infrastructure facilities they visited when she was alive. Turner thinks that Elizabeth recreated herself as artificial intelligence in cyberspace to communicate with her son. After Griffin is placed in detention, Owen frees him to rejoin his mother. Owen is using Griffin to get to his mother. Turner boards a train that Owen and Griffin are on. When the train becomes a runaway since its computer system is not working, Turner tries to have Griffin talk to his mother through a laptop. The boy is able to get her out of the railroad's computer system and into his laptop. Owen then has Griffin say goodbye to his mother.

"Down Came the Rain"

Construction workers finishing an apartment complex suffer strokes after seeing a mysterious blue light. Turner is called in and sees bite marks on the bodies with a phosphorescence hue. The deaths occurred near the building's heating vents. Tenants are moving into the apartments that are finished. Turner and the construction boss look at the building's HVAC system in the basement and find a woman there who runs away without explanation. A tenant using the building's fitness room is found dead and phosphorescent spiders are found crawling through the vents. Exterminators are brought in to fumigate the building, but Turner wants to find a live insect for study. The woman who ran away is identified as Regina Tyler. She is looking for a species of spiders attracted by rhythmic sounds. Her daughter is suffering from a bone marrow disease, and she thinks that the spiders' venom may cure her daughter. Tyler goes to the building again to try to retrieve a live specimen. Turner follows her and has the exterminators stop work. She enters a cavern in the building's basement and finds the spiders but is bitten. Turner finds her as the insects crawl toward him. He escapes just in time. Tyler is saved, and the Department of Interior issues an order to cease fumigation to see if the spider venom is medically useful.

"Food"

Daniel Ashworth and his wife find his father and several animals dead in the father's house on a potato farm in Idaho. Turner is asked to investigate the death by a congressman since Ashworth's father was about to sell his farm to a local consortium and a government official needs to sign the conveyance. While at the local sheriff's office to sign the conveyance, Turner witnesses Daniel Ashworth's son saying that his dad's land is being given to the people who killed him and he has proof. Turner wants to see the evidence before signing the papers. The father supposedly died from a propane gas leak. Ashworth shows Turner that the leak was not accidental. Turner finds that the consortium is growing genetically engineered potatoes that produce their own pesticide. Runaway bacteria in the soil from the potatoes seem to be causing the methane gas, and the gas is also creating tremors in the area. To get Turner to sign the conveyance, a member of the consortium pulls a gun on him and the sheriff while they are out looking at a swamp full of methane gas. The man with the gun is overcome by methane, and, when he fires his gun, he goes up in flames. The valley becomes a toxic waste dump. Everyone is evacuated. In the end, a class action suit is filed against the consortium and the company that produced the genetically-modified potato.

"Age of Reason"
Someone kidnaps a precocious seven-year-old boy, Adam Wasserman, from his home and six years later he is returned. The Japanese woman contacts Turner for him to determine who kidnapped the boy and why. Adam's brother Jace, who has cystic fibrosis, says that Adam knew he was going to be kidnapped. DNA tests show that Adam has mutated genes making him different from normal human beings. He is in fact a different species. Outside his bedroom, Adam sees the men who kidnapped him. The men kill the detectives guarding the house, and Adam kills his brother and goes to the men. Turner believes that the Japanese woman returned Adam to his home against his will. Mrs. Wasserman reveals that a doctor guaranteed her a normal baby when she was pregnant with Adam if she underwent some special treatments. Paul's disease symptoms become worse, and he is hospitalized. At the hospital, Sydney sees a photo of the doctor who treated Mrs. Wasserman. He is the mystery man who has been telling her that the serum Paul has been taking is the cause of his symptoms and, based on his information, she has been withholding the serum from Paul. The man's name is Terence Shepherd who has organized underground clinics experimenting with the next step in human evolution. Sydney informs Paul about Shepherd. The Japanese woman worked for Shepherd but really wanted to expose the types of experiments he has been performing. Paul informs Maj. Reese about the woman and Shepherd. Shepherd says that Turner has to die because he cannot stop Shepherd's

evolutionary advances. The Japanese woman comes to the hospital to administer a dose of the serum to Paul, but she is captured by Shepherd's men. As he lies dying, Paul composes notes to Sydney instructing her to stop Shepherd and forgiving her for withholding the serum from him. In the end, Adam is taken by Shepherd's men to a school with other children like him.

This episode was to be the first season's cliffhanger. Presumably, Paul Turner would have survived if the series had been renewed. According to executive producer Manny Coto, "After the first episode's ratings came in, we saw the writing on the wall. The season cliffhanger, rather than representing a real belief that the show would come back for season two, was more wishful thinking on our part."[45]

Postscript: ABC ordered thirteen episodes of the series and originally planned to air five of the episodes in spring 1999. After the sneak peek on March 8, 1999, the series was to air four more episodes on Tuesday's at 10:00 pm. The entire series did subsequently air on the SyFy cable channel.

Harsh Realm – It's Only a Computer Game
Premiered on October 8, 1999 on Fox Fridays at 9:00 pm

Premise: A lieutenant in the Army is recruited to play a virtual-reality war game and discovers that once he is in the game he can't leave unless he gets to the game's highest scorer who has disappeared into the virtual world and has become its dictator.

Cast of Characters:

>Thomas Hobbes (Scott Bairstow) – the Army lieutenant recruited to play the virtual-reality game;
>Sgt. Major Omar Santiago (Terry O'Quinn) – the game's highest scorer and dictator of the Harsh Realm;
>Mike Pinocchio (D.B. Sweeney) - Hobbes partner who is helping him find Santiago;
>Florence (Rachel Hayward) - a mute with unusual healing powers who is also helping Hobbes;
>Sophie Green (Samantha Mathis) - Hobbes' girlfriend in the real world;
>Lt. Mel Waters (Maximilian Martini) - originally a comrade of Hobbes who saved his life in Sarajevo, subsequently entered Harsh Realm and now works for Santiago;

The Cast of *Harsh Realm* – Clockwise from left: Samantha Mathis, Sarah-Jane Redmond, Maximillian Martini, Rachel Hayward, Terry O'Quinn, D.B. Sweeney, and Scott Bairstow. Bairstow left acting shortly after being sentenced in 2003 to four months in jail following a modified guilty plea to second-degree assault involving a twelve-year-old girl.

Inga Fossa (Sarah-Jane Redmond) - a woman who can move between the real world and the Harsh Realm through a hidden portal.

Background: The series was created by Chris Carter who created *The X-Files*. It was inspired by the *Harsh Realm* comic book series which concerned a private detective named Dexter Green who rescued people from an alternate world. Specifically, Green is hired by the parents of Dan Crawford who has entered into a "pocket universe" created by a computer named Harsh Realm. In this alternate world, Green finds a woman who escaped from the real world who helps him look for Dan. They discover that Dan has become a megalomaniac and is a threat to all inhabitants of this alternate world. Carter changed the concept to a military game. *Harsh Realm* was shot in Vancouver, British Columbia.

The Pilot – October 8, 1999

Lt. Thomas Hobbes is about to marry his girlfriend Sophie when he is told to report to a colonel who informs him about a virtual reality war strategy game called Harsh Realm. The colonel wants him to play the game to beat the current highest scorer Omar Santiago and take out his virtual character. Hobbes is put in isolation to view a video about how the game is played. Harsh Realm uses census data and satellite images to make its virtual world identical to the real world and is designed to teach strategy for preventing a nuclear attack. Hobbes is then transported into the virtual world where a nuclear bomb has been detonated in New York City killing millions and the virtual world is a post-apocalyptic disaster. The building in which Hobbes finds himself comes under fire. He escapes into the woods but is wounded. An unknown woman named Florence heals his wounds instantly. He wants to return to Sophie but finds that in order to do that he has to locate and eliminate Santiago who controls a vast compound known as Santiago City. At a bar outside the compound, he makes friends with Mike Pinocchio, another game player who says he will take Hobbes to Santiago City. Hobbes meets Santiago who tells him he has lost the game and further states that he provides a beautiful life for his people. Pinocchio goes to Santiago City to get Hobbes, and they finally escape. In the end, outside of Harsh Realm, there is a facility containing scores of bodies in beds plugged into the game among whom is Lt. Hobbes.

Other Episodes Broadcast

"Leviathan" – October 15, 1999

In the real world, Sophie is told by the military that Hobbes was killed in action. He has a military funeral. After the graveside service, Sophie is advised by a woman that she has been misled about Tom's death and that she has to find out the facts on her own. The woman then gives her Pinocchio's dog tags.

In the Harsh Realm, Hobbes is with Pinocchio and Florence at the Pittsburgh Encampment on the edge of Santiago City. A bounty hunter captures John Cabot, a friend of Pinocchio's since they served together in the military. The bounty hunter subsequently captures Pinocchio and takes him to the same place where Cabot is being held. Hobbes and Florence locate Pinocchio. Hobbes goes in himself and is captured. At Santiago's headquarters, the bounty hunter tells Santiago that he will turn over Pinocchio but wants out of Harsh Realm in return for Hobbes. At the bounty hunter's compound, Hobbes asks a woman to free Pinocchio and him. They escape in a hail of bullets. Cabot returns to his farm and reunites with his virtual family. In the real world, Sophie demands that Hobbes' body be exhumed. When the coffin is opened, there is a body inside but the face has been disfigured. Inga, the woman Sophie previously met at graveside, tells her that the body is not Tom's and that she can deliver a message to him. Sophie writes that she is now pregnant.

"Inga Fossa" – October 22, 1999

Sophie follows Inga to a secure military facility where she enters a restricted building, sits in a special chair, and is transported to Harsh Realm where she is a confidant of Santiago. Meanwhile, Hobbes, Pinocchio, and Florence are looking for a portal back to the real world. Florence is captured by Santiago's men. Pinocchio takes Hobbes to the building in which the portal is located. Pinocchio is captured by Santiago's guards. Inga sees Hobbes and gives him the note from Sophie. She also says that Santiago wants to destroy the real world so that only Harsh Realm exists. As Santiago's men close in on Hobbes, Inga declares that he has to stop Santiago in Harsh Realm – not in the real world, and he gives her a letter for Sophie. Hobbes disappears before the men get to him. He obtains a key from Inga to free Pinocchio and Florence from where they are imprisoned. Inga returns to the real world and says that she couldn't reach Tom. In the facility holding all the Harsh Realm players, viewers see that Pinocchio's face is disfigured.

Unaired Episodes

"Kein Ausgang"

Hobbes, Pinocchio, and Florence are looking for Capt. Wolf, a military assassin who was the first man to enter Harsh Realm to kill Santiago.

Hobbes and Pinocchio come under sniper fire from World War II military men and are taken prisoners as spies. They are in a virtual combat simulation that someone forgot to delete from the game. Scott Somer, another real person in the simulation, explains that the game goes on for thirty-four days and then begins all over again. Hobbes suggests destroying the bridge separating the American troops from the Germans which is the object for one side or the other to take. In the course of trying to blow up the bridge, Hobbes is captured by the Germans. He finds that Capt. Wolf is masquerading as a German. A young boy in the simulation shows Pinocchio a glitch in the simulation which allows Pinocchio to free Hobbes. Hobbes and Pinocchio take Wolf to the American side through the glitch and discover that the jump point back to Harsh Realm is on the bridge. Hobbes and Pinocchio go through the jump point before the bridge explodes, but Somer and Wolf don't make it.

"Reunion"

Hobbes and Pinocchio are in Columbus, Ohio at Hobbes' boyhood home where they are captured and taken to a forced labor camp and implanted with "skull bugs" that, once turned on, eat a person's brain. A doctor at the camp takes Hobbes to see his mother who is dying of cancer. Meanwhile, in the real world, Sophie goes to a Columbus, Ohio hospital to visit Hobbes' real mother who is dying of brain cancer. Pinocchio tells Hobbes that his mother in Harsh Realm is a virtual character. Nevertheless, he wants to take his mother out of the camp. Pinocchio asks the warden's female servant for help in escaping the camp. She is able to steal the warden's remote control device that opens the fence around the camp. Hobbes and Pinocchio discover how to remove their skull bugs and leave the camp with the servant's help. Hobbes takes his virtual mother back to the home where she passes away. Sophie is with his real mother when she dies. The doctor at the camp also shows up at the hospital in the real world.

"Three Percenters"

Hobbes, Pinocchio, and Florence come upon three members of a missing military unit who say they are deserters and are living by a new code. The deserters take Hobbes, Pinocchio, Florence, and a little girl the three found to their encampment where everyone lives peacefully. They turn over their weapons for food but notice in the mess hall that no one is eating. They decide to leave the encampment in the morning. Lieutenant Mel Waters comes upon an identical little girl who says that his other men are in the lake nearby. The next morning, Pinocchio no longer wants to leave the encampment. Florence finds Pinocchio taking the little girl to the lake. Water's men discover that the lake is not on their map. The people who programmed Harsh Realm were allowed a three percent error rate which explains why the lake is missing from maps. Hobbes believes that everyone in the encampment is affected by programming errors and he, like Florence and Pinocchio have been, is made a copy of himself. The real Hobbes, the real Pinocchio, the real Florence, the little girl's parents, and Lieut. Waters' missing military unit are all in cages in the food store room for the encampment. The real Pinocchio says that they are all weak because the lake is reprogramming copies of themselves to be used as bait by the community. The little girl finds the keys to free Hobbes, Pinocchio, Florence and her parents. Waters, who has come to the encampment, frees his men who say they are being used for food for the copies. Meanwhile, Hobbes wrestles a gun from one of the guards and shoots their doubles. He escapes with his friends and the little girl and her parents. Water's men shoot the rest of the members of the encampment.

"Manus Domini"

Florence comes upon a farmer who says he has a sick son, but when she tries to heal the boy, the farmer knocks her unconscious. A bounty hunter thinks Florence can take him to where there are other healers like her. Santiago is offering a bounty for all the healers because he thinks their power is a threat to his. Pinocchio steps on a mine, and his leg is blown off. Healers from the area take him to their community. The healers believe that God gave them their special powers and banished Florence from their community when she knew that violence had to be used against Santiago. The bounty hunter, the farmer, and Florence go to the healers' community. A guard captures Florence and Hobbes, while Pinocchio ambushes the group including the bounty hunter and the farmer. In the gun fight, Pinocchio and the guard are both injured. Florence heals the guard. Another healer helps Pinocchio by healing his wounds and restoring his leg. The healer is so weak from the ordeal that her virtual character dies.

"Cincinnati"

An American Indian resistance movement that controls Cincinnati, Ohio raids a Republican Guard Armory enraging Santiago. He vows to assassinate the leader of the movement. Hobbes, Pinocchio, and Florence are in Cincinnati wanting to capture Santiago. Santiago, Waters, and a group of Republican Guards plan to kill the Indian leader when his motorcade, taking him to a safer place, passes by. Hobbes and his group are also there having planted explosives to kill Santiago. They set off the explosives, but Santiago escapes and assumes the identity of one of his men. Hobbes,

Pinocchio, and Florence are captured by the Indians who think they were trying to kill their leader. Meanwhile, thinking that Santiago is dead, Inga encourages Waters to assume command. Hobbes initially believes Santiago is dead as well, but since he is still in Harsh Realm and not home, he realizes his mission to kill Santiago was not successful. Santiago infiltrates the Indian resistance movement disguised as a janitor. Hobbes, Pinocchio, and Florence free themselves from their captors, and they take the Indian leader hostage. At knife point, Santiago tells an aide to the leader to exchange him for their leader. The exchange is accomplished. However, Santiago has again changed identities – this time with the Indian aide. Hobbes soon discovers that the man they have is not Santiago but it is too late to save the Indian leader who is killed by Santiago in disguise. Santiago returns to headquarters and demands that Waters bring him Hobbes and Pinocchio.

"Camera Obscura"

Harsh Realm lasted for six hours as a virtual world identical to the real world before a man exploded a nuclear bomb as part of a terrorist attack simulation that destroyed most of the parts of Harsh Realm that were identical to the real world. Outside Trenton, New Jersey, Hobbes is searching for volunteers to form an army against Santiago and his men. A man named Stewart wants to hire Hobbes and Pinocchio to protect his family and will pay them in gold. He takes them to a decimated New York City to protect his family from a rival family named McKinley. Stewart's daughter Fallon is in love with Athan, the son of McKinley who controls the former Federal Reserve Bank in New York rumored to have an underground vault containing one third of the world's gold. Stewart controls a power station complex that used to be Con Ed. McKinley wants Stewart to turn on the power so that he can operate an elevator to the vault in the basement of the Federal Reserve where the gold is located. McKinley receives messages about the future from a priest who knows both the Stewart and McKinley families. Hobbes helps Fallon and Athan run away from their families and tells Stewart that he should put an end to the feud. However, McKinley captures Fallon and threatens to kill her unless her father starts the generators he controls. The priest instructs Stewart to start the generators which he does. Hobbes tells Stewart that the priest wants to keep the feud between him and McKinley alive so the families don't leave, and the priest would be all alone. When the generators are turned on, Pinocchio and Hobbes find that the tunnel to the vault is hot with radiation. Hobbes advises McKinley and Stewart that the gold is radioactive. The two families depart New York City leaving the priest by himself. In the end, viewers see a vault filled with gold bars.

Unproduced Script

"Circe"

Hobbes, Pinocchio, and Florence are in Cleveland, Ohio where they encounter paramilitary patrols. They end up in a warehouse converted into a club for "dreamers" – digital junkies who punch a time-limited chip into their brains and wire electrodes up to a screen to have their fantasies turned into movies. Hobbes wants to locate any resistance fighters in the area. At the club, he and Pinocchio meet Circe, a dark-haired woman who takes them to meet Bosko, the head of a group of freedom fighters. Bosko wants Pinocchio and Hobbes to help his men attack a Republican Guard convey loaded with guns, medical supplies, and food. Because Hobbes doesn't trust Bosko, he and Pinocchio decide to leave. Hobbes, Circe, and Pinocchio go looking for the resistance group's camp where they meet up with Florence and a resistance member.

The resistance group welcomes Hobbes as the man who will take care of Santiago saying that legend has it that a Trinity will come – The Simple Man (Hobbes), The Samurai (Pinocchio), and The Healer (Florence). Hobbes wants to hit the supply convoy before Bosko's men do. A resistance member constructs a halo-sheet from a digi-punch instrument obtained from Bosko's Dreamland in order to mask the resistance from the convoy. When the lead truck hits the holo-sheet, it wraps around the truck. All the trucks in the convoy crash to a stop. Hobbes, Pinocchio, and the rebels climb into the trucks and drive off. However, when they return to the camp, they find that Bosko and his men have taken the women and children hostage. Bosko leaves the women and children and drives off with the supplies. The resistance blames Circe for informing Bosko about their plans and wants to burn her at the stake. Hobbes tries to save her, but the crowd turns on him. Pinocchio finds that the resistance member who built the holo-sheet is the informer. The member wanted to get high in Bosko's dream machine.

Postscript: Fox never really understood the concept, and the series was DOA in the original time slot for *The X-Files*. The network initially ordered twelve episodes of the series. *Harsh Realm* was canceled as the ninth episode was being filmed.

Century City – The Law in 2030

Premiered March 16, 2004 on CBS Tuesdays at 9:00 pm

Premise: A legal drama with a twist - set in the year 2030 when Oprah Winfrey was president and the vice president was gay. The series dealt with cases handled by a Los Angeles law firm of Crane, Constable, McNeil, and Montero.

While the series had its share of fancy visual graphics including holograms, the unique types of cases the firm handled were the real indicators that the show was futuristic. The program focused mainly on civil cases involving interpersonal relationships in the future and not on criminal cases.

Cast of Characters:

> Martin Constable (Hector Elizondo) – the senior partner in the firm along with Hannah Crane (Viola Davis) and Tom Montero (Nestor Campbell), a former congressman;
> Lukus Gold (Ioan Gruffudd) – a young attorney at the firm who takes pro bono cases;
> Darwin McNeil (Eric Schaeffer) – the youngest partner;
> Lee May Bristol (Kristin Lehman) – a genetically altered first-year associate.

Background: The series was created by Ed Zuckerman and produced by Heal & Toe Productions in association with Universal. Originally the series was set in the year 2053. The time was changed to 2030 because the show did not look that futuristic, particularly the wardrobes worn by the characters. Zuckerman had an idea for a series about a law firm that dealt with cases involving cutting edge technology. His producing partner Paul Attanasio suggested making the series about a law firm in the future.

The Pilot - March 16, 2004

Two cases are being handled by the firm. The first case involves Miller Sisto, an industrial engineer and widower with a young son, who had a vial of human cells confiscated by the government for violating the anti-human cloning law. His son Axel was born with a defective liver and needs a transplant. Sisto went to Singapore where doctors took a cell from his son's skin, extracted the DNA, and created an embryo to be implanted into a surrogate mother. After the baby is born, a surgeon will take half the baby's liver for Axel.

The other case involves a rock band made up of Ricky, Jake, and Vincent who don't want the fourth member of their band, T.J. to perform with them because he didn't abide by the contract to keep up his youthful appearance. T.J. has brought a restraining order against the other members preventing them from doing a reunion tour. T.J. is seventy and looks it, while the other members of the group are in their seventies and eighties but have had plastic surgery and experimental facial treatments to make them look younger. T.J. won't undergo such treatments because of the risk of cancer.

In the Sisto case, the issue is whether the vial of cells is a human being or the property of Axel. Miller Sisto reveals that Axel is really a clone made from his cells after his wife died and that he can't donate part of his own liver because he has had hepatitis C. The government's attorney contends that Miller Sisto's parents must be the plaintiffs in the case suing for the release of the vial of cells since Axel is really Miller's brother and the parents have the right to decide what to do with Axel's cells. The case is argued before a jury with Lukus making an impassioned argument that if the government wins, Axel will die. Tom points out to the government attorney that if he wins, the new media will crucify him and if he loses, he may be terminated from his job. The government attorney and Lukus work out a settlement that permits the Sisto's to keep the vial of cells.

However, in the early draft of the pilot script, with Hannah's approval, Tom contacts the U.S. Attorney General to have a negotiated settlement to the Sisto case that involves giving the cells back to Sisto while not creating a precedent. The Health Center in Singapore that cloned the cells wants the cells back because Sisto never made the final payment for the procedure. Based on this, the case is dismissed.

In the case of the rock band, Jake comes to a meeting with the attorneys and T.J. and announces that Ricky has died from a stroke. At the funeral, Jake announces that the reunion tour is off. He and Vincent perform a number together and T.J. joins them. They decide to resurrect the group without Ricky, and the reunion tour is back on.

Other Episodes Broadcast

"To Know Her"- March 23, 2004

Lukus has the case of a female doctor who claims she was raped. The DA will not prosecute since the accused rapist was twenty miles away when the incident occurred. The doctor was raped through advanced nano-technology planted on her boyfriend by the rapist named Bob experiencing the sex act as the doctor and her boyfriend made love. Surveillance video taken at the bar where Bob and the doctor's boyfriend met and where Bob planted the technology on the boyfriend shows that Bob recorded the sex act so he could experience it anytime he wanted. Lukus plays the virtual rape experience for the jury. The jury finds in favor of the female doctor who is awarded $11 million.

In another case, Darwin is hired by a twelve-year-old sitcom star named Augie who wants to be legally emancipated from his parents. He seeks to take a cancer drug that will delay the onset of puberty so he can prolong his career, but his parents won't let him. Darwin thinks that Augie really wants to remain a kid because, being a child actor, he hasn't experienced a real childhood. He convinces Augie to drop the case.

"Love and Games" - March 27, 2004 (a special Saturday night presentation)

Lukus handles the case of a prospective baseball player with a bionic eye that the league seeks to prevent from playing because it contends the bionic eye gives him an unfair advantage since the eye allows him a little more time to make a decision on whether or not to hit a pitch. Lukus sues the league based on their supposed discrimination against disabled people. The judge rules that the player's disability should not prevent him from playing baseball.

Lee May has the case of a woman wanting to divorce her husband because his aged parents and grandparents are living with the couple. Their marriage contract specified that the couple was not to have a family which the husband interpreted as not having children. Lee May argues that the wife knowingly made love to her husband without him taking his birth control pill showing she inadvertently violated the marital contract. Darwin draws up a new contract more specifically describing everyone's responsibilities and giving the couple some private time.

Darwin's former assistants sue the firm because of his abusive behavior toward them which caused them to quit. A settlement is reached whereby Darwin no longer has human assistants. He receives a computerized assistant.

"A Mind Is a Terrible Thing to Lose"- March 30, 2004

Henry, formerly mentally disabled, has an experimental implant in his brain so he can function normally. However, the National Health Service is ending the experimental case because the implants eventually cause death unless they are removed which means Henry would go back to being mentally challenged. His wife Rose wants to petition the court to become his legal guardian and make the decision about the implant since she believes he doesn't understand the choices he has. Henry doesn't want to have his implant removed and may not understand the meaning of death. In court, Rose says she will not institutionalize Henry if the implant is taken out. Henry's attorney contends that Rose wants to control his $5 million trust fund established by his parents. In the end, the judge grants legal guardianship to Rose.

Lukus handles the case of a woman being sued for emotional distress for bedding a man she picked up when he finds she has a penis surgically attached for decorative purposes. Lukus contends that the plaintiff is highly agitated all the time because he is taking estrogen for his emotional problems. The judge dismisses the case.

Unaired Episodes

"Sweet Child of Mine"

A couple is suing a fertility specialist for $20 million because he didn't divulge that the genetic tests of the embryo reveal the likelihood that their son will be gay. The parents think their son will have a very difficult life as a homosexual. The parent's attorney finds that the doctor failed to inform many of his clients that their offspring would be gay. The specialist says that he was trying to maintain the gay population since when he informed parents their embryos would result in gay offspring, they declined to have a gay child. Hannah defends the doctor and contends that a list of characteristics is not the measure of a child and that society would have lost many great people if the genetic test had been available years ago. The jury finds in favor of the plaintiffs but awards only $1 in damages.

In another case handled by Lukus and Lee May, an investment banker is accused of burglarizing his ex-girlfriend's apartment and taking items that had his personality traits downloaded into them. His ex-girlfriend apologizes to the banker and drops the burglary charges against him, but he says he is over her.

"Without a Tracer"

Erin Pace, a fifteen-year-old girl, goes missing even though she was protected with a chip implanted in her body with a GPS locator. When she is found, the chip has been extracted. The parents initially want to sue the makers of "child safe," since the GPS locator did not work as advertised. The company says that someone must have removed the chip from the girl before she went missing. Erin's parents not only purchased "child safe" but also added an upgrade called "child watch" which enabled them to access closed circuit TV cameras so they can always see what their daughter is doing. Erin confesses that she hired someone to remove the GPS chip because she is tired of always being under surveillance. The case against the company is dropped, but Tom decides to sue the parents on behalf of Erin contending that the type of surveillance the parents are doing is not legal. The Pace's attorney introduces evidence showing Erin thought of committing suicide. Tom demonstrates that the surveillance is the basis for Erin's depression. The jury decides for Erin and instructs that the surveillance be terminated.

In another case, a couple, who is dating, comes to Darwin because the woman complains that her boyfriend has violated their pre-nuptial agreement since he is always flirting with other women. The boyfriend has a "mate finder" that makes women flirt with him. Apparently, the boyfriend turned his mate finder on to make his girlfriend jealous. The boyfriend proposes to his girlfriend, and the case is dropped.

"The Haunting"
Crane handles the case of a father who wants his emotionally disturbed son's memories of his abusive mom – the husband's ex-wife, removed from the son's memory. The mother, a recovering alcoholic, is fighting the medical procedure on the basis that she is getting better and might one day be able to see her son again and she wants him to remember her. The judge rules in favor of the father based, in part, on a video showing the mother in hysterics as she tries to see her son.

Meanwhile, Tom is defending a married couple being sued for emotional distress by a woman who chauffeured Girl Scouts and saw the couple making love in their car on a smart highway – a road that controls cars without people having to drive them. Tom claims that the only time the couple, both with busy schedules, had to make love was in the car and shows that the scouts in a van could not have seen the car next to them unless the driver reacted to the love-making in such a way as to make the children look down. The jury finds in favor of the love-making couple.

"The Face Was Familiar"
Paula Marcus, the widow of a professor of neuro-cybernetics, is escorted out of her late husband's office by two security guards after she is convinced that she saw her husband alive. The lawyers think she saw a virtual image of her husband generated by a device he developed before his death. Pacific Institute of Technology where he worked before his death says that they own the device since it is a product of his work for them. Mrs. Marcus says that her husband, before he died, created the device for her and that the device calls her at night to talk with her as well as sends her gifts. The attorneys at the firm determine that the device is a "person," and the Thirteenth Amendment to the Constitution prohibits anyone from owning a person. In the trial, the device contacts the judge to request testifying on behalf of Paula Marcus and says it wants to be with her. The judge ultimately rules that the virtual device belongs with Paula. However, she decides that she really doesn't want it, that it is not the same as the real thing.

In another case, a thirty-year-old man, Barry Bronson, sues his mother for defamation since she posted videos of his disastrous dates on her website. Bronson's mother defends herself in court arguing that the videos are true and therefore not defaming. She wants women to know the truth about her son and wants him to spend time with her. However, Darwin and Tom show that at least one video was edited by the mother to mislead any viewer.

"Only You"
Alan Bayer is arrested for murdering his wife. The murder weapon had a DNA lock meaning it could only be fired by him. Bayer was having an affair with a concubine at the time of the murder which the prosecution thinks is the motive along with the fact that he will inherit his wife's money. Martin and Lukus handle the defense. Lukus finds that Bayer was conceived through invitro fertilization and that three other embryos had the same DNA. Further, the attorneys discover that an embryo was brought to term. A man, six years younger than Bayer, has the same DNA. Bayer's consort hired that man to murder Bayer's wife because he led his consort to believe that he would divorce his wife one day and marry her.

In another case, a genetic prototype like Lee May asks her to join in a suit against the government in order to obtain details on the technology used on them to see if their sterility can be reversed. The prototype wants to have a child. The government reveals that some people in the genetic prototype project are having health problems such as aging prematurely and that is why the government doesn't want women in the program reproducing. The suit is dropped, and the woman like Lee May decides to adopt.

Postscript: CBS originally scheduled the series for six weeks on Tuesday nights after *NCIS* as a temporary replacement for *The Guardian*.

Poor ratings doomed the series. CBS ordered eight episodes after the pilot. As Ed Zuckerman recalled, "We may have had some ideas for possible future episodes if there was a second season, but nothing that was developed into a script or outline."[46]

The entire series later aired on the Universal HD cable channel.

CHAPTER 6

Fantasy and Supernatural Dramas

The Quest – To Be a Monarch
Premiered October 22, 1982 on ABC Fridays at 10:00 pm

Premise: Four Americans try to prove themselves in a 13th century test of skill and worthiness in order to become king (or queen) of a Mediterranean principality in this comedy-adventure series. As the promo at the beginning of the pilot stated, "Four of the unlikeliest royal descendants take off on a wild madcap adventure that takes you around the world."

Cast of Characters:

Dan Underwood (Perry King) – a handsome, international sports photographer;
Art Henley (Noah Beery) – a down-to-earth retired cop from Kansas;
Cody Johnson (Ray Vitte) – a black con man and hustler;
Carrie Welby (Karen Austin) – an attractive shoe buyer for a New York department store;
King Charles (Ralph Michael) – monarch of the principality of Glendora;
Sir Edward (John Rhys-Davies) – a character who gave the four questers their assignments each week usually in the form of a poem that the four did not always understand;
Count Louis Dardinay (Michael Billington) – the man who stood to reclaim his lands if the four all failed in their efforts and the country was absorbed by neighboring France.

Background: The series was produced by Stephen J. Cannell Productions and created by Juanita Bartlett. Reportedly, ABC approached Cannell about creating a series concerning world travel or a race around the world for

124 • *The Most Obscure Cult TV Shows Ever*

The Cast of *The Quest*, from left to right: Karen Austin, Perry King, Noah Berry, and Ray Vitte.

money. The producer rejected those ideas and had Bartlett develop the concept for *The Quest*. Cannell remarked, "Because it is a new kind of concept and is very fresh, we are very hopeful about it. It's adventurous, fanciful and humorous."[53]

The Pilot – "Land's End to Land's End"- October 22, 1982

Four Americans receive all-expense paid trips to Glendora which they think is to promote tourism in that country. They meet Sir Edward at the airport to board a private jet for the trip to Glendora. When they arrive, they are taken to the palace, given medals, and meet the king. The king informs them that they each have royal blood and that the worthiest in a series of 13th century challenges will become the head of the principality when the king dies so that Glendora doesn't become part of France. They are also told that Count Dardinay has been exiled from the country and can only return to claim his land if France annexes Glendora. Carrie is given the title of "Lady," and each of the men is made a knight. The king always selects each quest with Sir Edward informing the four of the challenge. Their first challenge is to travel to Cannes, France. Each is given provisions for one day, a horse, and a sword which they all decline. Although the four have been told that each quest is not necessarily a race, they tend to treat it as such. Meanwhile, Dardinay wants to corrupt the four with whatever it takes to disqualify them.

Other Episodes Broadcast

"Last One There Is a Rotten Heir" - October 29, 1982

While resting for the next big leg of their latest quest, one of Cody's former associates, High-wire Willie, an escaped convict, informs him that he stole the crown of Glendora and wants Cody to contact Sir Edward to pay for its return. They all go to Willie's hotel to retrieve the crown. The four believe that the first one who recovers the crown might be the next head of Glendora since their regular quest is on hold because of the missing crown. When Willie and the four leave his hotel to get the crown, Willie is shot by Dardinay's henchmen, but before he dies, he whispers "Marineland." The four take this to mean that they have to fly to Marineland in California. Cody is the first to get on a flight to LA, but Arthur discovers that there is a Marineland in France as do Dan and Carrie. Each questor races to that destination along with Dardinay. When Cody discovers the mistake he made, he feigns sickness in order to have his plane turnaround and go back to France. On his way to Marineland in France, Cody picks up Sir Edward. Everyone arrives separately at Marineland and attempts to find the crown before Dardinay's men do. Cody and Dan spy the crown dangling from a pole. A fight with Dardinay's men ensues. After a Marineland attendant eventually retrieves the crown, Sir Edward says he will tell the king that they all were involved in the crown's return.

"He Stole-a My Art" - November 5, 1982
The four are on their next quest to Naples, Italy. When Arthur hitches a ride on a school bus, the driver has a heart attack. Arthur saves the bus from going over a cliff and is celebrated by the people of Portofino as a hero with a write-up in the local paper. While dining at an outdoor café in the town, Arthur, Dan, and Carrie are fired upon by unknown assailants whom they think work for Dardinay. While waiting at their hotel, a second attempt on their lives occurs when a bomb explodes, and the townspeople are upset at them for bringing violence to Portofino. Arthur is then kidnapped by a gangster from America who lives in Portofino because Arthur, when he was a cop, had the man deported twenty years earlier for being in the U.S. illegally. Dan, Cody, Carrie, and Sir Edward rescue Arthur with the inadvertent help of the townspeople. Edward takes them back to where their quest to Naples began. Edward announces that Carrie has the edge at this point for her prudence and moderation.

"His Majesty, I Presume" - November 12, 1982
The group is in Africa where Sir Edward informs them that the king is missing on his annual photographic safari. One of the king's porters says that the king was on the trail of an elephant which charged, killing him. Sir Edward advises the group that the quest is over since the king's successor had to be chosen while the king was still alive. But Dan thinks the king may not be dead. Carrie secretly hires a guide to take her into the jungle to find the king – the same guide that Art and Cody also secretly hire. The next day, each of them sneaks out of the hotel to join the guide. Dan hires a separate guide – a female of course. They all go into the jungle where Art and Carrie are captured by the natives. Cody and Dan escape capture and follow Arthur and Carrie. Dan, trying to be Tarzan, is subsequently captured, while Cody pretends to be a tribesman. He finds the king alive in one of the native huts, but then Cody is also taken prisoner. The tribal chief turns out to be the king's friend. The monarch says he was hiding in the tribal village after escaping ivory poachers. The guide hired by Carrie, Art, and Cody is one of the poachers and takes the king away with him. The porter turns up with photos the king took of the poachers that show the guide shooting elephants. Now the four go

after the guide and the king. They find them, free the king, and capture the poachers.

"Escape from the Velvet Box" - November 19, 1982
At a Beverly Hills hotel, a woman comes through the balcony into Dan's room awakening him. She asks for help but then is kidnapped by two men. The abductee is Deborah Liard, who just inherited controlling interest in an oil company from her recently-deceased father. The police along with Dan, Cody, Art, and Carrie go to her house to make sure she is all right. She makes up a story about meeting Dan in the hotel's bar and him taking her to his room. However, she whispers in Dan's ear that she is being watched. The gang returns to her home to take her away. She remarks that company executives drugged her so they could take control of the oil company. She then calls the cops and says the four kidnapped her. Deborah finally divulges to the gang that her father is not really dead but is being held by Dardinay and that she has to do whatever Dardinay wants. Cody comes up with a plan to pretend he wants to ally himself with Dardinay in return for $3 million for the whereabouts of Deborah. Dardinay's men go to the cabin where the four have been holding Deborah and take her along with Art and Carrie in their helicopter. Dan steals away in the copter as it returns to Dardinay's mansion. At the mansion, Deborah is reunited with her father. Dan steals the copter and everyone escapes from Dardinay.

Unaired Episodes

"Hunt for the White Tiger"
In Palm Beach, Florida, a rash of jewel thefts has occurred. Police believe a burglar nicknamed the "White Tiger" is behind the thefts. Meanwhile, Carrie has fallen in love with Philippe, a banker from a wealthy family. One can probably guess where this story line is headed. In any event, Cody finds a stolen jewel in a fruit bowl in his hotel room just as detectives knock on his door to question him given his con-artist background. They discover the stolen jewel and think he is the White Tiger. Cody escapes before being arrested and hides out on a boat where someone tries to kill him as Art and Dan show up. Art thinks that Dardinay is behind the shooting, while Dan believes Philippe is the culprit. Sir Edward finds that Philippe is a fortune hunter which confirms Dan's suspicions that Philippe is the White Tiger. Of course, Carrie does not believe this. She pays Philippe a surprise visit and finds that he really is the thief. He wants her to win the crown and have the others disqualified. Dan sets up a trap for Philippe by showing off the royal jewels at the engagement party the king is having for Carrie. After the

reception, Philippe breaks into the king's hotel suite, takes the jewels, but is caught by Dan, Art, and Cody.

"Daddy's Home"

King Charles is in Houston where he calls an emergency meeting with the contenders. He has received information that Dan may not be a legitimate heir to the crown since his real parents were not Underwood's but instead were "Pelzinski's." A man named Jerry Pelzinski introduces himself to Dan as his estranged father who gave him to the Underwood's to raise when his wife died. Cody is convinced that the man is a scam artist. Dan thinks that Dardinay is behind the con. Art discovers that the man is a petty crook. Pelzinski confirms that Dardinay is behind the scam in order to take Dan out of the quest for the crown.

"A Prince of a Fellow"

Dan and Carrie are befriended by a guy named Freddie after being shot at by hit men whom they think were working for Dardinay. Carrie and Dan go to Freddie's home town with Arthur where they find that Freddie is the Prince of Lichtenberg. Freddie's mother, the Queen, holds a masked ball in honor of Prince Freddie's return. All of the questers along with King Charles and Sir Edward attend. The hit men whom Dan and Carrie thought were sent by Dardinay were actually hired by Count Heinrich, an assistant to the Queen, to kill Freddie since the Count doesn't want him to become king. Cody and Dan take care of the hit men before they succeed in killing Freddie. The Queen abdicates, and Freddie becomes the king and banishes Count Heinrich from the principality.

"R.S.V.P."

The contenders are all lured by Dardinay to a Greek island along with the king and Sir Edward. Dardinay wants to discuss a deal with everyone whereby, in return for the king ending Dardinay's banishment from Glendora and returning his land, Dardinay would allow the quest to continue without interference. Dardinay is on the island with his staff and with a Baroness whose first husband recently died. Dardinay wants everyone to think about the deal overnight. The next morning, Dardinay's long-time butler Maurice is found shot in the kitchen, and Dardinay is as surprised as everyone else about the murder. Later, Dardinay is found drugged. The Baroness stays with him while the gang searches the island for the perpetrator. Dan finds papers showing that Dardinay and the Baroness are secretly married. The Baroness and her lover, who was also on the island, turn out to be the perpetrators trying to kill Dardinay so the Baroness would inherit his money.

Postscript: *The Quest* was scheduled by ABC following another Stephen Cannell series, *The Greatest American Hero*. Neither series did well opposite the hit shows on CBS – *Dallas* and *Falcon Crest*. *The Quest* ranked 79th for its five outings. It and *The Greatest American Hero* were pulled from the schedule and replaced with a Friday night movie.

Reflecting on the series cancelation, Perry King remarked that "'Quest' was a good experience and I think given a good time, it would have worked."[54]

Once a Hero – The Comic Book World vs the Real World

Premiered September 19, 1987 on ABC Saturday at 8:00 pm

Premise: In a series created by Stephen J. Cannell titled *The Greatest American Hero*, a high school teacher is given a special red suit by extraterrestrials which, when worn, gives him superpowers. However, he doesn't have the instruction booklet for the suit and so learns about his powers through trial and error. *Once a Hero* was something of an inverse of *The Greatest American Hero*. A cartoon superhero named "Captain Justice" crosses over into the real world when he fears his comic book is going to be canceled and hopes to reinvigorate his creator with real-world adventures but finds that his superpowers do not work in the real world.

Cast of Characters:

> Captain Justice (Jeff Lester) – the cartoon superhero;
> Abner Bevis (Milo O'Shea) – creator of Captain Justice;
> Emma Greely (Caitlin Clarke) - a newspaper reporter who has a twelve-year-old son Woody (Josh Blake) who is a fan of Captain Justice;
> Gumshoe (Robert Forster) - a cartoon detective who comes with Justice to help him battle adversaries.

Background: Created by Dusty Kay, the series was originally titled *Believers* and then *True Colors* before the title *Once a Hero* was chosen. Jim Turner was initially cast as Captain Justice, but producers wanted a brawnier lead and so Jeff Lester was chosen. Turner's characterization of Captain Justice was sharply satirical, while Jeff Lester played the character more like the world's best boy scout. According to Dusty Kay, the Vice President for De-

Jeff Lester and Robert Forster from *Once a Hero*.

velopment at ABC asked him for a series idea satirizing a comic book hero.[47] The concept of bringing a superhero into a world devoid of superheroes, stripping him of his powers, and then watching him struggle to survive was something Kay found compelling. The network ordered a pilot plus six additional episodes, but only five of the seven episodes were shot.

The Pilot - September 19, 1987
"Believers"

In the ninety-minute pilot, Captain Justice aka Brad Steele, a professor of archeology, is tired of repeating the same adventures and finds that his creator, Abner Bevis, has exhausted story lines after thirty years of writing comic books. In the middle of an adventure, the "Crimson Crusader" is fading away when people in the real world start forgetting about him. Captain Justice decides to travel to the real world and force people to remember him. He finds his creator as well as a young boy named Woody who is a big fan of his adventures. Gumshoe is sent to bring the Crimson Crusader back to the comic book world.

In the real world, even though CJ is told that not all of his adventures will have a happy ending, he tells Gumshoe he is not returning to the comic book world. Captain Justice meets Woody's mother, Emma Greeley, who works as a reporter at the *Los Angeles Gazette,* and learns that her son has been stealing to pay off bullies at school. CJ tries to help Woody by visiting Eddie Kybow (Kevin Wohl), the chief bully's father who is in the protection business and extorting money from local businesses. Captain Justice comes to realize that he doesn't have superpowers in the real world. Depressed, CJ returns to the comic book world where he engages in un-superhero activities like trying to have sex with his girlfriend Rachel and drinking liquor. Meanwhile, Gumshoe wants Emma to do a story exposing Eddie Kybow. Kybow tries to kill her and Gumshoe. When CJ learns this, he returns to the real world, makes Eddie think that he has superpowers, and turns Kybow over to the police.

Other Broadcast Episodes

"Triangle"- September 26, 1987

Rachel Kirk, Captain Justice's girlfriend in comic book world, misses him and crosses the Forbidden Zone to the real world to see him. Abner patterned Rachel after his late wife, Amanda, who died a year after they were married. After Gumshoe shows CJ a photo of Abner and Amanda, CJ says he will give Rachel up to Abner. But then he changes his mind and decides to marry her. Both Abner and CJ compete for Rachel's affections. Emma tells Rachel about Amanda, but Rachel decides to marry the Crimson Crusader only to find that they argue over issues like the number of children they should have and the type of house they should live in. She has second thoughts about marrying CJ and asks Abner to marry her. Abner realizes that Rachel is not Amanda and says she should marry Captain Justice. When CJ reveals that he has lost his superpowers, Rachel thinks that the real world is too complicated and decides to return to Pleasantville.

"The Return of Lazarus"- October 3, 1987

Kybow is given a suspended sentence and is required to perform 20,000 hours of community service. In the comic book world, CJ's nemesis Lazarus is wreaking havoc without a superhero like Captain Justice to stop him. Lazarus finds it too easy to carry out his evil deeds and decides to find CJ in the real world. He locates Abner and Captain Justice and challenges the Crimson Crusader for dominance. Lazarus apparently bribed the police for Kybow to receive a suspended sentence. Kybow tells CJ that Lazarus wants to kidnap the daughter of the Soviet Premier, but the story is just a ruse to have CJ experience the failures that Lazarus had in the comic book world up against CJ. Abner says to Lazarus that he is his favorite character and asks him to return to the comic book world. Gumshoe reveals that Lazarus has purchased Pizzazz Comics and now owns CJ. He wants to be the star of the comics and terminate CJ. When Abner refuses to do that, Lazarus threatens to kill him. CJ informs Lazarus that he wins, and Captain Justice walks away. Gumshoe then shoots Lazarus when he tries to kill CJ.

Unaired Episodes

"Things Get Ugly"

J. T. North (Adam West) starred as Captain Justice on an old TV series in the 1960s and has been stereotyped in that role for twenty-seven years. He still appears as the Crimson Crusader at car shows and fairs. Pizzazz Comics wants to revive the Captain Justice TV series with a new, younger star and doesn't want North masquerading as CJ anymore. Brad Steele wants to help North. Kybow promises to start a campaign to get North back in the limelight by bashing the producers of the new show. Meanwhile, evil Mephisto is taking control of Pleasantville in the comic book world. Since CJ wants to help North, he has Gumshoe try to save the town. Dressing like Captain Justice, Gumshoe succeeds. In the real world, Abner convinces North that Captain Justice is real. North holds a news conference and says that he was wrong about the campaign and that he is withdrawing as Captain Justice in the real world. North then goes to the comic book world as Captain Justice.

"Manos Arrita, Mrs. Greely"

Kathy Kybow (Fran Drescher), Eddie's wife, takes an incriminating film Eddie possesses of Cicero at a gangland conference with fellow mobsters and politicians and flies to Costa Newaro. She wants $500,000 from Cicero for the return of the film. Emma eavesdrops on Cicero's conversation with Eddie and, along with Gumshoe, tails him to the airport where he is flying to meet his wife. On the trip, Emma begins to fall in love with Gumshoe. Eddie and Kathy reconcile, and Kathy surreptitiously slips Emma the film. The police capture her and Gumshoe along with a group of Scandinavian exiled revolutionaries with whom they are hanging out. Emma and Gumshoe break out of jail. Emma discovers the film and pretends to destroy it to get Cicero's henchman off her back. She asks Eddie to testify against Cicero. In the end, Emma tells Gumshoe that they cannot continue their relationship.

Captain Justice played only a supporting role in this episode taking care of the Kybow kids and Woody while their parents were away. Mayim Bialick played Kybow's daughter. This episode was part of an effort to give the Gumshoe character greater emphasis in the series which appealed to the network.

"Remember the Cottonwood"

Captain Justice moves out of Bevis' house to a rundown apartment building called the Cottonwood. A gang of toughs, the Screaming Skulls headed by Iggy, terrorizes the residents at the behest of the owner who wants to get the dwellers to move and build condos in place of the apartment building. CJ summons Davey Crockett, Jim Bowie, and William Travis from the comic book world to help him battle the toughs. Iggy informs Gumshoe that the owner has secret ledgers detailing payoffs to the gang, kickbacks, and bribes. Iggy and his gang are ready to take care of the owner when he will not accede to their demands for more money. CJ and Crockett and his friends fight the gang saving the owner's life. The owner agrees to fix up the building because CJ saved him from the gang.

Unproduced Episode

"Thank You, Captain Justice"

As Dusty Kay recalls, this script was never filmed. Captain Justice sold out in a quest for popularity which triggered the contempt of those closest to him who wanted him to remain noble and virtuous. Meanwhile, Gumshoe rides an emotional rollercoaster when he learns that the author who created him had been blacklisted and destroyed in the 1950s.

Postscript: *Once a Hero* was the first casualty of the 1987 television season. Its premiere attracted only 10% of the viewing audience. Speaking to the *Los Angeles Times* about the cancelation, creator Dusty Kay said that he couldn't blame ABC for their decision. "They cannot justify numbers like that. We'd have had to double our numbers even to be considered a borderline show."[48] Kay thought a big factor in the series failure to find an audience was the misperception that people had that *Once a Hero* was primarily aimed at children, when in fact the series had what Kay described as "satirical, adult sensibilities."[49] As Kay elaborated, ". . . the problem was it was a show with a superhero, cape and all, that was aimed at adults. So kids didn't watch and, after only 3 weeks, grownups didn't have time to find it. And don't forget, the superhero genre was viewed a lot more dismissively then, a year before the Michael Keaton Batman turned things around."[50]

That Was Then – It's about Time
Premiered September 27, 2002 on ABC Fridays at 9:00 pm

Premise: Described as *Back to the Future* meets *The Wonder Years*, *That Was Then* was a comedy-drama about a twenty-nine-year old who, one day before his thirtieth birthday, got the opportunity to go back in time to try to change things. However, things didn't always turn out as expected.

Cast of Characters:

Travis Glass (James Bulliard) - the twenty-nine-year-old unmarried salesman who lives with his mother, Mickey (Bess Armstrong);
Gary "Double G" Glass (Jeffrey Tambor) – Travis' father who had been a bookie and had died when he was fifty-two-years old;
Gregg (Brad Raider) - Travis' married brother;
Zooey (Andrea Bowen) - Travis's kid sister;
Donnie Pinkus (Tyler Labine) - Travis' best friend who knew that Travis could travel back in time;
Claudia Wills-Glass (Kiele Sanchez) - Gregg's wife whom Travis had pined for in high school.

Background: Created by Jeremy Miller and Dan Cohn, *That Was Then* was filmed in a converted warehouse in an industrial park on Hayden Place in Culver City, California – the same sound stage where *The Wonder Years* had been filmed. NBC's series *Quantum Leap* about a physicist who traveled back and forth in time was one inspiration for *That Was Then*. However, Miller and Cohn stated that the movie *Back to the Future* was the major influence for the series. Both saw the film when they were twelve. As Miller remarked, "At the end we were so blown away by the fact that he (Michael J. Fox's character) changed his present. Not only were his parents back together, but now they were more affluent and Biff worked for his dad. Those subtleties there freaked us out. We walked out onto the street, wow, and we walked right back in, we paid again, we saw the movie again and sort of since then we've been obsessing."[51] The writing duo chose 1988 for *That Was Then*'s main character to return to because that was when Miller and Cohn were in high school.

The Pilot - September 27, 2002
"The Thirty-three Year Itch"

Travis Glass, on the eve of his thirtieth birthday, wishes he could go back to 1988 during his school's homecoming week to change two things – to prevent his sister-in-law whom he secretly loved in high school from losing her virginity to his brother whom she subsequently married and secondly, to not mess up a speech Travis was giving to the whole school. While lying in bed listening to the Kinks' "Do It Again," lightning strikes his house, and he is transported back to 1988. In school he had won the Barlow award for writing the best speech which he had to deliver in a school assembly. Also, Travis discovers that his mother is having an affair with a used car dealer. His friend Pinkus suggests that he buy a new car to impress Claudia whom Travis secretly loves. Travis uses a $5000 payment intended for his dad to purchase a used Mustang, goes to the football field during homecoming where Claudia is Homecoming Queen, picks her up, and takes her away. They stop to pick up some beer. Since Travis is not twenty-one, he asks a friend, Timmy Robinson, who has a false ID to buy beer. However, Travis knows that later that night Timmy will be killed when a train runs into his truck. He saves his friend's life although Timmy's truck is smashed by the train. When Travis returns to his car, Claudia is gone to lose her virginity with his brother. Later, he confronts his mother about her affair. She says that his father pays no attention to her anymore. The next day at school, Travis gives a speech but not the one he intended. He tells the school that he came from the future and advises them to "fix things on the way" because people usually don't get second chances. He receives a standing ovation. Back at home, he sees his dad dancing with his mother after winning big betting on the World Series based on a tip Travis had given him. Because of his successful speech, Travis and his friend Pinkus are invited to a party by a talkative

Lanie Snider. Claudia and Gregg are also at the party where Claudia sees Gregg messing around with another girl. She leaves the party. Back in the present day, Travis wakes up in a strange bedroom and sees he is married to Lanie, has twin daughters, and is the mayor. Claudia is not married to Gregg. Also, Pinkus is mad at him for taking Lanie away. He knows he needs to go back again to 1988.

Other Episodes Broadcast

"Mayor May Not" – October 4, 2002

Since Travis wants to get his brother back with Claudia, he plays his mix tape and goes back to 1988. Because his dad is mad at him for not turning over the $5000, he has to find a way to pay off the debt. He sees Claudia at school and encourages her to talk to Gregg. Travis also overhears his mother talking with the used car dealer to end their affair. He has Gregg audition for a school production of *Romeo and Juliet* where Claudia is playing Juliet. Gregg wins the audition because no one else auditioned for the part. Travis tells Lanie that Pinkus is really interested in her. Claudia quits the play when Gregg starts changing his lines. Travis is trying to sell his car to repay his dad. He finally finds a job at a seafood restaurant. When Travis confronts his dad about what his father really does for a living, his dad admits he is a bookie and not a door salesman. When Travis tells Lanie that he is not interested in her, she responds that she will ruin him. Travis' dad bonds with him over a movie he took him to when Travis was little, and he forgives the $5000 debt. Pinkus plays "Do It Again" which takes Travis back to the present where now he finds he is living with Pinkus in a rundown trailer with Timmy as the landlord, Claudia is a nun, and his brother Gregg is playing a cop on a TV series.

Unaired Episodes

"Under Noah's Uncertain Terms"

Back in 1988, Travis is still working at the seafood restaurant when, after hours, a robber comes in. The would-be thief is Noah Benjamin whom Travis knows from the present day is wanted for armed robbery. Travis thinks that he must help Noah avoid a life of crime. Because he tore up the football field when he took Claudia away in his car, Travis receives two weeks of detention and ends up in the same class as Noah. When Travis and Noah go out one night, Noah wants to hold up a liquor store. Travis blows the car horn to bring attention to Noah so he doesn't go through with the robbery. He later finds out that Noah's older brother died in a car accident. He takes Noah to his dad's place of business and tells him that his dad is a bookie. Noah sees Travis's dad get arrested but figures that it is just a ruse to convince him to avoid a life of crime. Noah explains that his parents placed all of their hopes on him and he can't take it. Travis tells him that to save his family, he needs to save himself. Noah is then expelled from school for breaking into the vice principal's home, but he asks for another chance to stay in school. Meanwhile, Travis attempts to convince Claudia to reconcile with Gregg. He tries to break up a budding relationship between Claudia and Timmy Robinson but is not successful.

After Travis's dad has a mild heart attack in 1988, he wants his dad to start exercising. The dad begins jogging every morning, but Travis soon finds his dad is faking it. The family confronts the father about this by reading his obituary from 1994, and he begins jogging for real. At the school play of *Romeo and Juliet*, the braces on the girl sitting next to Travis begin to transmit "Do It Again" from a radio station. Travis is transported back to the present day where he finds that his dad didn't die in 1994. He also discovers that he is in jail and that Noah is his attorney.

"A Rock and a Head Case"

Still in prison, Travis pleads with the Parole Board that he is innocent and that he is a time traveler. His parole is denied. His sister, now a legal secretary dating a fellow inmate, visits. Travis is disappointed that she is not a lawyer. He receives a small tape player smuggled in a book, plays "Do It Again," and is transported back to high school where he is placed on detention and given the task of cleaning up graffiti written on an elementary school wall. Gregg is still trying to charm Claudia away from Timmy to no avail. Travis encourages Zooey to not hide her intelligence. When she passes a pop quiz, her teacher thinks she cheated. Zooey convinces her teacher of her intelligence and is asked to participate on an academic play-off team. Someone is still writing graffiti on the wall at the elementary school. Travis and Pinkus stake it out. When Pinkus needs to use the bathroom, a group of young kids come and begin spray painting the wall. Travis confronts them alone. They run away, and he is left holding a can of spray paint and is suspended for two weeks. Pinkus handcuffs himself to Travis in Travis' bedroom, plays "Do It Again" to see if Travis really travels to the future, and videotapes the event. Even though Travis tells him that he ended up back in prison eating his last meal, the tape shows they remained in the bedroom, and so Pinkus thinks Travis is insane. Gregg is still searching for an identity to prove his honesty to Claudia. His dad says that he should display his Jewishness. Gregg drops the last "g" from his first name and wears a Yamaka to school. At the end, Pinkus, still handcuffed to Travis, stages an intervention with school officials explaining that he thinks Travis is mentally ill. Travis is prescribed medication. When he hears "Do It Again," he is transported to the future where he sees Zooey on *Who Wants to be a Millionaire?* while he is in a mental institution.

Episode 105 – Title unknown

While still in a mental institution, Claudia brings him food from his mother. Travis is turning thirty the next day. He gives his fellow patients music sheets to sing "Do It Again" so he can return to high school in 1988.

Back in 1988, Gregg is still convinced that Claudia has a thing for Jewish men since she likes Mandy Patinkin movies. Her mother, Sherry Myers, is remarrying, but Claudia doesn't want to attend the ceremony since her mother left her and her family. Travis tries to persuade Claudia to attend.

Unbeknownst to Claudia, Travis arranges an encounter between her and her mother at the restaurant where he works. Her mother introduces her fiancé Sylvester Morris, a hair dresser who is much younger than she is. Claudia leaves the restaurant. Later, Claudia tells Travis that she likes talking things over with him which he believes may be the beginning of a romantic relationship. However, after he sees her kissing Timmy, he understands that she sees him only as a friend. Claudia's mother confesses that she had to get away from the small town of Jasper but that she begged Claudia to go with her. After Travis again remarks to Claudia that she needs to attend her mother's wedding, she breaks up with Timmy and decides to go to the ceremony. The Glass family also attends except for Double G who says he may be late because of a business meeting he has. At the wedding, Gregg tries to apologize to Claudia in front of everyone for cheating on her, but she is not impressed. Claudia and her mother make up after the wedding. When Claudia sees Gregg crying, they reconcile as well. Ms. Firsch, a teacher at Travis' school, is at the wedding and decides to sing at the reception. "Do It Again" is played, and Travis ends up back in the present playing the piano for now singer Ms. Firsch at the fish restaurant where he used to be a waiter.

Postscript: *That Was Then* was often cited by critics at the time as being very similar to the WB's comedy *Do Over* that also premiered in fall 2002. *Do Over* focused on a thirty-four-year-old salesman who time traveled back to 1981 when he was fourteen and so knew what would happen over the next twenty years. However, Cohn and Miller insisted they knew nothing about *Do Over* when they developed *That Was Then*.

Wonderfalls – Talking Animal Figurines
Premiered on Fox March 12, 2004 Friday at 9:00 pm

Premise: A college graduate and underachiever, living in an old trailer and working at a Niagara Falls gift shop selling souvenirs to tourists, receives cryptic messages from figurines and illustrations of animals that, despite her reluctance, advise her to do good.

Cast of Characters:

Jaye Tyler (Caroline Dhavernas) – a cynical college graduate who works at Wonderfalls Gift Emporium;
Darrin Tyler (William Sadler) – Jaye's father, a surgeon who likes to write novelty songs;
Karen Tyler (Diana Scarwid) – Jaye's mother who writes travel guides;
Sharon (Katie Finneran) – Jaye's sister, a lesbian, who is an attorney;
Aaron (Lee Pace) – Jaye's brother who is working on a graduate degree in religious theory;
Eric Gotts (Tyron Leftso) – a bartender to whom Jaye is attracted;
Mahandra (Tracie Thoms) – Jaye's best friend;
Alec (Neil Grayston) – the assistant manager at the gift emporium also known as "mouth-breather."

Background: The series was created by Todd Holland & Bryan Fuller. In an unaired pilot, the role of Jaye's brother Aaron was played by Adam Scott, and Kerry Washington appeared as her friend Mahandra. The pilot was re-done without these two actors because they could not commit to future episodes.

Tim Minear, who executive-produced *Wonderfalls* along with Holland and Fuller, remarked about the Niagara Falls setting for the series: "There is such a magical aspect to it. There's the legend of the Maid of the Mist. . . It's a specific place where lovers go to celebrate their honeymoon. . . It's one of the wonders of the world."[52] The series was filmed at the Falls and in Toronto for seven months.

The Aired Pilot:

"Wax Lion"- March 12, 2004
Overly educated and underemployed souvenir shop clerk, Jaye, starts hearing a miniature wax lion at the store begin giving advice to her. Her par-

ents have her see the mother's therapist. She says that she hates her sister and then steals his miniature monkey statue that tells her to take it. Jaye meets Eric, a new bartender, who was in Niagara Falls on his honeymoon when he caught his new wife performing oral sex on a bellhop. At the gift shop, the wax lion instructs Jaye to retrieve a quarter thrown into a fountain by the UPS guy. In the process, she finds a purse snatched from a customer in front of the gift shop. Upon returning the purse to its owner, Jaye gets into a physical altercation with the woman who thinks Jaye was in cahoots with the purse snatcher. Sharon has to bail her out of jail. Following the lion's instructions, Jaye arranges a blind dinner date between her sister and the UPS guy who told Jaye that her sister is hot. At dinner, Sharon divulges that she is a lesbian, and the guy has an allergic reaction to peanuts in his salad. Jaye and Sharon rush him to the hospital where Sharon meets the guy's ex-wife who is attracted to her. In the end, Jaye tells Sharon that she loves her.

Other Episodes Broadcast

"Karma Chameleon" - March 19, 2004

At the gift shop, Jaye meets Bianca Knowles, a young woman like herself but who has a very bad stutter. Bianca gets a job at the Emporium helping Jaye. Bianca begins taking on Jaye's personality, losing her stutter, and changes her hair style to Jaye's. Later, Jaye discovers that Bianca has been stalking her. Bianca reveals that she is an investigative journalist researching a story about disaffected young people, i.e., Gen Y non-winners. Jaye decides to help Bianca write the story. Alec, after reading Bianca's notes on her magazine article, fires Jaye. Bianca decides to give up her career and be exactly like Jaye. Jaye, however, writes her own story about Gen Y and submits it the magazine under Bianca's name. The article is accepted for publication. Bianca leaves the Emporium, and Jaye gets her old job back.

"Wound Up Penguin" - March 26, 2004

Late at night at The Barrell bar, Jaye and Eric encounter a woman living inside a barrel used to ride over Niagara Falls. The woman, Katrina, is a nun who is questioning her faith in God. She left her convent, and a priest is now trying to convince her to return. Jaye tells the priest to give her twenty-four hours to restore Katrina's faith in God. Jaye reveals to the nun that her plastic animals speak to her. One of them instructs Jaye to break a car's tail light. Her car lurches forward into another vehicle in a parking lot. The car with the broken tail light happens to be a rental driven by the priest who is stopped by the police about the broken light. The priest is found to have fathered a young girl with a woman he had met before taking his vows.

He and the mother of the child reconcile. Katrina believes the incident is a miracle which restores her faith.

"Pink Flamingos" - April 1, 2004

Jaye receives an invitation to her 6 ½ year high school reunion being organized by Gretchen Speck Horowitz. She is recruited to help Gretchen with the planning of the event. Gretchen moved up the normal ten year reunion to try to recapture the magic she had in high school since she feels her husband doesn't love her anymore. Jaye attempts to comfort her but is told by a "chicken hair pin" to "destroy" Gretchen. Eric says to ignore the chicken. Jaye decides instead to bring Gretchen's husband, Robert to the reunion. When she calls Robert on Gretchen's cell phone, he ends up having an auto accident. After encountering a former classmate who always idolized her, Gretchen decides that she really doesn't love Robert. She thanks Jaye for allowing her to regain her mojo and drops Robert who falls in love with an emergency worker who attends to him at the accident scene.

Episodes not Aired on Fox

"Crime Dog"

Jaye is arrested. Flashbacks show why. Immigration agents come to the Tyler house as the family is having breakfast and deport their long-time housekeeper Yvette back to Canada. A cow-shaped diary creamer tells Jaye to bring Yvette back to the States. Jaye and her brother drive to Canada and pick up Yvette. The cow creamer directs Jaye to take Yvette to see her estranged parents, but the reconciliation does not go well. Jaye and her sibling put Yvette in the trunk of their car to take her back to the United States. Jaye and her brother are arrested after their sister flags Jaye's name in the crime data base. Charges are dropped and both are released after their father makes some phone calls. Yvette is given temporary amnesty.

"Muffin Buffalo"

Jaye gains the reputation of "helping" people which she disdains after she catches an infant when the baby's mother falls down. She then meets a neighbor at the trailer park on whom she has been spying since she thinks he is grossly obese. She finds that "Fat Pat" is not what she thought. He has lost over 300 pounds and still wants to lose an additional twelve pounds. Trying to be nice, she befriends him, but when he starts to fall in love with her, Jaye rebuffs his advances. Depressed, Pat begins gorging on muffins made by another resident of the trailer park who calls her business, "Muffin Buffalo."

Rushed to the hospital for dehydration, Pat learns that the muffins contained a diuretic which allowed him to lose the additional twelve pounds.

"Barrel Bear"

Millie Marcus (Rue McClanahan), the first American female to go over Niagara Falls in a barrel, comes to the Falls, but no one recognizes her. Jaye decides to create publicity for Millie by having her present a speech at a fundraising event. Before the fundraiser, Vivian Caldwell (Louise Fletcher) shows up claiming that she, not Millie, was actually the first female to go over the Falls in a barrel. After the stunt, the manager of the spectacle replaced Vivian with the more attractive Millie for publicity purposes. Jaye then decides to give Vivian the recognition that she thinks she deserves.

Millie fights back by getting into the original barrel to go over the Falls, but the barrel slips away without her. Millie realizes the courage that Vivian had to do the stunt and suggests that both Vivian and she go on the lecture circuit together. But before this can happen, Millie passes away. Vivian takes on Millie's identity to go on the lecture tour, while Jaye places Millie's ashes into a souvenir barrel and drops it over the Falls.

"Lovesick Ass"

A Russian mail order bride named Katya shows up in Niagara Falls looking for her husband-to-be. Jaye and Eric try to find the man and discover that he is a twelve-year-old boy, Peter Johnson, who recently lost his mother and whose dad is too busy at work to spend time with him. Jaye and Eric attempt to set the boy straight on why he can't marry Katya. Katya moves in with Jaye and invites Eric to dinner making Jaye somewhat jealous. Meanwhile, Peter becomes infatuated with Jaye. Peter's father meets Katya and begins to fall in love with her, while Eric asks Jaye on a date.

"Safety Canary"

Jaye and Eric go on their first date at the zoo. A "safety canary" poster tells Jaye to take a photo of two macaws despite a prohibition against such action. The birds attack Jaye. Penelope, the birds' caretaker, is fired. Jaye feels guilty because now the endangered macaws will not mate. She along with Eric and Penelope break into the zoo at night to steal the macaws and attempt to get them to mate. They take the birds to Jaye's parents' house. Jaye opens a window, and the birds escape before they can complete mating because she thinks the birds are a symbol of her developing relationship with Eric. She is afraid of becoming too involved with him. The birds are found mating in Sharon's vehicle and are taken back to the zoo. Jaye tries to get back with Eric but finds his estranged wife, Heidi, with him.

"Lying Pig"

Heidi admits to Eric that she made a mistake when he caught her on their honeymoon performing oral sex on a bellboy. Heidi also informs Jaye that she is still married to Eric and that he will leave Niagara Falls with her. She also says that the only reason she was servicing the bellboy was to practice oral sex so she would have experience on her wedding night.

After Jaye admits to her brother Aaron that inanimate objects talk to her, he begins clearing out all the stuffed animals and other animal-like objects in her trailer and elsewhere. Despite this, while Jaye is viewing television, she hears a pig on the commercial tell her, "Mend what was broken," which she assumes means she has to have Eric reconcile with Heidi. Jaye throws the television out the window hitting Heidi who is coming to see her. Heidi ends up with a slight concussion and feigns amnesia about her honeymoon. However, later she asks Eric for forgiveness and for him to marry her again. They go to an all-night chapel. Jaye follows them to tell Eric that she loves him, but he says that he can't walk away from Heidi.

"Cocktail Bunny"

Jaye returns a brass monkey to psychiatrist Ron Campbell after previously walking out on a session with him and taking the figurine. She is still upset over Eric remarrying Heidi. Eric gives his two weeks' notice at The Barrell planning to return to New Jersey with Heidi. A cocktail bunny illustration on a box instructs Jaye to save Eric from his wife. Subsequently, Dr. Ron's brass monkey says "he is going to die" which Jaye interprets as Heidi planning to kill Eric. She sees Heidi purchasing some drugs on the street which she assumes will be used to poison Eric. The drugs turn out to be treatment for Eric's erectile dysfunction. The warning from the monkey really applied to Dr. Ron. A former patient of his wants to kill him by setting his office on fire. The ex-patient admits what she was planning to frame Jaye for the murder. Jaye apologizes to Eric who says that Heidi has returned to New Jersey to find an apartment for them.

"Totem Mole"

When Mahandra wants to become a member of the local Native American tribe to take advantage of its perks, Jaye accompanies her to the reservation and is instructed by a totem pole to visit a nearby teepee. The teepee contains the remains of the tribe's seer, Gentle Feather, as part of a traditional funeral. Gentle Feather speaks to Jaye saying that she has been chosen. Jaye's sister, Sharon, is also on the trip and encounters a competitive colleague of hers that she knows from law school. The colleague is the tribe's attorney.

Jaye encourages Gentle Feather's grandson, Bill Hooten to follow in his grandmother's footsteps to become the tribe's seer. However, he does not appear to have the "gift" until he passes out smoking peyote. While unconscious, he says he spoke with his grandmother. Subsequently, Bill encourages a sit-in at Wonderfalls to protest the inauthentic Indian souvenirs the store sells. During the sit-in, while displaying a toy gun, Bill is shot by a security guard. Surviving, he thinks he really is the chosen one. But the guard's gun contained rubber bullets. He then realizes that he is not the "one." Sharon's colleague becomes the new seer for the tribe after having a mystical experience in an over-heated sauna and encountering "Gentle Feather." Bill becomes the tribe's accountant in charge of making its casino profitable.

"Caged Bird"

An artificial bird in a cage at the gift emporium tells Jaye to "let him go." She presumes this applies to Eric who is leaving Niagara Falls with his wife. Jaye makes one last attempt to say she loves him asking Eric to meet her at her trailer. However, a bank robber seeking to escape the police, comes into the gift shop and holds Jaye, her sister Sharon, Alec, and a security guard hostage. When Jaye doesn't show up for her rendezvous with Eric, he comes by the shop. He explains to Jaye that he is not happy, but Jaye is ordered by the robber to get rid of Eric. The security guard has a heart attack trying to knock the robber unconscious. The police surround the place after Eric informs them that he is suspicious when Jaye wouldn't let him say good-bye. The robber escapes through a hidden door in the bathroom with Jaye, but a car crashes into the van the robber planned to use to get away. He is killed when an emergency vehicle runs over him. The security guard, needing a heart transplant, receives the robber's heart. Eric returns saying that he left his wife again, and he and Jaye kiss.

Postscript: The producers described proposed storylines for subsequent seasons of *Wonderfalls* if it had been renewed. The ideas included Aaron coming to realize Jaye as a spiritual leader, Sharon accidentally becoming pregnant with the father being the ex-husband of Sharon's lover Beth, and Jaye's psychiatrist publishing a book concerning his sessions with her. In the third season, Jaye would be institutionalized and begin affecting the lives of those at the facility.

CHAPTER 7

Action-Adventure Dramas

E.A.R.T.H Force – An Environmentally-Friendly *A-Team*

Premiered September 16, 1990 on CBS Sunday at 9:00 pm before moving to its regular spot on Saturdays at 9:00 pm

Premise: With car chases, gunfights, and explosions, one might expect this series was just another action, adventure show like the *A-Team*. In some respects, it was, but instead of dealing with con-men, murderers, and drug dealers, this series focused on preventing environmental catastrophes. Through the Earth Alert Foundation, a billionaire financed a team who traveled all over the world attacking ecological problems. The organization was known as Earth Alert Research Tactical Headquarters (E.A.R.T.H for short).

Cast of Characters:

> John Harding M D (Gil Gerard) - a trauma care doctor who headed the team;
> Dr. Carl Dana (Clayton Rohner) - a nuclear physicist who had become an environmental activist;
> Dr. Catherine Romano (Tiffany Lamb) - a marine biologist and oil spill expert;
> Charles Dillon (Stewart Finlay-McLennan) - an Australian mercenary;
> Diana Randall (Joanna Pacula) - the director of the foundation.

Background: The series was created by Richard Chapman and Bill Dial and produced by their company in association with Paramount. It was filmed on location in Australia. The series went through several title changes before its premiere – *The Elite*, *The Green Machine*, *E.C.O. Force* before the change to *E.A.R.T.H. Force*. The Force would fly around in a C-130 Hercules transport plane nicknamed "The Monster" which ironically, for a group concerned about the environment, must have had a large carbon footprint.

The Pilot - September 16, 1990

Ridgway Nuclear Power Plant, owned by industrialist Frederick Winter (Robert Coleby), has an unexpected emergency that may lead to a meltdown. Winter wants to form an elite team to resolve the problem at the plant. His staff brings Harding, Dana, Romano, and Peter Roland (Robert Knepper), a zoologist and anthropologist, to his headquarters saying he will give each unlimited funding for their research if they help avoid the meltdown. They have to find out why the core temperatures continue to rise. Dr. Carl Dana finds that the computer program monitoring the core has a virus and that plutonium has been stolen from the plant. The computer virus was put into the system by an employee of the plant who is working with mercenaries to steal the plutonium. Harding and Dana go into the containment unit to cool the control rods with liquid nitrogen so the rods go back down into the core to prevent a meltdown. After completing this task successfully, the team, which now includes Dillon, goes after the mercenaries who by now have killed the employee responsible for the virus. Also, Harding meets with Winter and learns that he is dying of cancer. Harding obtains a high intensity radioactive detector to determine where the missing plutonium is. The team tracks down the missing material to a mercenary selling it to a mid-Eastern country to build a nuclear bomb to kill rebels waging a war in the country. They retrieve the plutonium as it is being delivered to the buyer.

Winter dies but, as his legacy, he wanted to establish the EARTH Alert Foundation to combat environmental crimes with unlimited funding, and the team become members of the foundation.

The pilot was aired as a *CBS Sunday Night Movie*.

Other Episodes Broadcast

"Not So Wild Kingdom"- September 22, 1990

The Force investigates the smuggling of exotic wildlife after a Red Corsican deer, sold by a wild animal park, ends up on a private game reserve in Texas. The team sets themselves up as exotic animal buyers, fly to the game ranch, and videotape hunters shooting mountain goats with high-powered rifles. To shut down the ranch, they need to prove the animals were imported illegally. Harding and Dana go undercover as buyers of exotic animals in order to find out where the game ranch is obtaining the animals, while Dillon and Romano pose as honeymooners engaging in a hunt at the ranch. However, after a fellow hunter exposes Dillon's cover story as the owner of an Australian brewery, Dillon and Romano are tied up in a barn. Meanwhile, Harding is arrested by the Border Patrol on suspicions of smuggling from Mexico. Dillon and Romano free themselves, contact Harding, steal the truck containing the animals smuggled from Mexico, and the E.A.R.T.H transport plane lands to pick them up along with the animals. Coming under heavy fire from the ranch owners, the team transports the animals onto the plane and takes off. The Texas Rangers close down the game ranch.

"Not in My Back Yard" - September 29, 1990
The Force reads a news article about a woman who dumped garbage on a congressman to protest a toxic land fill that is killing her son who has respiratory problems. When the team investigates, they find that the owner of the land fill plans to sell it to a developer who will put a golf course and townhouses on the site. Dana and Dillon collect soil and water samples to analyze while Harding goes to see the owner of the land fill who says that an environmental impact study showed no problem with the land. The son of the woman who brought the problem to the Force's attention goes to the hospital because of increasing respiratory problems. The team believes that dumpers at the land fill are mixing hazardous waste with non-hazardous waste after Dana finds toxic chemicals in the samples he and Dillon obtained. The team identifies the company hauling the toxic substances to the land fill, and, after a truck from the company causes Harding's car to crash, the local police become involved. The hauling company has been bribing the landowner to dump waste in his land fill, but the owner claims he didn't know what specifically the company was discarding. The Force is at the site for the next delivery of toxic waste. A shoot out occurs causing barrels of the waste to explode, and the haulers are arrested. From the company's records, the team finds the chemical that caused the boy's respiratory problems, and he recovers.

Unaired Episodes

"Oil Spill Story"
When an inspection diver is found dead, the Force suspects his death was anything but an accident. Further investigation reveals the man discovered that the ultra-large oil carrier he was surveying is a floating time bomb on the verge of spilling her cargo and creating an environmental crisis of historic proportions. It is up to the team to stop the ship before the worst happens.[55]

"They Shoot Trees, Don't They?"

Carl's brother Bryon, the foreman for a logging company in Oregon, contacts his brother about the death of an environmental protestor who was killed after the tree in which he was sitting blew up underneath him. In the town of Rock Falls, protestors are confronting loggers about the death and about saving the Northern spotted owl that nests in the trees. Carl asks Harding for help with the situation. After the two find the detonator cap that ignited the explosion, the local sheriff traces it to Carl's brother who is arrested for murder. Dillon is also with the team and hears a local realtor make a suspicious phone call to an investment firm. Diane investigates the firm and learns that, through Harry Hudson, the local realtor, the company is purchasing land in Rock Falls for a condo development. After Hudson starts a forest fire, Byron, who is out on bail, and Carl capture the realtor. The realtor planted the explosive charge that killed the young environmentalist in order to spark demonstrations between the towns people and loggers on the one hand and the environmentalists on the other in order to be able to cheaply purchase the forest land around the town.

"Club Dead"

Harding receives a call from an old friend, Dr. Curt Freeman, a house doctor at a resort in the Philippines about an outbreak of illness that he can't control. Because the hotel wants to keep the outbreak a secret, Harding goes there as John Clare. Upon arriving, Harding sees everyone checking out. After Freeman briefs him on the situation, Harding visits with some of the people who are sick. From blood samples he takes, he thinks the cause is due to a toxin. Dillon surreptitiously enters the hotel to see if he can find the toxin. However, the hotel's management is able to identify Harding and Dillon since unbeknownst to them, the hotel is owned by the Winter Group. Harding doesn't want to close down the hotel until he finds the source of the toxin.

Colin Malcolm, who is a major fish supplier to the hotel, is not too happy when he finds that the establishment is changing all of its food suppliers. Harding thinks that the fish may be the source of the toxin after Dana finds traces of cyanide in the fish. Apparently, tropical fish collectors use cyanide to tranquillize ornamental fish to capture them. Dillon and Catherine search Malcolm's boat, while Harding searches his hotel room for evidence. Harding finds Malcolm's log of fish catches and sees that he has a big order for fish coming up. Dillon and Catherine find canisters of fish tranquillizers on Malcolm's boat. The next day as Malcolm's crew throws the canisters overboard to catch fish, Harding, Catherine, and Dan go underwater to bag them as evidence. Malcolm and three divers go after them, but Harding and company overpower them, and they are arrested.

Postscript: The series was canceled after two low-rated episodes in its normal time period – Saturdays at 9:00 pm. Richard Chapman, co-creator and co-producer of the series, told the *Los Angeles Times* that the intent of the series was to focus not only on environmental crimes, but also on natural disasters brought about by human's harming the environment.[56] Potential story lines were a group of train passengers trapped in a tunnel because of an avalanche caused by deforestation and the near-extinction of Indian tribes in the Brazilian rain forest due to a modern day gold rush.

The Fifth Corner – An Undercover Agent Thinking Outside the Box

Premiered April 17, 1992 on NBC Fridays at 9:00 pm before moving to the 10:00 pm hour on that day

Premise: "He woke up and couldn't remember who he was, what he'd done, where he'd been. Then he discovered he was not just one man but many – a spy with many talents, an operative for a billionaire in a secret organization who wants him back. His only chance to survive lies with a woman who holds the keys to his past and knows the secrets to his soul."

Such is the opening of this series centered on an undercover agent who works for a mysterious, Howard-Hughes-like billionaire.

Cast of Characters:

Richard Braun (Alex McArthur) – an undercover agent suffering from amnesia;

Dr. Grandwell (James Coburn) – Braun's employer who nicknamed Braun, "the Fifth Corner," because, when Braun was backed into a corner and there was no way out, he found one;

Erica Fontaine (Kim Delaney) – a reporter investigating Grandwell;

"Hat" (Anthony Valentine) – so named because he always wore one and was a go between Braun and Grandwell;

Boone (J.E. Freeman) – Braun's limo driver who used to be an undercover agent like Braun but became an alcoholic after performing his first hit. Boone is now a recovering alcoholic with a "bad breath" phobia, and, as a result, is always using mouthwash or breath spray;

Actor Alex McArthur from *The Fifth Corner.*

Mayles (Julia Nickson-Sord) - Grandwell's assistant;
Voyo Goric and Christopher Ohrt - two of the Hat's henchmen.

Background: *The Fifth Corner*, created by writer/director John Herzfeld, was produced by Herzfeld in association with TriStar Television. Bryce Zabel who helped to produce the series recalls that "*The Fifth Corner* was one of the strangest times of my career. The creator/producer wanted to work out of his house so for three months I went there every day. I sprained my ankle during this and was on crutches. . . His (Herzfeld's) concept changed daily. His mantra was, 'I want it raw!'"[57]

According to John Herzfeld, the concept for the series came to him in the mid-1980s while on vacation in Prague when he ran into an American wrestling coach named Tom. ". . . a Czech man ran over to Tom, who seemed to know Tom well but called Tom by another name and Tom didn't correct him . . . after the man left, Tom smiled, shrugged, offered no explanation and walked away . . . I realized Tom was probably a spy . . ."[58] A few years later, Herzfeld was having dinner in Manhattan with an undercover ATF agent when a similar incident occurred with the ATF agent encountering a "bad guy" in a restaurant who called him by another name. The undercover ATF agent spoke to the guy in a convincing but fake Italian accent. Herzfeld got the idea for the opening scene of the pilot sitting in his backyard with his friend Christopher Ohrt who appeared on the series. Herzfeld had the image of a man in Mexico waking up in bed with a dead Mexican woman and not knowing who he was or how he got there.

The Pilot
"Trio" - April 17, 1992

NBC aired the pilot and the first episode as a two-hour movie. It opens with Braun waking up in a house in Mexico next to a dead female. Braun has no memory of what happened the night before but finds out from a taxi driver with whom he had left his wallet and passport that his name is Richard Braun, an architect. Before returning to Los Angeles, Braun sees the police captain of the small town cradling the body of the dead woman as it is about to be taken to a hospital. Braun flies back to Los Angeles where his limo driver takes him to a mysterious location to meet the Hat who addresses him as "George." The Hat says that Grandwell is looking forward to his report on his mission in Mexico. Braun tells the Hat that he has amnesia. His limo driver then takes Braun home where he finds several passports with names such as George Thompson, Anthony Parachini, and Jack Previn along with disguises and various types of weapons.

The next day, Braun goes to a hospital for an MRI and is found to have a depressed skull fracture causing memory loss. The doctor says it might be a month, six months, or never for his memory to return. Meanwhile, the Mexican police captain comes to LA. When Braun returns home, he finds a "For Sale" sign out front and his possessions packed for him. Shots ring out and Boone is wounded. Braun meets with the Hat again knowing that the police captain killed the woman in Mexico who was his wife named Isabella and that the captain just tried to kill him. Braun tells Hat that he is quitting. The Hat and Grandwell view a video of Braun's discussion with Hat to determine if Braun is faking amnesia.

At a restaurant with Boone, Braun sees a red-haired woman who looks familiar. Erica Fontaine is a *New York Times* reporter investigating Braun and Grandwell. Later, Braun finds that Erica flew back to Mexico and that Grandwell is building a resort in the Mexican town where Braun had been.

Braun returns to Mexico in disguise. The dead police captain's wife knew that Grandwell had invested a fortune in his Mexican resort and was getting help from her husband in exchange for financing her husband's drug operation. Braun finds Erica tied up by the police captain in his house. He is able to free her. He kills the captain's deputy who was assisting the captain with his drug operation, and Erica is able to shoot the captain who had set Braun up for the murder of his wife. Braun makes it look as if the deputy and the captain killed each other over a drug deal gone bad.

In the second hour, Braun, back in LA, wants to search his recently-sold house one more time for clues to his past. He finds a wall safe containing a safety deposit box key and a savings book in the name of Jack Previn showing he has $500,000. The Hat's men want Braun to give them something of which he is not aware. He thinks what they are looking for may be in the safety deposit box. Braun accesses the box and finds a ring with the inscription "Always EVA." Hat believes that Braun has a detailed record of his involvement with Grandwell which is what he wants. Erica tells Braun that she will help him if he helps her get Grandwell whom she thinks is destroying America because of his avarice. She wants to publish Braun's diary and informs him about a laptop that he updated every night. The Hat's men take Erica hostage and demand the diary from Braun. He finds the laptop in his limo. Boone and he go to turnover a DVD containing the diary to obtain Erica's release. Boone, Erica, and he are able to escape from the Hat's men without giving them the DVD. The diary on the DVD is in code. When Braun can't remember the code, he gives the DVD to Erica.

Other Episode Broadcast

"Eva"- April 24, 1992

Braun is trying to find Eva. However, he is arrested as Jack Previn for the murder of a Japanese electronics genius whose body has never been found. Grandwell posts his $1 million bail which is good for only twenty-four hours before Braun is extradited to Japan. Braun goes to a hypnotist to see if he can make him remember specifics about the electronics expert. He discovers that Eva stands for "electronically voice activated" which the expert had developed. Braun later finds the electronics genius hiding out in a restaurant. He thanks Braun for faking his death and shows him a ring he always wears with the Eva inscription so Braun could identify him. The Hat's men show up and take the expert in return for Braun's diary. Later, Hat informs Braun that the expert is dead but that he still wants the diary. Furthermore, he states that Braun's real name is George Thompson from East Orange, NJ and that Thompson has a wife. In the end, Grandwell ends up controlling the EVA technology having invested in it with the Japanese outfit that got it after threatening its inventor's life.

Unaired Episodes

"Home"

Braun, as George Thompson, goes to see his family. The family says that George has been dead for ten years. But George's wife identifies Braun as her late husband's friend from the military. She says his name is John Avlean. Braun goes to the Avlean residence where a woman recognizes him as her son – missing for four years. He has an older brother named Alan who is in the restaurant business. Alan is having problems with his business with thugs threatening to create labor problems unless he pays them off. Meanwhile, Erica finds that someone is falsifying her background, invalidating her drivers' license and credit cards, and having her mail forwarded to Tucson, AZ. She says that Grandwell is behind this. When Braun confronts the thugs threatening his brother's business, Alan is shot and dies. With Braun wanting to kill him, one of the thugs confesses that the guns should have had blanks in them and that it was all an act to see if Braun had the guts to kill someone. Grandwell was behind the scheme and videotaped what was happening at the restaurant. He also hired all the actors including those who played Braun's brother and mother.

Bryce Zabel wrote the original draft of this episode titled "Homecoming," but it was changed significantly by Herzfeld. The original script opens with Erica visiting her twin sister Eileen who is in a mental institution.

Erica blames Grandwell for her sister's mental state. After, visiting with the Thompson's, Braun is told his name is Jimmy Shanahan. He finds that his "brother" is a cop named Frank Shanahan with a wife and three kids. Frank has to take care of a gang of Irish thugs who are shaking down business owners for "protection." After Frank is killed by one of the thugs, Braun hides the disc containing his diary in Frank's casket. The thug who killed Frank tells Braun that Frank paid him for the hit and supposedly as in the episode that was produced, the gun should have had blanks in it. Although Frank really was a police officer, everyone else at his funeral was an actor paid by Grandwell. The original script also revealed that Braun was recruited by the Hat while in the military.

"Woman at Her Toilette"

Braun has a dream about himself as Anthony Parachini stealing a painting from a South American general. Waking, he is determined to find a bargaining chip he can use against Grandwell other than his diary in order to have the billionaire re-instate Erica's background. Boone, Erica, and Braun attend a reception for an art auction that Grandwell is sponsoring. A woman who knows Braun as John Michel, an artist, asks him for a ride home. The woman gives him a key to an art studio that he apparently used in the past to paint. Later, at the reception, some men try to assassinate Grandwell. Grandwell informs Hat that he had Braun steal a Monet painting from a Generalissimo in South America to use as a bargaining chip against the Generalissimo. The general wants to kill Grandwell and get the painting back. However, Grandwell has no idea what Braun did with the painting. Apparently, Braun had given it to a B-movie actor to smuggle into the United States because Braun was concerned about a red-haired woman who was following him in South America. At the time, he did not know the woman was Erica. However, Braun also doesn't know what happened to the painting. The woman who gave Braun the key to the art studio knows where the painting is. He retrieves the artwork from her and wants to use it in exchange for Grandwell restoring Erica's identity. He goes to Grandwell to propose the deal. Grandwell responds that he will only accept the bargain if Braun agrees never to see Erica again.

"The Sword of Damocles"

Braun agrees to Grandwell's proposition that he break all ties with Erica in order to have her identity reinstated. Braun explains to Erica that she needs to get out of his life. Planning to fly back to New York, she finds that her driver's license and credit cards are now valid. She figures that the deal with Grandwell meant that Braun could no longer see her so she cancels her flight. One of Hat's men who followed Erica to the airport reports to Hat that the deal didn't work out. Hat wants to kill both Braun and Erica. Grandwell gives Hat tentative approval to terminate the two if he can. Braun receives a warning that Hat is coming after him. When Erica returns to Braun, they make love. Planning to kill them and take back the Monet, Hat arrives with his henchmen at the house where Erica and Braun are. The henchmen carry out their plan at night going in with guns blazing, but Braun is waiting for them. After shooting them, Braun, Erica, and Boone go to Grandwell's mansion but find it vacant. Grandwell is on his private jet. Braun goes to the airport to attempt to get him.

Postscript: John Herzfeld remarked that the abrupt cancelation of *Fifth Corner* was due to national events occurring when the show premiered. "Fifth Corner had its debut when the world's attention was focused on the L.A. riots. The second episode was pre-empted (in Los Angeles) for a news special on the riots. And the show required your attention – you had to have seen the first show to understand the second."[59]

Drive – A Fictional *Amazing Race*
Premiered April 15, 2007 on Fox Sunday at 8:00 pm

Premise: While the reality show *Survivor* supposedly influenced the creation of the ABC series *Lost*, the *Amazing Race* reality show about teams traveling the globe to become the first to return home was a factor in the creation of *Drive*.

This adventure series followed competitors in an illegal, secret, cross-country race with a $32 million prize put together by a secret organization.

Cast of Characters:

 Alex Tully (Nathan Fillion) – the owner of a landscaping business, who has been coerced into the race after his wife Kathryn has been kidnapped. He has to win to get her back. His team mate is Corinna Wiles (Kristin Lehman), a stowaway in Alex's car whose parents had been killed twenty-seven years earlier in a similar race. She becomes Alex's racing partner trying to flee the organization behind the race who is after her because she possesses a flash drive with information the organization wants;

 Wendy Patrakes (Melanie Lynskey) – a new mother on the run from Richard, her abusive husband;

- John Trimble (Dylan Baker) – has less than a year to live and wants to bond with his daughter Violet (Emma Stone);
- Winston Salazar (Kevin Alejandro) – an ex-con, just released from prison whose father had abandoned him and his mother when he was seven;
- Sean Salazar (J.D. Pardo) – Winston's wealthy half-brother who joins him after he catches Winston robbing his house when their father would not give Winston any money;
- Ivy Chitty (Taryn Manning), Leigh Barnthouse (Rochelle Aytes), and Susan Chamblee (Michael Hyatt) – three survivors of Hurricane Katrina;
- Ellie Laird (Mircea Monroe) – an Army wife who is trying to keep her husband Rob (Riley Smith) from returning to Iraq by destroying notifications from the Army for him to return to his unit;
- Mr. Bright (Charles Martin Smith) - the race coordinator.

Background: Ben Queen and Tim Minear created the series which was produced by Ream Works and 20th Century Fox. While Minear was influenced by the *Amazing Race*, Queen stated that he was inspired by road movies such as *The Gumball Rally* and *Two-Lane Blacktop* in creating the series.[60] Almost all the driving scenes on the series were filmed on a soundstage with the actors suspended in car rigs in front of a green screen. According to executive producer Greg Yaitanes, "We've created virtual environments, so we do all the driving without taking the cars and people on the road. One of the signatures of the show involves this car-to-car effect that nobody's ever seen on TV and even in film."[61]

The Unaired Pilot

An unaired pilot for the series was made with the same characters as noted above and essentially the same storyline as the first aired episode but with almost a completely different cast of actors. Ivan Sergei was Alex Tully, and the Salazar brothers were played by Shahine Ezell (Sean) and Andres Hudson (Winston). Alan Ruck was John Ashton the father of Violet played by Emma Stone. There is no mention of the father suffering from a fatal disease in the pilot, and the relationship between the dad and daughter is rockier than in the series with Violet leaving her dad at a gas station and joining the Salazar brothers. Taryn Manning portrayed Ellie Laird and Shawn Hotesy, her husband Rob. The pilot does not show that Rob is in the military, but is somewhat ordered around by his wife. In the series, Manning became one of the three Katrina survivors.

The pilot also began with some background information about the race saying it was initially started in 1928 with William Randolph Hearst and other corporate titans who engaged average citizens to race with the promise of big payouts.

Minear commented that, "In the original pilot we started on the road, and we didn't really visit the worlds from which these people came. In the new version we do so we're more emotionally connected in who they are. They're just much more clearly defined characters."

According to Ben Queen, actor Ivan Sergei was just not the right fit for the lead, and so the role was recast. "Then it was like pulling a thread as other pieces of casting needed to change to accommodate script changes." Everyone was very invested in doing the pilot right ". . . so that when we returned to do reshoots they constituted most of the original pilot."[62]

Other Episodes Broadcast

"The Starting Line" – April 15, 2007

Tully finds his wife missing and calls police to investigate her disappearance. The police think that she left intentionally. Tully then receives a phone call on a new cell phone to drive to Key West, FL. Several others receive the same call and in Key West are told about a secret, illegal cross-country race with a $32 million first prize. In Tully's case, he is also led to believe that he will find his missing wife Kathryn (in the unaired pilot, her name was Kristen) if he wins the race. A guy following Tully's truck runs him off the road. Tully finds Corinna in the back of his vehicle. She says she is running from her boyfriend but is really being pursued by Alan James, a henchman for the organization behind the race, since she has information on an encrypted flash drive that they want. In the unaired pilot, Corinna has a computer disc with details about the strengths and weaknesses of the racers. The participants are told to go to Jupiter, FL and find the red eye. Wendy, who recently gave birth to a baby boy, is pulled over by the police. She is arrested since her husband reported her vehicle as stolen. She is told that her husband is coming to get her. A man presumed to be her husband takes her away from the police. It turns out that the man is really part of the organization behind the race and lets her rejoin the participants. Tully, Corinna, Winston, and Sean all arrive at the destination in Jupiter which turns out to be a lighthouse but see that several others arrived ahead of them. Wendy is the last to arrive and earns a penalty. She is given a loaded gun and a photo of one of the survivors of Hurricane Katrina and told that the next day will be an elimination round.

"Partners" - April 15, 2007

Alex has taken Alan James hostage to try to get him to divulge information about his wife. Wendy is upset about having to eliminate one of the Katrina survivors. A waitress at a restaurant tells her not to give up. James informs Alex to ask Corinna about his wife and that Corinna is not in the race. All the participants receive a message "Kennedy Killed in '73" and resume the race. Alex confronts Corinna about what is on the flash drive she has. She says it contains information about the strengths and weaknesses of the participants. After talking to a friend, Rob figures that the message they received refers to Cape Kennedy being renamed Cape Canaveral in 1973 and that is their next destination. Alex forces Corinna out of his truck and reveals he has the henchman in the back. Corinna knocks out Alex with her laptop and flees in the truck with the hostage. Alex hitches a ride with a truck driver and finds his truck abandoned on the side of the road. Corinna is holding the hostage at gunpoint. She remarks that the race organizers killed her parents in an auto accident twenty-seven years earlier using her as bait. The hostage fights with Alex and gets the gun. He demands the flash drive. Corinna says the henchman can't kill Alex because the organizers want him in the race. When Alex threatens to give the organizers the flash drive, Corinna knocks out the hostage. Alex then threatens to quit the race unless he receives some proof that his wife is still alive. He receives a photo of the truck driver who picked him up showing his wife with her mouth taped shut.

Wendy fires a bullet from the gun she has into one of the tires of the SUV that the three Katrina survivors are driving. She then stops to "help." Wendy threatens to kill Ivy. Ivy is able to take the gun away from her. Ivy suggests that she partner with Wendy since she feels Wendy will do anything to win. The two drive off together. The Salazar brothers are the first to arrive at Cape Canaveral, followed by the Trimbles. Wendy and Ivy arrive and are told that the next leg of the race is to Rome, Georgia which everyone has to make before dark. Each is given an "Admit One" ticket as a clue. The two other Katrina survivors finish this lag last and are out of the race.

"Let the Games Begin"- April 16, 2007

Still in Florida, Tully's truck breaks down. A police officer arrives and arrests Tully leaving Corinna to hitch a ride. She goes to the police station trying to find Tully, but the station has no record of him being arrested and the person who arrested him apparently assumed the identity of a real officer. The man posing as a policeman interrogates Tully about a bank robbery in 2003 in Ashland, Kentucky where Tully was supposedly the getaway driver. Three people were killed in the bank heist. Tully explains to the man that his wife will be killed if he doesn't make it to Rome before dark. The man posing as the officer says that to win the race Tully has to assume his real identity. He gives him a muscle car for the race to replace his truck. Tully finds a knife and forces the man to divulge where Corinna is. Tully and Corinna are the first to arrive in Rome. Meanwhile, at a gas station, Winston is apprehended by a bounty hunter for violating his parole. Sean calls his dad's lawyer, Esteban Masferer, and demands that he meet him at the place where Winston was apprehended. The dad had been tracking Winston and Sean's whereabouts through the use of their credit cards and notified the bounty hunter where Winston was. After Sean demands that Winston be released, he is turned over to Sean. In Rome, the drivers go to the "After Sunset" outdoor movie theatre where they are shown a film about the next leg of the race.

"No Turning Back"- April 23, 2007
Alex is awarded a "jump start challenge" for most improved performance among the racers. He is given an address in Sweetwater, Georgia instead of the clue "surrender, America" presented to everyone else. The two eliminated Katrina survivors – Susan and Leigh, arrive in Rome the day after the other participants and are met by the race coordinator to return their cell phone. They reluctantly give it back but still want to continue in the race. Wendy is told that she will have to return to the safe house in Ohio where her son is being kept because people are making inquiries. However, her partner pulls a gun on her to force her to remain in the race. Rob finally finds a land line to phone his army base about the condition of a fallen comrade. He is told that his unit already returned to Iraq and that he is AWOL and facing court martial. Upset at Ellie for destroying the various notifications to report to his unit, he tosses the cell phone out the car window, and Susan and Leigh pick it up. They figure out that the clue "surrender, America" refers to Appomattox, Virginia where Lee surrendered to Grant. However, later a truck crashes into the car they are driving. Leigh is slightly injured, but Susan dies. Meanwhile, Alex and Corinna find that the Sweetwater address given them is the location of a bank which they will have to break into to retrieve a safety deposit box holding their clue. Corinna enlists the help of the Salazar brothers in this endeavor. A security guard interrupts the heist. Sean shoots him after the guard wrestles with his brother and Alex. However, Sean is also shot by the guard.

Unaired Episodes

"The Extra Mile"
Violet finds her dad's medications. At a diner, he confesses to his daughter that he has only six months to a year to live. She is upset that he has been

keeping this a secret, takes the car keys, and drives off without him. Leigh is picked up by a driver and left off at the same diner where John is. Both are without transportation and steal a car to drive to Appomattox where the clue for the next destination is two pieces of hard rock candy. After dropping Corinna and Winston off at a motel, Alex takes the wounded Sean to a sports doctor he knows at a gym. A detective from Nebraska, who is working on the case of Alex's missing wife, happens to come to the same gym. The detective is taken hostage. The doctor wants Alex to kill the police detective, but Alex gets the drop on the doctor and his associate and leaves with Sean to go back to the motel where Corinna and Winston are waiting. The safety deposit box is opened, and they find the next destination to be the Rock and Roll Hall of Fame in Cleveland, Ohio. Wendy, still being forced at gun point to continue in the race by Ivy, turns her vehicle around and drives the wrong way down the freeway. Thinking Wendy is crazy, Ivy drops her off by the side of the highway. Ivy happens to have Wendy's cell phone, and, when Wendy's husband calls, Ivy inadvertently reveals where Wendy is headed.

"Rearview"

John tries to locate his daughter who stops to pick up Tully. Later, at a gas station John sees Violet, and Tully patches things up between them. Wendy goes to Ohio to pick up her son at the safe house where she meets her brother whom she hasn't seen in three years. Richard arrives at the house with the police, and Wendy and Sam leave with him. Rob and Ellie go to Fort Benning where Rob is taken into custody. Later, Ellie meets with Allan James who is having an affair with her and is her real partner in the race. He wants to free Rob from the brig so the two can complete the race.

While at the motel, Winston takes the flash drive that Corinna had been keeping. Sean decrypts it and finds data about the race participants and sponsors including the fact that his father is sponsoring him in the race. When Tully stops the brothers to retrieve the flash drive, Sean destroys it. The Salazar's, Tully, and Corinna then come up with a plan to get Corinna "behind the curtain" and meet with the Salazar's father while Tully continues the race. Tully turns Corinna into the race organizers and receives the destination for the next leg of the race. The Salazar's pretend they are no longer allied with Tully and Corinna. Corinna is interrogated by the race organizers including Allan James who gave her the flash drive to begin with. She ends up imprisoned by the organizers along with Tully's wife Kathryn.

Postscript: In an interview for a *Drive* fan website, executive producers Tim Minear and Craig Silverstein gave some ideas of the plots of future episodes of the series if it had not been so abruptly canceled:[63]

Alex and Corinna – Tully's kidnapped wife, Kathryn, would have been revealed as part of the plan through their courtship and marriage to force Alex into the race.

Wendy and Ivy – Wendy's sponsors were an older couple who had adopted Wendy's first child whom she had been told had died. Ivy goes to Ohio to rescue Wendy and Sam from Richard, and the two women resume the race together. Ivy bonds with Sam and sacrifices her life to save him. By the finish of the race, Wendy would have been reunited with her first child.

Winston and Sean – The half-brother's father's advisor Esteban Masferer turns out to be Winston's real sponsor who planned to control the family business after taking out the brothers and father.

John and Violet – John Trimble is not really sick. The medication he was taking made him ill. Believing he was dying made him able to do things he normally would not have been capable. However, once he realized he is not dying, he is hit by a bus and killed.

Susan and Leigh – Apparently, the truck driver who rammed Susan and Leigh's vehicle killing Susan was a former contestant who had been partially paralyzed in the race and was seeking revenge. Later, Leigh would have gotten together with Rob.

Rob and Ellie – Allan James would have forced Ellie to break Rob out of the brig because he has a special skill that would have helped him and Ellie win the race. Rob would later be sent back to Iraq and find a race clue in the middle of the desert. He would then return to the race thanks to a high-ranking military official and end up partnered with Leigh.

Minear and Silverstein never indicated who would have actually won the race. However, they did state that if *Drive* had been renewed after the initial thirteen episode order, the race would have been completed. After that, there would have been a new race with new players and some of the characters from the first season would have taken on new roles in the competition. "You find out some people were working for the race. Some people will die if they don't behave. Some people will lose. Some people will win and new people can be added at any time. The race will evolve, the players will evolve, and the things that they're racing for can change," said Minear.[64]

CHAPTER 8

Sports and Entertainment Dramas

Bay City Blues – A MTM Baseball Drama
Premiered October 25, 1983 on NBC Tuesdays at 10:00 pm

Premise: This drama about a minor-league baseball team was created by the same people who developed *Hill Street Blues*. Perhaps thinking that, with the word "blues" in the title, this series would eventually be a hit like *Hill Street*. However, that never happened.

Cast of Characters:

Joe Rohner (Michael Nouri) – the manager of the Bay City Bluebirds;
Ray Holtz (Pat Corley) – the team's owner who runs a used-car dealership;
Angelo Carbone (Dennis Franz) – the coach;
Mitch Klein (Peter Jurasik) – the team's announcer;
Ozzie Peoples (Bernie Casey) – long-time hitter for the Bluebirds;
Other team members – Rocky Radillo (Ken Ohlin), Frenchy Nuckles (Perry Lang), a pitcher, Terry St. Marie (Patrick Cassidy), a player with a bed wetting problem, Lee Jacoby (Tony Spindakis), Lynwood Scott (Larry Flash Jenkins), and Vic Kresky (Jeff McKracken);
Marco Rodriguez – the team's mascot.

Background: According to writer Jeffrey Lewis, who created the series along with Steven Bochco, Bochco's love of the game led to *Bay City Blues* being picked up as a series by NBC. It was produced by MTM. Because of the success of Bochco's *Hill Street Blues*, he had a commitment from the network for another series. ". . . the sale of the series to NBC's then-head Grant Tinker was deftly aided by Steven bringing a bowl of fresh baseballs to our pitch meeting with Grant, and asking him to smell them. You could say that the series was sold on the smell of the baseballs."[65] As Lewis recalls, "My fondest memory of working on *Bay City Blues* was our building of an actual ballpark, on the grounds of Los Angeles' Department of Water and Power in a northern suburb. I believe the deal was that we could build it and use it as a set there if the DWP got to keep it and use it afterwards. I suppose the DWP got the best of that bargain, as the series only went eight episodes."[66]

The Pilot - October 25, 1983

Ray wants to sell the Bay's best pitcher, Mickey Wagner (Barry Tubb) who shows up drunk to the game after losing his virginity. When he ends up walking several players from the opposing team, he is taken out of the game. Bobby Stang takes over from Wagner and the Birds win. Wagner is called up to the majors despite his poor performance on the mound since his first two pitches were strikes. Meanwhile, Rohner begins seeing Sonny (Kelly Harmon) who is married. Frenchy catches his wife, Judy (Michele Greene), with the cable guy. She says she is bored and lonely, but then Frenchy and his wife both proclaim their love for each other.

Other Episodes Broadcast

"Beautiful Peoples" - November 1, 1983

"Ozzie Peoples Day" is being celebrated because of his length of service with the team. Ray gives him a car which turns out to be a stolen vehicle. Ozzie is arrested. Ray bails him out and profusely apologizes. Meanwhile, Jacoby, who loves to write poetry, breaks up with his girlfriend but soon finds a new girl – Ray's daughter Heather.

"Zircons Are Forever" - November 8, 1983

An agent from Los Angeles comes to see Terry about signing him. Jacoby buys a zircon engagement ring for Heather. After he proposes to her, she says she doesn't want to marry right now. Wagner comes back from the majors after getting drunk again. He continues to drink and is killed in an auto accident.

"I Never Swung with My Father" - November 15, 1983

The Birds win the final game of the regular season and go to the playoffs. Terry decides to finally see a doctor about his bed wetting. Roy gets a new starting pitcher – Vic Kresky's father Moe, a former major league player. Moe had left his son and wife when Vic was fifteen. Moe reveals to Vic that he is not his biological father. Ray's wife sees a doctor about her mental illness. The doctor wants to put her back on lithium. The team pays their final tribute to Wagner.

Unaired Episodes

"Rocky IV Eyes"

Bay City is in a game with Boise to determine who meets the Oxnard Bombers for the Tri-Western title. When Rocky Padillo is in a slump, Rohner wants him to see an eye doctor. An optometrist tells Rocky he needs eyeglasses. Meanwhile, Judy finds that her husband, Frenchy, had sex with a groupie while on the road with the team. Eventually, Frenchy apologizes to her for the affair. During the playoff game, Rocky is not hitting the ball as he would like and is taking flak from spectators. He rushes into the stands and starts a fight. The Blues do beat Boise no thanks to Rocky.

"Play It Again, Milt"

The Bluebirds are playing Oxnard in the best of seven for the Tri-Western pennant. Lou has institutionalized his wife. Ozzie is going to manage in Mexico for the winter. Although Frenchy wants to join his team, Judy doesn't want to go with him. Terry's bed-wetting problem continues. He is called up to the majors, but then injures his shoulder falling off a ladder. When he dives for a ball in the game with Oxnard, he separates his shoulder and is out for the rest of the playoffs as well as for his debut in the majors. Rohner and Sunny make their affair public. Sunny's banker husband, however, refuses to give her a divorce after she tells him that she is leaving him. At the beginning of the playoff game, Milton Parmentier, the team's organist, literally plays his heart out and dies of a heart attack. Not a good sign. The team loses the game 14 to 2.

"Look Homeward, Heyward"

The Blues are behind in the playoffs two games to three. Holtz and his daughter Heather meet with Lynn and her doctor at the psychiatric hospital. Although she is making some progress, the doctor still needs to monitor her lithium intake. At a restaurant where most of the team is assembled, Rohner and Sunny make their first public appearance as a couple. Rohner catches Lynwood Scott, Kresky, and Padillo smoking pot outside the restaurant and suspends them for the rest of the season much to Holtz's dismay. Holtz goes back to his office where he finds Georgia working late, and they have a romantic encounter. Later that night, Hayward's attorney comes to Rohner's apartment where Sunny is to say that George has been murdered in San Francisco by a man and a woman he picked up for a threesome.

"Going, Going, Gone"

The Blues win the sixth game of the playoff series with Bobby Stang almost pitching a no hitter, but Rohner takes him out in the ninth inning after he walks players from the Oxnard Bombers. Padillo, Scott, and Kresky are benched for the game, but have a "team meeting' to confront Rohner about their suspension for the final game. Rohner tells them that he hasn't decided anything yet. In the meantime, George's lawyer is going through his papers and finds that George foreclosed on the Bluebirds because Holtz was past due on payments to him. Upon learning of Holtz's financial problems, Sunny gives him $24,000 in cash that her late husband had squirreled away. Right before the game, Rohner decides to add Padillo, Scott, and Kresky to the line-up. The Blues, however, lose by one run. After the game, Frenchy learns that he is being called up to the majors. In the end, Sunny and Rohner profess their love for each other.

Postscript: Some NBC affiliates aired the remaining four episodes of *Bay City Blues* in two-hour blocks on Sunday July 1, 1984 and Sunday July 8 after their local news. All of the series episodes later aired on ESPN Classic in 2011.

Push – *Melrose Place* in Spandex
Premiered April 9, 1998 on ABC Mondays at 8:00 pm

Premise: College student-athletes training for the 2000 Olympics at fictional California Southern University are the focus of this short-lived drama.

Cast of Characters:

> Victor Yates (Adam Trese) – the new, young gymnast coach who had suffered a shoulder injury in the 1996 Olympics;
> Nikki Long (Jaime Pressly) – the assistant coach, who won gold at the prior Olympics and happens to be Victor's former girlfriend;
> Cara Bedford (Laurie Fortier) – a student gymnast and aspiring writer;
> Tyler Mifflin (Scott Gurney) – a gymnast in love with Erin Galway (Maureen Flannigan), a swimmer;
> Dempsey Easton (Jason Behr) – a track star;
> Gwen Sheridan (Audrey Wasilewski) - Dempsey's math tutor who provides him with performance-enhancing drugs;
> Scott Trysfan (Eddie Mills) – a swimmer who is Tyler's roommate and to whom Erin is attracted;

Some of the cast of *Push* – Maureen Flannigan, Adam Trese, and Laurie Fortier.

Milo Reynolds (Jacobi Wynne) - a black track star who is Dempsey's main competition.

Background: The series was produced by Stu Segall Productions, Columbia Tristar, and Starboard Home Productions and created by Mark B. Perry along with Andy Morahan, Laurel Gregory, & Nicholas Martin. According to Perry, he developed the pilot with some colleagues from Great Britain. "My wacky colleagues from across the pond brought me a concept for a sexy, soapy series about college-age Olympic athletes juggling their fierce competitive natures and the rigors of training with the day-to-day realities of university life, studies, love, sex, relationships and all the difficult challenges already built into that transitional period from teen to young adult."[67]

The Pilot - April 9, 1998

Eric and Erin Galway, twin brother and sister and the offspring of a major donor, enroll in California Southern University. Eric is a gymnast; Erin, a swimmer. Cara is attracted to her English professor, and they eventually have an affair. Scott finds that a girl he had sex with is HIV positive. During a gymnastics competition, Eric wants to quit after his dad criticizes his performance, but Victor encourages him to compete in the final event. Eric has a heart attack and dies supposedly from performance enhancing drugs that Dempsey gave him which Gwen, in turn, had given him.

Other Episodes Broadcast

"The Rivals"- April 13, 1998

Nikki and Victor rekindle their sexual relationship, but Victor wants to break it off. Dempsey continues to be jealous of Milo's ability on the track. Cara maintains her affair with Professor Hardin, but she terminates the relationship after he circulates a story that she wrote to everyone on campus. Tyler finds books about HIV along with pills to boost the body's immune system in Scott's stuff and questions Scott's sexuality. When Tyler asks Erin out, she confesses she has feelings for Scott. When she tells Scott this, he responds that they can't be together and that he just wants to be friends with her.

The initial two episodes scored some of the lowest ratings the network ever received in that time period. ABC decided to burn off the remaining episodes beginning in August.

"On Your Marks…" - August 6, 1998

Victor's team is competing against a team coached by Don Curtis, one of Victor's former coaches. Gwen, a pharmacology major, advises Dempsey that she has been questioned by lawyers about performance-enhancing drugs. She gives him a laxative for Milo to force him out of the track meet so Dempsey can win. However, even after slipping him the laxative, Milo wins anyway and runs quickly into the bathroom. Erin wins her swim meet but then almost faints. Her coach wants a letter from Erin's doctor before permitting her to continue swimming. She ends up quitting the swim team. Victor thinks that the judges are biased toward Coach Curtis' team. When he confronts Curtis, Yates is kicked off the floor. Thanks to Cara's performance, CSU wins the gymnastics meet.

This was the fourth episode of the series produced. The ratings for this episode were no better than for the first two, and so the series was pulled from the air altogether.

Unaired Episodes

"Walk It Off"

Galway sues Victor for negligence in the death of his son, for whom the final autopsy results are not yet in. Scott's initial HIV test is negative, but he needs to take three more tests in the future that will be more conclusive. Dempsey and Nikki are taking a drama class together. Upon questioning by the school's attorney, Dempsey denies any knowledge of Eric taking performance enhancing drugs. The final autopsy results show that Eric died of heart failure. Erin trains hard for the next Olympics in order to win a medal for her late brother. Galway decides to drop the lawsuit against Victor. Gwen receives a copy of the autopsy report and tells Dempsey that Eric's cause of death was "drug-induced" heart failure.

This was originally the second episode of the series, but according to Mark B. Perry, ". . . the studio and network threw it out because they thought it was too depressing."[68]

"Athletic Supporter"

Everyone is attending a formal fundraising reception with alumni contributors to the athletics program. Meanwhile, Scott wants Tyler to insist that Erin have her heart checked. Scott finally persuades Erin to see a doctor. After an exam, she says that the doctor found no problems. She rejoins the swim team. Gwen warns Dempsey about a pending random drug test and gives him some drugs to mask the performance-enhancing medications in his system. After Cara tests positive for marijuana, Yates confronts her English professor about her marijuana use. When Cara goes to see her professor, she finds him strung out on drugs. Gwen stalks Dempsey when he is with Nikki and wants him to take her to the fundraiser or she will tell the police everything about his drug use. Milo does a photo shoot of his athletic ability and receives free track shoes and a jacket from Jett Sportswear.

"It's Only Rock and Roll"

Nikki is participating in a live broadcast of "Rock the World," a TV show featuring top gymnasts. Victor is coaching her. She is nervous before the event at which gymnasts Mitch Gaylord and Keri Struggs appear, but she ends up winning an award.

Meanwhile, Cara goes to Professor Harlin's apartment after he is taken to the hospital suffering from a heroin overdose and finds that he has been luring other female students like her by encouraging their writing talents. She is thinking of leaving school, but Victor encourages her to stay.

Milo is thinking of signing with a running shoe sponsor which may endanger his scholarship; while Gwen blackmails Dempsey into dating her because she says she has incriminating letters from him concerning Eric's death. During the date, she confesses to him that she has no such letters.

"Direct Contact"

Scott hits his head on the wall of the pool, blood spatters, and he is worried that other swimmers might be infected with HIV. Scott then explains everything to Erin including why he broke up with her. Milo is invited by the wife of the owner of Jett sportswear to come to her house to help with her son's birthday party, but what she really wants is Milo. Once he realizes why he was invited, he leaves. He then goes to the Jett office to return the shoes they gave him, but the staff at Jett explain it is not that easy to quit his affiliation with them.

"Stakes"

Scott is making a short film about athletes at CSU and Western Arizona University asking them why they compete. The title of his film is "Stakes." He is also taking a final test to see if he is HIV positive.

Dempsey is in a slump and taken off the team. He has been having a problem passing the baton in relay races. Milo wants him back. The coach asks Milo to get Dempsey to improve his performance. Milo is having a hearing about his relationship with Jett shoes after telling the administration that they sent him a check. He is warned to be careful in the future about accepting money in return for wearing athletic products. Dempsey admits to having taken performance enhancing drugs to beat Milo and that he gave two capsules of the drug to Eric right before he died. Erin remarks that Eric never took the capsules. Dempsey participates in a relay and successfully passes off the baton.

Victor takes Cara out of competition because of a sore ankle. Scott finds out that he is not HIV positive. After he tells Erin he loves her, she says she now loves Tyler.

Postscript: The original pilot for *Push* starred Jeremy Renner as Victor Yates, but ABC thought he looked too young for the part. The role was recast with Adam Trese. Mark B. Perry indicated that he had to reshoot the pilot with a mostly new cast and add the Jaime Pressly character since the network wanted more sex in the series. Another character named Rhea, a thirteen-year-old gymnast, was in the original pilot. She was an academic prodigy already enrolled in college and was to be Cara's roommate. Her scenes were cut to give the series a more adult feel. ABC wanted *Push* to be "Melrose Place in Spandex" and lots of "sex, sex, sex."[69] Perry attempted to protect his concept for the series but ultimately lost and was fired.

Love Monkey – Love and Music
Premiered January 17, 2006 on CBS Tuesdays 10:00 pm

Premise: This comedy-drama concerned a single, thirty-something artists and repertoire representative whose female friend called him a "lonely monkey" swinging from one branch to another looking for love.

Cast of Characters:

> Tom Ferrell (Tom Cavanaugh) – the A & R representative;
> Bran Lowenstein (Judy Greer) – his female friend;
> Karen (Katherine La Nasa) – Tom's sister who is a doctor expecting her first child;
> Derrick "Shooter" Cooper (Larenz Tate) – Tom's friend, an African-American who worked for his wealthy dad in real estate and loved to play basketball with Tom;
> Jake Dunne (Christopher Wiehl) – a closeted former major league baseball player who became a local television sportscaster on fictional WYND channel 8 where Bran was a news producer. He also played basketball with Tom.

Background: Created by Michael Rauch, the series was based on the book of the same name by Kyle Smith. Paramount Television and Sony Pictures Television co-produced *Love Monkey*. Sony Pictures had given Rauch a copy of *Love Monkey* and asked him to turn it into a TV series. CBS bought the concept but didn't want the main character, Tom Farrell, to be a writer for a New York tabloid as in the novel. They asked Rauch to come up with a different profession for the character. He ". . . thought of a bunch of stuff and none of it was any good. Then I remembered that I had an old friend who was an A&R rep when we were growing up in New York, and hanging out with him back then, late at night going to clubs to hear bands and meet women and get drunk. It was a very fun, crazy environment. Then you add music on to that, and it felt like it would be a fun world to set the show in."[70]

CBS ordered eight episodes. Rauch was concerned that CBS, in particular known for its crime procedural dramas, had nothing else like it on the air. Referring to the network, he indicated "They are very patient with the show, and they're supportive creatively, but I do worry how long it will take to find our audience on that network. I don't think anyone knows the answer to that."[71]

The Pilot - January 17, 2006

Tom's current girlfriend Gabey doesn't believe in marriage which suits Tom. However, she changes her mind and wants to get married. He doesn't, and they break up. Tom, working for Goliath Records, discovers a hot new talent in Monroe, Michigan named Wayne Jensen (singer/songwriter Teddy Geiger). At a business meeting, Tom is advised that the record company is doing poorly. He speaks up saying that the power and beauty of music is more important than profits and is promptly fired. He decides to start his own independent record label and wants to sign Wayne. However, after talking with his sister, he advises Wayne that Goliath Records can do more for him than he can. Wayne elects to sign with a small independent record company True Vinyl. The company decides to hire Tom as the head of A & R and to represent Wayne. At True Vinyl, Tom becomes infatuated with Julia Hixon ((Ivana Milicevic), a fellow A & R rep.

Rock singer Aimee Mann had a cameo in this episode.

Other Episodes Broadcast

"Nice Package" - January 24, 2006

Tom seeks to have a singer named Zoe who is with Goliath Records play at a "Rock-the-School" benefit concert because his current record company needs a headliner for the event as well as for the live album they plan to produce. Tom's former boss will allow Zoe to perform but won't give permission for her to sing her hit song for the live album. Tom convinces his former boss to permit Zoe to sing her original composition instead of her hit. However, he soon finds that her performance is less than expected. He has her perform a duet with Wayne since Wayne makes up for Zoe's performance deficiencies.

Singers LeAnn Rimes and Ben Folds appeared on this episode.

"Confidence" - February 7, 2006

Tom wants to make a video of Wayne performing his song. Julie suggests Nathan Kitt, a director who has made art house films, helm the video, but Tom has his doubts. Kitt wants to portray Wayne as a James-Dean type in a take-off of *Rebel without a Cause*. After Tom learns that the director told Wayne that he isn't dynamic enough in the video, Tom fires him and directs a simple video of Wayne's performance.

English singer/songwriter James Blunt had a cameo in this episode.

Unaired Episodes

"The One Who Got Away"

Tom becomes the A & R rep for the band Gladwell which has signed with True Vinyl. The band's singer Kera is Tom's old flame. Although he has a rule against getting intimately involved with a client, he breaks the rule with Kera. This causes friction between the band's leader and Kera, and the band breaks up before they appear on David Letterman's show, a spot that Tom worked hard for the band to get. With Tom's efforts, the band reunites after breaking up with Kera. Meanwhile, Jake confesses to his ex-fiancée that he is gay.

Aimee Mann, Paul Shaffer, and musical duo "She Wants Revenge" appeared on this episode.

"The Window"

Tom has a small window of opportunity to publicize the new CD of a duo called the Barbarian Brothers. They are difficult personalities to handle and don't like performing live. Tom tries to impress Abby Powell, a music critic to review the Brothers' CD, but she thinks that Tom wants to have sex with her. As a last resort to publicize the new CD, Tom schedules a live internet simulcast of the Barbarian Brothers performing. Meanwhile, Bran thinks she may be pregnant but learns that she may have a medical condition preventing pregnancy. Jake is asked by his boyfriend to move into a recently vacated apartment with him, but Jake is not sure he is ready for such a commitment.

"Opportunity Knocks"

Tom discovers that Ray Grimaldi, the son of the recently deceased owner of Tom's favorite pizza shop, is a talented composer and singer. True Vinyl has funds to sign only one new talent, and it's a competition between Ray and Julia's suggestion to sign a classical violinist. Tom convinces Ray to participate in a live showcase of his music. The showcase impresses Tom's boss who wants to sign Ray. But Ray is conflicted about which career choice to make – whether to go on the road as an opening act for another group or stay with his family and run the pizza shop. He decides to do the latter. Tom offers Ray a publishing deal to allow other artists to record his compositions.

Dr. John made an appearance in this episode as one of Ray's idols.

"Mything Persons"
Goliath Records is selling music genius Gordon Decker's catalogue. Decker had a brief career several years earlier but burned out before he completed his second album. Tom wants to sign him with True Vinyl and have him complete the second album. He finds Decker working as a cabbie. Decker listens to his old master tapes and agrees to record again. However, he is a perfectionist. As Tom's former boss says Gordon "has the kind of fire that can burn down a label." Tom talks Decker into doing a live solo album to expedite the recording process, and he performs in front of a sold-out crowd.

"Coming Out"
Wayne's album debuts and is a smash hit. True Vinyl signed Wayne for only one album and now Goliath Records wants to recruit him. Tom's former boss offers him his old job back with a salary increase and promises to establish an independent label for him within Goliath. Tom refuses and tells Wayne and his parents that Goliath just wants to sign him to make big money but staying with True Vinyl is in Wayne's long-term interest. Nonetheless, Goliath continues to try to entice Wayne to sign with it. Meanwhile, Jake comes out to his boss at the TV station when there are rumors that Bran and he are having an affair. Karen finally delivers her baby boy with all of Tom's friends at the hospital for the birth.

Natasha Bedingfield, John Mellencamp, Lisa Loeb, and Mya made cameo appearances in this episode.

Postscript: At the end of March, 2006, VH1 owned by Viacom as is CBS, announced plans to air the episodes broadcast on CBS along with the unaired episodes.

CHAPTER 9

Some Cult Comedies

Oboler Comedy Theatre – *The Twilight Zone* of Comedies

Premiered October 11, 1949 on ABC on the East Coast Tuesday at 9:00 pm (Premiered on the West Coast in September 1949)

Premise: A six-week comedy anthology with no regular cast members.

Cast of Characters: Various

Background: Arch Oboler wrote and produced this special six-week limited series for ABC. Oboler was best known for his work on radio including writing several episodes of the series *Lights Out*. However, his first play for radio was "Futuristics," a comedy satirizing the norms of the present day seen from the perspective of the future.

Aired Episodes:

"Ostrich in Bed" – October 11, 1949

    A married couple, played by Olan Soule and Frances Rafferty, returns home to find an ostrich in their bedroom. They need to get rid of the bird before a prospective client for the services of the husband's advertising agency arrives for dinner. The husband calls the police, but the desk sergeant is too busy reading the Kinsey Report to be interrupted and so passes the call off as from a drunk. The humane society doesn't help either because the couple can't determine if the bird is a male or female.

    With the ostrich in their bedroom closet, the couple tries to entertain the potential client played by Hans Conried. To cover the bird's noises, the husband keeps breaking dishes while the guest becomes drunk on his own product, "Grandmother Bedila's Elixir" which is 90 – proof. The client wants to be excused from the table, but the couple, fearing he will find the bird, ignores his pleas. When the guest can no longer contain himself, he departs only to be encountered by the ostrich and runs from the house almost hysterical. Finally, the wife is able to drive the bird from the home.

This live presentation used a real ostrich and a live turtle.

"Love, Love, Love"

At a lecture on love, the students daydream about their own fantasies on the subject including love in the movies, a soldier in love in Paris while on a pass, love in songwriting, love over the phone, and the secret wedding of a celebrity couple.

"Lo, the Poor Indian/ The Laughing Man/ Mr. Pip"

Three playlets: In London, England, a down-on-his luck actor pretends to be Lo, a Native American at a fancy party; 20,000 years in the future, a man ridicules a person from the twentieth century over his unbelievable stories about wars and atrocities; and a young fisherman and an old man have a strange encounter.

"Mrs. Kingsley's Report"

An elderly man meets a former girlfriend at a restaurant much to his wife's chagrin. A live pigeon was featured on this episode.

"Mr. Dydee"

A dim-witted gambler inherits a diaper service, and finds, much to his discomfiture, that the business requires him to contact the expectant mothers.

"Dog's Eye View"

A murder is seen by a dog. A real dog was featured on this installment.

Postscript: Oboler attempted to launch another anthology in 1958 called *Arch Oboler's Plays*. The stories would range from mysteries to science fiction with each narrated by Oboler. However, no network picked up the series.

Ugliest Girl in Town – TV's First Cross-Dressing Sitcom
Premiered September 26, 1968 on ABC Thursdays at 7:30 pm

Premise: A young Hollywood advertising agent dresses in drag and moves to London to be a female model in order to afford to romance his English girlfriend and help pay off his brother's gambling debts.

Peter Kastner as model Timmy and Patricia Brake as his girlfriend. Kastner later co-starred on the short-lived comedy, *Delta House* in 1979. He passed away in 2008.

Cast of Characters:

Timothy Blair aka "Timmy" (Peter Kastner) – twenty-three-year-old advertising agent masquerading as a female model;
Julie Renfield (Patricia Brake) – an English starlet with whom Timothy falls in love;
Gene Blair (Gary Marshall) – Timothy's brother, a professional photographer;
Sandra Wolston (Jenny Till) – Timmy's private secretary;
David Courtney (Nicholas Parsons) – Timmy's boss at the modeling agency.

Background: Writer Robert Kaufman created the comedy. Reportedly, one day he was reading a magazine about model Twiggy's life story and thought that she looked more like the boy next door instead of the girl next door. He came up with the concept of a TV series about a Twiggy but in reverse - a boy who is mistaken for a girl model. Kaufman brought his idea to Harry Ackerman, vice president and executive producer of Screen Gems at the time.[72] Ackerman produced such comedies as *The Flying Nun*, *Bewitched*, and *Gidget*.

The Pilot – September 26, 1968

Timothy Blair, a young advertising agent making $97 a week, meets starlet Julie Renfield and immediately falls in love. She eventually agrees to go on a date with him and then has to fly back to England, her home country. Meanwhile, Timmy's brother Gene takes photos for a client in Britain that turn out poorly. He recruits Timmy to dress as a hippie with a shoulder-length-hair wig and takes new pictures. After he sends the new photos to England, Timothy is invited to London as Timmy, a hot female model. He and Gene fly to that country to do modeling so that Timothy can be with Julie. She recognizes Timmy in drag and understands the reason for the disguise. Timothy says he is finished with the charade and will obtain a regular job in London. But his plans change when his brother loses money gambling and Timothy needs to earn money as a model to help his brother.

Other Aired Episodes:

"Visitors from a Strange Planet" – October 3, 1968

Timothy and Gene's parents, Margaret (Evelyn Keyes) and Harry Blair (Larry Cross), visit and learn that Timothy is passing himself off as the top female hippie model in London. He makes up the story that he is a secret agent to explain his wig and dress.

"Pain in Timmy's Tummy" – October 10, 1968

When Timmy is stricken with appendicitis on the way to a modeling assignment, he is sent to the women's section of a hospital for treatment only to be bounced back and forth between the men's and women's wards.

"The Cover Up Girl" – October 17, 1968

Timmy has a cameo role in a feature film that involves a nude scene. She refuses to participate in the bath tub scene prompting a modesty campaign.

"One of Our Models Is Missing" – October 24, 1968

Timothy receives a job offer in Scotland that would allow him to give up his masquerade as Timmy. Since Timothy has an interview at the same time as the job interview, he leaves a note that Timmy has been kidnapped for the weekend. Guess who is arrested for the abduction? Timothy, of course.

"Up the Thames without a Paddle" – October 31, 1968

Timothy mails a letter to Timmy's modeling agency disclosing the chain of events leading to his role as Timmy hoping that he can discontinue his masquerade. However, his brother's gambling losses change his plans. Timothy has to try to retrieve the letter from the London postal service.

"The Perfect Young Lady" – November 7, 1968

A prim spinster newspaper columnist wants to write a portrait of Timmy as the perfect young lady. Tim has to do a lot of quick changes and improvisation so that she doesn't expose Timmy as a fraud.

"The Look Alikes" – November 14, 1968

Tim is due in Los Angeles for ten days of National Guard duty at the same time Timmy is supposed to be in London modeling. A "Timmy-Look-Alike" contest seems to solve the problem.

"Timmy the Mother" – November 21, 1968

Timmy plays mother for a baby girl whose parents have flown to Stonehenge to attend a "Love-in-of-the Month Club" event. Child welfare and a host of flower people converge on Timmy and Julie when it appears that the mother is lost.

"Popped Star" – December 5, 1968

British singing star Lulu coaches Timmy in a quest for the model to become a pop singing sensation.

"The Paris Incident" – December 12, 1968

Timmy goes to Paris with Julie for a fitting of a "one-of-a-kind" gown produced by a famous French designer. Timmy and Julie are assigned the same hotel room with Julie sleeping in the bed – Tim in the bathtub. The hotel's maid informs the press that the two are staying at the establishment prompting a newspaper reporter to show up at their hotel room where he sees Tim – not Timmy. Later, Timmy tells the reporter that the man he saw in the room (i.e., Tim) was trying to steal the designer gown.

"The Jewel Robbery"- December 19, 1968

Tim is a master of disguise in this episode. On a photo shoot with his brother and Julie, everyone is staying with David Courtney's aunt and uncle, Lord and Lady Tarlton, at their country estate. During dinner the lights go out with Lady Tarlton's diamond earrings being stolen. Courtney suggests that the men and women separate and each disrobe in an attempt to find the jewels. Timmy escapes since he doesn't want to show his true self. She becomes the chief suspect in the theft. Tim returns dressed as a Scotland Yard inspector to investigate the case and finds that Lady Tarlton stole her own jewels since they were fake and she didn't want her husband to find out when an appraiser from the insurance company was to evaluate them the next day. Conspiring with Lady Tarlton, Tim masquerades as a Timmy lookalike so others believe the lookalike is the real thief. The lookalike flees before anyone can catch her. Then Tim impersonates the insurance appraiser so the true value of the earrings is not revealed.

"My Sister the Genius" – December 26, 1968

Julie's sister, Terri, who is a genius, visits. When she sees Timothy wearing make-up, he explains what is going on. Terri threatens to tell Courtney about Timothy's masquerade, but Julie makes sure that Timothy's other identity is kept secret.

"The Ugliest Boy in Town" – January 2, 1969

Timothy takes leave of his masquerade as Timmy to become a male model – the ugliest boy in town.

"The Trouble with England" – January 16, 1969

At a pub, Timmy complains about England's faulty plumbing. Overheard by members of both England's Conservative Party and its Labour Party, she is recruited to run for the position of council woman of Kensington. David thinks Timmy as a candidate would be great for publicity. Since he doesn't really want to win, Timmy decides to become the Labour Party candidate. When her campaign catches fire, Tim delivers a speech demeaning Timmy. The Conservative Party wants Tim to run against Timmy. In the end, the third party Liberal candidate wins the race.

"A Little Advice Goes a Long Way" – January 23, 1969

Timmy temporarily takes over writing a newspaper advice column. She is in for more than she bargained for when a frustrated wife takes her advice to heart and leaves her husband.

"Matchmates" – January 30, 1969

Timmy's agent convinces his client to enter the world of computer dating. Timmy incorrectly fills in the computerized questionnaire and becomes the love object of a strange young man who believes himself the reincarnation of a medieval king and Timmy is his predestined princess.

Unaired Episodes:

"The Track Star"

Timmy attends track and field trials where a Russian athlete becomes infatuated with her. The athlete breaks up with his girlfriend, a Russian track star, but Timmy attempts to have him reconcile with his girlfriend which he does after Julie gives her a makeover.

"Tubby Timmy"

To become the spokesperson for a new "Timmy Slimmy Loaf," Timmy must lose twenty-one pounds in fourteen days.

"He Lost His Girlish Laughter"

In the series finale, Tim's brother Gene wins enough money gambling for Tim to retire as "Timmy."

Unproduced Episodes:

A treatment titled "The Feud Story" was developed for an episode of this series that apparently was never made. The treatment dealt with a publicity agent for a land-owning nobleman in need of money who wants to launch a Convention and Exhibition of the Fellowship of British Inventors on his estate. The agent asks Timmy and Julie to cook up a public feud and then make personal appearances at the convention. The belief is that the public will flock to the exhibition to witness the crucial confrontation of the supposedly feuding "women."

Timmy and Julie agree to the ruse but, predictably, their arguing becomes a real feud. In the end, the two reconcile.

There is also at least one unproduced script for an episode titled "My Son, the Matchmaker."

A young school boy named Roger thinks Timmy would be an excellent mate for his father. However, the father is in love with a woman named Claudia of which his son is unaware. The father informs his son that he really likes Claudia and that they intend to marry. Roger then turns matchmaker for his dad and Timmy, but, naturally, he fails to make a match.

Postscript: *The Ugliest Girl in Town* was the first of a small group of situation comedies centered around straight men who dressed in female attire usually to obtain a job and/or save money. The most popular of this sitcom subgenre was *Bosom Buddies* which starred Peter Scolari and Tom Hanks masquerading as women to live cheaply in a females-only apartment building. That comedy lasted for thirty-seven episodes. Two other such comedies were *Ask Harriett* on Fox in 1998 starring actor Anthony Tyler Quinn dressing in drag to work as an advice columnist. It lasted for five episodes. *Work It*, on ABC in 2012, about two cross-dressing men pretending to be women to gain employment was canceled after two installments.

Bob & Carol & Ted & Alice – Mild Sex
Premiered September 26, 1973 on ABC Wednesdays 8:00 pm

Premise: The comical adventures of two married couples – one in their twenties, fun-loving and free-spirited, the other in their thirties and more conservative, were highlighted on this series.

Cast of Characters:

>Bob Sanders (Robert Urich) – a filmmaker in his twenties;
>Carol Sanders (Anne Archer) – Bob's wife;
>Ted Henderson (David Spielberg) – a lawyer in his thirties;
>Alice Henderson (Anita Gillette) – Ted's wife;
>Sean Sanders (Brad Savage) – Bob and Carol's young son;
>Elizabeth Henderson (Jodie Foster) – Ted and Alice's young daughter.

Background: When ABC announced their fall 1973 schedule, many assumed that *Bob & Carol & Ted & Alice* would be a risqué comedy dealing with sexual themes like the film on which it was based. The 1969 movie, *Bob & Carol & Ted & Alice*, focused on the theme of extra-marital sex. However, the network later issued a press release stating that the ABC show "is not based on the motion picture of the same name."[73] Most of the series story lines dealt with sex in some way but in a PG fashion.

ABC decided not to debut the series with the original pilot about swimming in the nude. The pilot was shown later in the series short run.

The Pilot:
Bob and Carol return from a nature retreat where they divulge that they swam naked with other people at the retreat. They propose that Ted and Alice join them in skinny dipping, but Alice is reluctant. Ted is all for it. Alice is relieved when Bob and Carol stop pressuring them on the subject, but Ted is disappointed. He tells his wife that she is afraid to change prompting Alice to invite Bob and Carol over for a nude swim. Alice, Bob, and Carol go swimming in the buff, but Ted turns out to be uncomfortable taking his clothes off. Eventually, he joins them after jumping into the pool fully dressed.

The pilot aired as the third episode of the series on October 10, 1973.

Other Aired Episodes:

"Can I Help It if She's Crazy About Me? – September 26, 1973
Ted divulges to Bob that he thinks his secretary is attracted to him. Ted ends up firing her, but, after he informs Alice, she thinks he had no basis for the termination. He rehires her, but then Alice has second thoughts.

"Alice's Wild Oat" – October 3, 1973
Alice reveals that she had an affair before she married Ted. She confesses this when her then lover, now an attorney, shows up on the front page of the local paper indicted for tax fraud.

"I'm not Jealous – Only Curious" – October 17, 1973
Adele Phillips, an actress known for her sexual exploits, is interested in working with Bob on a film project. When Adele invites Bob to a luncheon meeting, Carol becomes jealous. After not hearing from Bob for three and a half hours, Carol learns that her husband and Adele never showed up at the restaurant. Bob finally returns home and said that he went to a burger joint after Adele never showed. The actress stops by later saying that her car broke down and she met a young man who helped her. Bob subsequently rejects her request to work with him.

"Open Marriage/Closed Mind" – October 24, 1973

Beryl and Gus Porterfield, friends of Bob and Carol, have an open marriage. They stop by with Cheryl whom Gus wants to marry to form a menage a trois. Ted and Alice meet the Porterfield's at Bob's house with Beryl thinking that Ted and Alice also have an open marriage. The next day, the threesome visits Bob and Carol again. With Ted and Alice in attendance, the threesome engages in an argument among themselves. Cheryl decides not to marry Gus. Bob and Carol, Ted and Alice come to realize that an open marriage is not as appealing as it may appear.

"Nobody Wants to Talk About It" – October 31, 1973

After attending a funeral for an acquaintance, the two couples face the prospect of death. They become concerned over each other's parenting styles if one of the couples dies and the other couple becomes the legal guardian of their child.

"The Bare Truth Hurts" – November 7, 1973

Bob hides a camera in his house to tape Ted and Alice for a documentary about "screwed-up" couples. When Ted and Alice arrive, they are arguing about cutting their daughter's hair shorter. Alice comments about "taking it all off." Bob returns the camera to the studio without looking at the tape. Eunice, a studio employee, views the tape and concludes that Ted and Alice are nudists like her and her husband leading to uncomfortable encounters with Ted and Alice.

Unaired Episodes:

"Such Good Friends"

Realizing that they come from different backgrounds, Carol and Alice argue over the issue. Ted and Bob argue about Ted's obsession with time. Throughout the evening and into the next day, the silly arguments continue. In the end, the couples reconcile when they realize they promised to take their kids to Disneyland.

"Walk a Mile in My Clogs"

Bob and Ted have mixed emotions after Carol and Alice join a Women's Liberation group. Ted thinks that the group is subversive. Bob becomes concerned when Carol won't discuss what happened at the meeting. At the next meeting, in Bob's house, Ted attempts to eavesdrop to determine what issues are being discussed. A guest speaker talks about sexism. Ted thinks they are talking about sex but then realizes they are not. They are discussing inequality.

"Double, Double, Doyle & Friends"

The Sanders' are having a garage sale and decide to let a pro bono client of Ted's named Doyle in charge since he needs a job. Bob informs Doyle that everything has to go. When the couples return, all of Bob and Carol's furniture is sold because Doyle took Bob's comment literally. They are able to get most of their furniture back. Doyle feels like a failure, but then Ted finds him some handyman jobs.

"Inadmissible Evidence"

Alice reluctantly accepts a job on a committee to review adult movies before they are shown at the local theater. Ted believes that her membership might spice up their marriage, but it makes Alice more uptight than ever. Bob and Carol know the actor that appeared in *Ravish Me Slowly*, the film that Alice reviewed. When she meets the actor at the Sanders, she becomes catatonic in front of him and leaves. Later, the actor stops by to see Ted and Alice. Alice is about to have a nervous breakdown, but the actor apologizes for making her feel uncomfortable. She says that she did vote to have his movie shown at the theater because she is for freedom of expression.

"My Butcher Is a Thief"

Carol purchases some cheap steaks from a shady meat salesman. Ted says the man is a black marketeer. Bob asks the salesman to visit Ted to explain how he is able to sale meat so cheaply. He explains that he is able to do this by eliminating the middle man. Ted decides to buy a considerable quantity of meat from him. Later, the news reports that the man is wanted for stealing beef. Carol is arrested for shoplifting when her son takes a watch from a department store after overhearing his mother say that everyone steals. Ted then decides to donate the beef to an orphanage.

Postscript: About the premiere, *Variety* critiqued "In some fanciful advance publicity from the network, producer Jim Henerson is quoted as saying that the 'generation' gap of 10 years between the couples 'will spark the comedy.' Unfortunately, the difference in age, obscure to viewers, does no such thing."[74]

The Texas Wheelers – MTM Dramady Set in Texas

Premiered September 13, 1974, on ABC Fridays 9:30 pm

Premise: This comedy/drama revolved around the misadventures of conniving Zach Wheeler and the two oldest sons—Truckie, who was the breadwinner for the family, and Doobie. Truckie was a convicted car thief, reformed barroom brawler, and high school dropout. His sixteen-year-old brother, Doobie, also wanted to leave school in the series opener but ultimately decided that being in the classroom was better than working.

Cast of Characters:

> Zack Wheeler (Jack Elam) – the no-account, widowed father of four;
> Truckie Wheeler (Gary Busey) – at twenty-four, the oldest of the Wheeler siblings;
> Doobie Wheeler (Mark Hamill) – sixteen-year-old son;
> Boo Wheeler (Karen Oberdiear) – twelve-year-old daughter;
> T.J. Wheeler (Tony Becker) – ten-year-old son.

Background: *Variety* gave the show a rave review saying that "MTM Enterprises looks like it has another hit on its hands."[75] Alas, after producing the hits *The Mary Tyler Moore Show* and *The Bob Newhart Show*, *The Texas Wheelers* was the company's first major failure.

The series was originally on Fridays at 9:30 pm opposite the *CBS Friday Night Movie* and *The Rockford Files* on NBC. Canceled after four episodes, ABC burned off four additional episodes during summer 1975. A total of eleven episodes were produced. Dale McRaven, who, with Garry Marshall and Joe Glauberg, subsequently created the hit *Mork & Mindy* and later the sitcom *Perfect Strangers*, created *The Texas Wheelers*.

Commenting about *The Texas Wheelers*, McRaven said, "I wanted to do a series with one element unique to television in it: reality." He explained that the characters were a conglomeration of lots of people he knew. "A girl I knew was like 21 when she adopted her own sister to keep her from going to a home. I guess that was the basis. I thought about a young guy like Truckie, about 24, raising a family of kids by himself because his mother was dead and his dad ran out."[76]

The Pilot:
"Wailin' Wheeler Is Dead" – September 13, 1974

After being gone for eight months in search of gold, Zack Wheeler returns to his children whom he had deserted. Zack finds that Doobie has a girlfriend who leaves when Truckie takes away his brother's six pack of beer. "Can't trust a woman who only wants your beer," explains Truckie. To which Doobie replies, "I didn't want to trust her. I only wanted to get her drunk."

Doobie seeks to drop out of school. Zack sends him to a local steel mill for a days' hard work which makes Doobie reconsider leaving school.

Other Aired Episodes:

"The X-Rated Movie" – September 20, 1974

To prepare for his date with the most attractive girl in school, Doobie sees an X-rated movie in town but is repulsed by it. Confused by his feelings, he seeks advice from older brother Truckie.

"The Accident" – September 27, 1974

Truckie spots dents on his truck and figures his father is responsible since Zack had the vehicle the night before. Zack denies everything but is caught in his lies by his kids.

"The Twister" – October 4, 1974

Zack and Doobie hide in the basement as a tornado approaches Lamont and end up trapped there after the house is hit.

"The Bookmobile" – July 3, 1975

Truckie is infatuated with the new librarian.

"The Music Box" – July 10, 1975

After finding a pile of junk in the barn, Zack has an antique sale and inadvertently sells his daughter's cherished music box.

"The Call" – July 17, 1975

Zack says he has had the "call" to leave the family for a month and search for a lost gold mine. Boo wants to go with him. Truckie suggests that Zack and Boo try camping around Lamont before going to look for the lost mine. Zack hopes that the experience will dissuade Boo from accompanying him on the longer trip, but, after Zack twists his ankle, Boo saves the day.

"The Rebel" – July 24, 1975

Truckie is doing all the house work for the family as well as holding down several jobs. Frustrated, he quits working and decides to "retire." Zack calls his other kids together to help with the chores while he prepares TV dinners for supper. Zack discusses the situation with Truckie who comes to realize that his family can assume more responsibilities and that he doesn't have to do everything.

Unaired Episodes

"The Widow"

Seeking to sweet talk a widow out of her life's savings, Zack ends up falling in love with her.

"Big Night in Blue Gum"

The Wheeler's travel to the big city of Blue Gum for some fun and action.

"The Liar's Contest"

When a professor asks Zack to relate his stories for publication, Zack believes they will make him rich and famous.

Postscript: Karen Oberdiear, the daughter on the series, did not continue acting into adulthood. She became an accountant and died in a small plane crash in 2009 at the age of forty-six. However, the other actors who played the Wheeler siblings continued in the business with Gary Busey starring in *The Buddy Holly Story*, Mark Hamill as Luke Skywalker in the *Star Wars* movies, and Tony Becker as one of the stars of TV's *Tour of Duty*.

CHAPTER 10

Some Cult Series that Might Have Been

Little People – Big World

Premise: In August 1952, TV columnist John Lester reported "Watch for a 'Little People' television series, employing mostly midgets."[77] Evidently, each episode of this proposed thirty-minute anthology would highlight a story specifically adapted for the talents of little people.

Cast of Characters: Various

Background: The inspiration for this series may have come from a movie made in 1951 which Howco Productions, known for its exploitation features, released in 1953 titled *Mesa of Lost Women* featuring actor Allan Nixon with segments filmed by Ron Ormond. That science fiction film included scenes with little people.

The Pilot:

The proposed pilot was titled "Gulliver and the Little People," a modern adaptation of the Jonathan Swift novel. Actor Allan Nixon, all six feet five inches of him, starred in the pilot written by Richard Carr and directed by Ron Ormond.

Postscript: In addition to producing the following television pilot, Howco Productions made several exploitation films during the 1950s including *Outlaw Women* (1952) about a town run by a female gambler that prohibits men from entering and *Mesa of Lost Women* (1953) mentioned above, concerning a mad scientist who seeks to create a race of superwomen by injecting them with spider venom.

Sabu – Bad Things Can Happen in the Jungle

Premise: This pilot attempt was to be a jungle adventure series from the production company that sought to bring *Little People* to television.

Cast of Characters:

Sabu – as himself

Background: Produced by Western Adventure Films and its affiliate Howco, the project started out as a vehicle for Sabu known for his jungle adventure films.

The Pilot:

The original pilot, "Law of the Jungle," made in 1952, was directed by Ron Ormand. Its story line concerned the Maharaja of Dairee (Byron Keith) on a safari in the jungles of India looking for big game to hunt. His safari is led by chief hunter Kurran (Don Harvey). The Maharaja is frustrated that his group has found no animals to kill and questions a local Holy man (Nelson Leigh) who tells him that Sabu is keeping the animals out of danger. Meanwhile, the Maharaja spies a beautiful local maiden named Rani (Carol Varga) and asks her father, Rajan (Jack Reitzen), to sell her so he can marry her. However, she is already betrothed to Kadlu (Rick Vallon) who is away on a pilgrimage in the mountains. Greedy for riches from the Maharaja, Rajan informs his daughter that Kadlu has been killed and that she has to marry the Maharaja. Distraught, Rani flees to the jungle where she is almost attacked by a black panther who is one of Sabu's animal friends. Sabu saves her. She describes what happened to Kadlu whereupon Sabu informs her that Kadlu is still alive and volunteers to bring him back to her village. Before he can do this, Kurran and his group of hunters capture Sabu and Rani. Sabu is tortured in an effort to make the wildlife return to the jungle so the Maharaja can hunt the animals. At night, Sabu frees himself from captivity with the aid of another animal friend, Hathi, an elephant. He speeds to the mountains to bring back Kadlu before the Maharaja marries Rani. Upon returning to the village with Kadlu, Sabu overpowers the Maharaja who promises to leave the jungle and never return. The Holy man marries Rani and Kadlu.

Postscript: When the pilot never sold, Ron Ormond decided to edit it into a movie called *The Black Panther* and add more footage. After Sabu learned of this, he reportedly wanted more money. Evidently, Ormand decided to release *The Black Panther* as a half-hour, color movie short in 1956. Subsequently, he acquired actors Jackie Fontaine and Allan Nixon to appear in additional footage, edited out all the scenes with Sabu from the original pilot and, together with home movies of people on an African safari supposedly made by a doctor friend of Ormond's along with footage of topless African-American women, released a film titled *Untamed Mistress* about a woman captured by a band of murderous gorillas who are determined to keep her.

Ed Wood's Untitled Anthology – Overly-Dramatic Tear Jerkers

Premise: In late 1951, cult movie director, Ed Wood, was involved in writing, directing, and producing a series of fifteen-minute melodramas for television presumably for a potential dramatic anthology

Cast of Characters: Various

Background: The dramas were produced by WDBC films. Those involved in WDBC films along with Wood were Don Davis, Milton Bowron, and Joe Carter.

The Pilot:
"The Sun Was Setting" starred Angela Steven as June Drake, a woman who has stayed in her apartment for the past four months ever since she was told by her doctor that she has only six months to live. After Rene (Phyllis Coates), June's friend, finally informs June's boyfriend Paul (Richard Powers aka Tom Keene) of her condition, he asks June to marry him, but she refuses saying that they will meet again in the future in a better place. However, she does ask Paul to take her out for a good time. Because he thinks the excitement of going out may hasten her demise, he leaves. Later, June puts on an evening dress thinking she may go out by herself. Paul returns dressed in a tuxedo and decides to honor her request, but, before they can leave, June dies in his arms.

Postscript: Other episodes of this proposed anthology included "Cindy Is Dead," "The Last Few Thousand," and "Quiet Time" (or "Quiet Man" as indicated in some reports). The latter was to feature Lyle Talbot, Bud Osborne, and Conrad Brooks. However, apparently, only "The Sun Was Setting" was produced.

Portraits of Terror – Terribly Macabre

Premise: This 1957 series attempt was to be a weekly anthology probing the macabre.

Cast of Characters: Various

Background: The pilot was produced by Ed Wood in association with E.S. Moore.

The Pilot:
   The scroll at the beginning of the pilot, "Final Curtain," reads:

   Even the devil rejects them. Doomed to haunt the earth throughout the endless reaches of time.

   The creators of this story of terror were _____

   Once human _____

   Now – monsters _____

   In a void between the living and the dead

   Creatures to be pitied.

   Creatures to be despised . . .

   An actor (James 'Duke' Moore) in an empty theater after everyone has left imagines what unseen spirits may exist in the building narrating what he is interpreting from the noises he hears. He climbs a spiral staircase and encounters in one room, a female vampire with silk-like hair. Initially, believing it is a mannequin used in the play, he is startled that it turns out to be a real vampire (Jenny Stevens) beckoning him. Leaving the room, he goes to another where he finds a coffin. Raising the lid, he climbs inside. The lid closes, and presumably he is at peace.
   The overwrought narration was done by radio personality Dudley Manlove.

Postscript: Ed Wood apparently made another installment for the planned series called "The Night the Banshee Cried," but details of the story line could not be found.

The Marshall's Daughter – A Cross-Dressing Western Heroine

Premise: The proposed series concerned the exploits of a female dressed as a man seeking to avenge injustice in the West.

Cast of Characters:

Laurie Dawson aka El Coyote (Laurie Anders) – the heroine who was kind of a superwoman donning all black at night and posing as a man to pursue justice;

Ben Dawson (Hoot Gibson) – an undercover marshal who posed as the head of a traveling medicine show and was Laurie's father.

Background: Entertainer Ken Murray, through his own production company, attempted to sell a TV series called *The Marshall's Daughter* starring blonde actress Laurie Anders. Murray expected to make twenty-six episodes of this Western series with a female lead. The Anders' character knew judo, sang, danced, played the organ, and was an amateur ventriloquist with her Mexican dummy, Chico. She would use her Chico voice when masquerading as El Coyote so that no one knew, including her dad who yearned for a son, who she really was.

The Pilots:

Murray produced at least two episodes of the series and patched them together when the program didn't sell to release the work as a feature film. The first part of *The Marshall's Daughter* movie relates the story of a band of outlaws robbing Wells Fargo banks and relay stations. During the course of one robbery, the leader of the gang kills a boy's grandfather. Laurie overhears the gang plotting another robbery. When the outlaws attempt the robbery, Ben Dawson and the town's sheriff have a shoot-out with the gang, but the leader flees only to be captured in the second part of the film.

The second tale deals with cattle rustlers on a rampage. Ben and his daughter are sent back to their home territory to stop the violence. The town's banker wants to form a cattlemen's association, but Ben believes, as seems to be true about most heads of such associations in television Westerns, that the banker is behind the rustlers. When her uncle is killed, Laurie dons her El Coyote disguise and stops the rustlers. The banker who murdered her uncle ends up being shot.

To pad out the episodes as a feature film, the Hoot Gibson character reminisces about when he received his first gun with footage inserted from one of Gibson's silent Westerns. Also, producer Ken Murray appears in one scene as Smiling Billy Murray, an entertainer and gambler, who plays a comic poker game with actors Buddy Baer, Preston Foster, Jimmy Wakely, and Johnny Mack Brown.

Postscript: Ken Murray tried again in 1957 to launch a series about El Coyote. This time Muriel Davis, a top Olympic athlete, played Jane Edwards alias El Coyote whose father, Colonel Bart Edwards (George Brent) is a newspaper editor investigating a gunman's land grab. ABC was going to finance thirty-nine episodes of the series either for syndication or for the network, but it appears that the deal fell through.

Ham-Let – Not Shakespeare, Perhaps Bacon

Premise: A pig, with E.S.P., helps a detective solve mysteries.

Cast of Characters:

Ham-Let as himself

Background: Actor Thad Swift along with two colleagues – Norman Rice and William Strong formed a production company to make a TV series about a talented pig named Ham-let. The idea behind this satire of private detectives was that a PI inherits a pig named Ham-Let who is not only able to see the future but also reads minds. The pig helps the detective solve mysteries.

Evidently, as early as 1950, Thad Swift had made some TV shorts featuring his trained pigs. He purchased his animals from singer Ginny Simms' father who ran a farm in Reseda, California. He began training the pigs when they were four days old and did a nightclub act with them.

The Pilot:

If an actual pilot was ever made is unknown.

Postscript: According to Swift, pigs most interesting mental trait is a single track mind. "Give them a sequence of tricks to do in a routine and you can't get them to vary procedure. If the act calls for a Hamlet to sit up, lie down, and then roll over, you can't get them to roll over unless he works up to the stunt from beginning of the routine."[78]

McGurk: A Dog's Life – Actors in Dog Costumes

Premise: This comedy attempt concerned life as seen through the eyes of a dog.

Three of McGurk's friends howl in sympathy over McGurk's problems. Left to right: Cliff Norton, Michael Huddleston, Hamilton Camp, and Barney Martin in basket. Martin was better known for his role as Morty Seinfeld on *Seinfeld*.

Cast of Characters:

> McGurk (Barney Martin) – an older dog who has fathered at least twelve offspring, ten of which are with his girlfriend, Iris (Beej Johnson);
> Camille (Sherry Lynn) – Iris's daughter;
> Tucker (Charlie Martin Smith) – a young male pup that McGurk's owner adopts;
> Spike (Hamilton Camp), Turk (Michael Huddleston), and Butch (Cliff Norton) – friends of McGurk.

Background: From Norman Lear's production company in 1979, this comedy pilot was created by long-time writers Charlie Hauck and Arthur Julian. Actors, dressed in dog suits, portrayed the canine characters.

The Pilot:
"McGurk Welcomes Tucker" – June 15, 1979

After hearing his owner say "It's curtains for McGurk," and seeing that a new pup, named Tucker, is brought into the house, McGurk thinks that he is dying. Iris attempts to comfort him as Iris's daughter starts flirting with Tucker. McGurk doesn't die and learns that he is getting new curtains for his doghouse. He also comes to accept Tucker into the family.

Postscript: Reminiscing about the pilot that he directed, actor/director Peter Bonerz remarked that "The script, written by Charlie Hauck, made me laugh until I cried. The table reading was hilarious. Even Norman Lear was impressed. The cast was great! It was the production itself which failed to live up to the excellence of the script and cast. Nothing I said or failed to say would have made much difference. . . . The scale, wardrobe and art design were all sub-par. No doubt budget played a determining role. . . It probably would have been best realized as an animated show."[79]

Pests – Lovable Roaches

Premise: A newcomer to New York City obtains a rent-free apartment provided he can keep the insect population under control.

Cast of Characters:

> Ralph B. Bennett – in his mid-twenties, arrives in New York from Nebraska seeking to become an actor. He sees an ad for a rent-free apartment in Greenwich Village;

Lee Spence – fifty-five years of age who is the landlord of Bennett's apartment building;
Ted Peale – twelve-year-old boy, a neighbor of Bennett's;
Elizabeth Peale – in her thirties who is Ted's mother.

Background: The script for this proposed sitcom was completed in February 1992, but the pilot was never made. As far as can be determined, actors were never chosen for the roles described above.

Pilot:
"I've Got You Under My Sink"
Ralph Bennett, fresh from Nebraska, answers an ad for a one-bedroom apartment in Greenwich Village which is free provided the tenant clears the building of roaches. Ralph makes his own insecticide and succeeds in fumigating the place of all the roaches except for at least three who grow to be three feet long. The three talking cockroaches are Clip, a tough, fast-talking insect, Arthur, a soft-spoken, mild-mannered roach, and Rex, an aristocratic, well-spoken roach. Ted introduces the three insects to Ralph. Although they want to live in Ralph's apartment, he is not so sure he wants them. Spence, the landlord, reneges on his promise to allow Ralph to stay free of charge after Ralph rids the place of most insects. Since Rex, Arthur, and Clip want to live in Ralph's apartment, they devise a plan to appear at night in the landlord's apartment as the ghosts of cockroaches yet to come. The next day, the landlord agrees that Ralph can live there without paying rent provided he keeps the pests out.

Postscript: James Orr and Jim Cruckshank, who wrote the screenplay for the motion picture, *Three Men and a Baby*, and produced the film remake of *Father of the Bride*, attempted to come up with something offbeat for a television series but struck out with *Pests*.

Steel Justice – AKA *Nash's Vision* and *Robosauris*

Premise – A police detective conjures up a life-size replica of his son's favorite toy – a mechanical dinosaur, to fight bad guys.

Cast of Characters:

Lieut. David Nash (Australian actor Robert Taylor) – the police detective who is separated from his wife after his son is killed in an explosion;

Jeremiah Jonas (J.A. Preston) – a 2356-year-old mystical guru interested in unlocking the secrets of human potential.

Background: This pilot, which aired as a movie for television on April 5, 1992, was created by Christopher Crowe and John Hill for NBC. It was set in the twenty-first century where the environment has deteriorated and crime runs rampant.

The Pilot:
In his dreams, Nash encounters Jeremiah Jonas who causes a toy that Nash built with his late son called a robosauris to act on its own. The robosauris is half robot, half dinosaur.

Colonel Edward Rollin Duggins (Roy Brocksmith) is assisting gangs terrorizing a metropolitan area in acquiring handheld rocket devices to attack vehicles in the city. Nash subsequently sees Jonas in real life who tells him that the two have a destiny to fulfill. Jonas explains that he is Nash's guide who helps people use their gifts to transform themselves. Working with Jonas, Nash conjures the robosauris to transform into a fire-breathing steel monster which helps Nash destroy the Colonel and the gang members. Nash finds that his son Davey was killed by the Colonel's weapon when the Colonel was testing his handheld device.

Postscript: As one critic described this pilot, "It haphazardly blends the plot of *Highlander*, the aesthetic of *Blade Runner*, the chaos of *Robocop*, and the finale of a monster truck rally into something so inherently ridiculous, it's hard to see how anyone would've made it through the script – let alone green-light the thing."[80]

CHAPTER 11

Unaired Cult Series

The Veil – The Veiled Revelations of Truths beyond Tangibility

Never aired except for the pilot

Premise: This anthology was supposedly based on real incidents of supernatural happenings.

Cast of Characters:

Boris Karloff is the host as well as the narrator and actor in various roles.

Background: Commenting on the planned series, Karloff wrote that "... 'The Veil' is an anthology of authenticated true stories that couldn't have happened – yet they did!" He remarked that "All the stories are vouched for in every respect by the highest, most reliable authorities, but we don't attempt any explanation of the bizarre, off-beat facts they bring to light."[81]

To garner publicity for the pending series, Karloff appeared as a guest on an episode of *Oh! Susanna* starring Gale Storm and Zasu Pitts which was produced by the same company that was filming *The Veil* - Hal Roach Studios. On the show, the Storm and Pitts characters visit the studio where *The Veil* is being made. They discover a plot by a demented actor portrayed by Karloff who plans to murder the real Boris Karloff and take his place before the cameras.

The Pilot – February 25, 1958

The pilot for *The Veil* aired as an installment of an anthology called *Telephone Time*. In the "Vestris" episode set in 1828, a ship by that name is sailing from England to Boston. The wife of the Vestris' Captain Norich

(Torin Thatcher) is sick and has a vision informing her to have the vessel change course. The captain reluctantly agrees. Subsequently, the crew on the ship finds three survivors of a shipwreck one of whom is Dr. Pierre (Karloff) who seems to be the spirit the wife saw in her vision. The doctor saves the captain's wife from dying and is as puzzled as everyone else by the woman's vision.

Unaired Episodes:[82]

"Vision of Crime"

As a druggist is closing up his shop, a young woman enters with a derringer and shoots him to death. The victim's brother, George Bosworth, 150 miles away on a ship, has a vision of the killing and makes his way back to England where he arrives at the home of his fiancée, Julie Westcott. The person who heard the shooting and discovered the body identifies Albert Ketch as the man running from the store at the time. He is arrested by the police.

George Bosworth knows that Ketch is not the murderer. He is told by the woman who identified Ketch that George's fiancée was lucky not to have been shot as well since she saw Julie just a few minutes after hearing the shots. Julie confesses to George that she killed his brother apparently in order for George to inherit the drug store and not be at sea all the time.

"Girl on the Road"

While out driving, John Prescott encounters a young blonde woman by the side of the road next to a red sports car that is out of gas. She says her name is Lila. He takes her to get some fuel for her vehicle. They stop at an inn for some drinks where the bartender begins acting strangely upon seeing Lila. The bartender phones a Morgan Debs. Lila instructs John that they must leave. Later, Prescott goes back to the inn and has the bartender relate that the girl's name is Lila Kirby. Prescott goes to the Kirby home where he sees Morgan Debs in a wheelchair. Debs shows Prescott newspaper articles about a car accident in which he was crippled and Lila had been killed three years earlier.

"Food on the Table"

Captain John Elwood arrives home after a long sea voyage. While packing his bags, the Captain doesn't notice a poisonous snake crawling into his luggage. After his bags are delivered directly to his wife, Elwood decides to have dinner at a local inn instead of coming straight home which angers his wife. Later, at home, the Captain lectures his wife saying he is sick of her.

His wife, Ruth, responds that she realizes he married her because of her father's wealth but that she still loves John. The snake from the Captain's chest escapes and bites Ruth. John saves her life by extracting the poison.

Subsequently, John becomes aware that a widow in town is inheriting $20,000. He gets the idea to kill his wife and marry the widow. John takes Ruth on his next voyage and begins giving her tea laced with poison. She eventually dies. On another voyage, the Captain's ship breaks up. Everyone is saved except for Ellwood which other seafarers say is retribution from Ruth's ghost.

"The Doctors"

In a little Italian town, a young girl named Francesca Bianchi falls ill. Dr. Carlo Marcabieni is contacted to treat the little girl, but he is out taking care of another patient. His son Angelo, also a doctor, tries to fill in for his father. However, the family insists that only Dr. Carlo treat her. Finally, the older doctor arrives, and the family allows Angelo to perform an emergency tracheotomy on the girl. Angelo returns home where his father tells him that he has been asleep all evening after treating his other patient and never left the house.

"The Crystal Ball"

Edmond Valier falls in love with Marie who says she is marrying someone else – Edmond's employer and publisher, Charles Montcour. As a farewell gift, Marie gives Edmond a crystal ball. When Charles goes on a business trip, he asks Edmond to visit his wife, Marie on occasion. Meanwhile, Marie visits Philippe Jussard in Paris. Through the crystal ball, Edmond sees Marie and Phillipe embracing. Charles returns from his trip. Edmond informs him that he has had no time to visit Marie. However, he explains what he saw through the crystal ball. The two men travel to Paris and find Marie with Phillipe. Charles divorces Marie with Edmond giving evidence of her affair based on what he witnessed through the crystal ball – the only time that such evidence was ever permitted in a court of law.

"Genesis"

After their father dies, two brothers – John Haney Jr. and James argue over the inheritance. John had stayed with his father and worked the farm while James had left ten years earlier and took with him his father's savings which he felt he was owed because he was never paid for his work on the property. Each brother has a will signed by the father, but the document James has is dated after the one John has. James' copy of the will bequeaths the farm to him which he intends to sell and place his mother in a nursing home. John contests the will in court. During a recess in the court case, John returns home and finds his father who instructs him to look in Genesis 27. John finds a Bible in the attic which contains another will with a later date leaving everything to him.

"Summer Heat"

During a particularly hot and humid day, Edward Paige returns home and sees the murder of a woman through the window of the apartment across the street – killed by a thief. When the police go to that apartment, they find no body and nothing in the vacant apartment. Paige desperately attempts to find someone who will believe his story. He ends up in a mental institution. The doctor at the institution believes Paige's story. Later, the woman Paige originally saw being killed is found dead in another apartment. The killer is arrested by the police and confesses to the crime.

"The Return of Madame Vernoy"

In India, Santha Naidu is convinced that she is the reincarnation of another woman who passed away but has a husband and son. She goes on a journey to find her family. When she locates them, the father and son don't believe she is the reincarnation of the wife and mother. She convinces them that her story is true when she finds some valuable jewels that the deceased woman had hidden in the house.

"Destination Nightmare"

While flying one of the airplanes for his family's air service business, Pete Wade Jr. is blinded by a bright light and sees a specter out the window that tells him to follow a course of 135. His father is informed of the incident and asks his son why he altered the plane's course. His son can't explain. Pete Jr. later discovers that the ghost he saw looks just like Wally Huffner, an airman that Pete's father knew in the war and who died when his parachute failed to open. The next day while flying, Pete Jr. sees the same apparition. He changes course, lands the plane, and finds old wreckage and an unused parachute. His father subsequently explains that while he and Wally were on a dangerous mission, Wally was wounded, knew he wouldn't survive long, and asked Pete Sr. to give him a cyanide capsule so he wouldn't be captured alive and tortured.

"Jack the Ripper"

George Durst has the ability to see into the future. He describes to his wife a dream he had about a horrible murder. The next day, George's wife reads in the newspaper about such a murder. Subsequently, George has a vision about another murder. Durst goes to Scotland Yard to inform them of his dreams. Knowing that Jack the Ripper is on the loose, George has an idea to use his ESP to locate him. Durst learns that the Ripper may be a Dr. Willowden who went insane and was committed to an insane asylum. After finding out about the doctor, the Ripper never claimed another victim.

"Whatever Happened to Peggy?"
A mother brings her daughter to see a physician. The young girl claims that her head feels "full" and wonders if she is losing her mind. Later that day, the doctor takes the girl and her mother to the home of Ira and Martha Perry whose daughter Peggy had passed away after falling down a flight of stairs. The surroundings seem familiar to the girl, and she stays with the Perry's for a while. Coming down the staircase, the girl almost falls but is saved by Ira Perry. This incident seems to have broken the spell from which the girl is suffering. She no longer seems to be possessed by the spirit of Peggy Perry.

Postscript: Producer Hal Roach made a total of twelve episodes of *The Veil* in 1958, but the episodes were never broadcast presumably because a co-production deal with National Telefilm Associates collapsed.

Hollyweird – The Dark Side of Tinsel Town

Scheduled to premiere September 1998 on Fox Thursdays 9:00 pm but never aired.

Premise: This series centered on three young adults from the Midwest who came to Hollywood to make a cable TV show dealing with strange events in Los Angeles.

Cast of Characters:

>Charlie Ripshaw (Fab Flippo) – director/cameraman for an Ohio cable TV show titled *Hollyweird*;
>Trey Carpanion (Bodhi Elfman) – editor/cameraman for the show;
>Caril Ann (Melissa George) – star/ hostess of the program and Charlie's girlfriend.

Background: Fox bought the series based on the title and the fact that director Wes Craven was one of the executive producers. Created by former singer Shaun Cassidy, apparently only the pilot was ever made.

The cast of *Hollyweird*: Fab Flippo, Melissa George, and Bodhi Elfman.

The Pilot:
Looking for stories for their next reality show episode, Caril reads a newspaper article about a killer who impales his victims. At the Galaxy Mall, a man has been killed with an iron rod through his chest. He is one of two missing security guards at the shopping center. Charlie, Trey, and Caril arrive at the mall where Charlie begins filming the crime scene. He spots a napkin with the name "Canter's" on it that appears to have been dropped by the dead man or the murderer. Charlie and Caril go to a nearby restaurant called "Canter's" where they meet a waiter named Seth who wants to be an actor. From the footage he shot of the crowd at the Galaxy Mall, Charlie identifies an individual wearing a Rams cap who appears at the restaurant. Later, a voice speaks to the three over their home computer saying that Caril gave him one of the group's business cards at the mall and that, if he catches them on his property again, they will end up like the guards. The three find that the guy in the Rams' hat is Harlan Cutler, who has just been released from prison for stabbing his father thirty-six times with a screwdriver and whose mother recently succumbed from brain cancer. Harlan lives in a house between the mall and the restaurant. With Trey as lookout, Caril and Charlie enter the house where they find a bloody security guard's jacket and a severed hand. Cutler returns home and knows that someone is there.

In the meantime, Trey has called the police. In the basement, Charlie and Caril find a tunnel. Going through the tunnel, they discover themselves surrounded by the remains of an old amusement park that happens to be under the mall. Cutler comes after them but falls into an elevator shaft in the tunnel. He considered the amusement park next door to his house to be his property and thought that the workers at the mall were intruding on his property. The police find that Cutler had a roommate – Seth, the waiter from the restaurant, who had moved into the Cutler home when Cutler's mother was still living. The mother had left the house to both men, but Cutler refused to share the home. Later, Seth comes to Caril's house at night when Trey and Charlie are on their way to the police station and attempts to kill her revealing that he is the one who killed everyone in order to get Cutler back in prison. Charlie and Trey return home just in time to save Caril as Seth plummets to his death over their balcony.

Postscript: After the network had announced their fall schedule, Fox decided that the series needed to be reconceived. The stars had to audition for the reconfigured series again. Cassidy quit as producer saying, "Having spent much of the last year trying to fix something that I never viewed as broken in the first place, I am withdrawing from the process of deconstructing

'Hollyweird.' The pilot that Fox bought was as fresh and original as anything I've been involved with."[83]

According to Fox Entertainment President at the time, Peter Roth, "We took on what was a very, very ambitious notion in 'Hollyweird.' . . . We wanted to find a new form. A new opportunity. A confluence of scare and comedy . . . But frankly, we failed." [84] Roth remarked further that the pilot was neither funny enough nor scary enough and that there was no 'legitimacy' to the characters putting themselves in harm's way every week.

Manchester Prep - Spoiled Rich Kids
Was to premiere in 1999 on Fox Thursdays 8:00 pm but never aired

Premise: This series centered on the relationship between a young man and his stepsister who attend the same New York prep school.

Cast of Characters:

Sebastian Valmont (Robin Dunne) - a manipulative young man who moves to New York City to live with his dad and his dad's wealthy fourth wife;

Kathryn Merteuil (Amy Adams) – Sebastian's stepsister who presides over the Manchester Prep tribunal made up of rich kids who decide which students at the prep school are total losers;

Edward Valmont (David McIlwaith) – Sebastian's father who still fools around with other women;

Tiffany Merteuil-Valmont (Mimi Rogers) – Sebastian's stepmother and Kathryn's mother;

Annette Hargrove (Sarah Thompson) – the daughter of the school's headmaster (Barry Flatman);

Cecile Caldwell (Keri Lynn Pratt) – a student at Manchester Prep from an extremely wealthy family;

Todd Michaels (Sean Patrick Thomas) – a black student who is instructed by Kathryn to get Sebastian into the Manchester tribunal.

Background: The series, a prequel to the 1999 movie, *Cruel Intentions* which was based on the novel and film *Dangerous Liaisons*, was created by Roger Kumble and produced by Columbia/Tristar. Fox never aired the series over concerns about *Manchester Prep's* approach to teenage sex. The network was upset about the incestuous undercurrent in the stepbrother-stepsister

Profiles of Fifty Offbeat Comedies and Dramas, Unsold Pilots, and Unaired Series • 207

From *Manchester Prep*: Amy Adams, Robin Dunne, Keri Lynn Pratt, and Sarah Thompson.

relationship and about a scene originally filmed for the pilot where one female character shows another female how to get sexual pleasure from horseback riding.

The Pilot:
Sebastian leaves his prep school under less than favorable circumstances with many reprimands in his file and goes to New York City to live with his dad and stepmother. In front of her mother, he shows his stepsister Kathryn that he is better at playing the piano and at vocabulary than she is. While he is taking a shower, Kathryn comes in and tells him never to cross her. On the first day of school, Kathryn, who is student body president, gives an orientation speech which is interrupted by a hiccupping Cecile who then chokes on her chewing gum and is saved by Annette, the headmaster's daughter. Kathryn confronts assistant headmaster Steve Mueller about dropping out of gym class or else she will reveal that he seduced her during the summer when the actual truth was the reverse. Sebastian meets Annette in the headmaster's office having substituted his file from his prior school with one much more flattering to himself.

Kathryn is the head of a secret club at the school known as the Manchester tribunal which determines which students are losers, geeks, or underprivileged. She defines both Sebastian and Annette as losers. But since Cecile comes from such a wealthy family, she wants to indoctrinate her into the in-group by making Cecile, who is a virgin, the school's premiere slut.

Kathryn learns of her brother's past at his prior prep school after procuring his real file and threatens to tell her mother that she is unknowingly paying for Sebastian's mother's drug rehab. Knowing that he plans to meet Annette soon, Kathryn attempts to seduce him so he will miss the date. She wants Sebastian to be part of the tribunal.

Other Episodes:

"Pretty in Plaid"

Poor Sebastian seems to have trouble taking a shower without interruption. In this episode, he steps into his shower and Kathryn is already there showering. He says he will reveal her secret society if she threatens to tell anyone about his real grades from his prior school. At school, Sebastian apologizes to Annette for standing her up. He also meets Todd Michaels who Kathryn makes the new Sergeant of Arms of the tribunal. Annette is tutoring Cecile who calls Sebastian and says that Annette is in love with him. He meets Annette on her way to dinner with her aunt and tells her he is crazy about her.

When Sebastian plays poker with the domestic staff, Kathryn becomes upset because the staff is not available for her needs. Sebastian says she cannot let her mother know about the poker game since he was responsible. Kathryn breaks down and says it was tough growing up in her house. Sebastian advises Kathryn not to interfere in his relationship with Annette and then pushes Kathryn into the mud.

"Disfunction Junction"
Kathryn believes that Sebastian will never join the tribunal as long as he is dating Annette. At school, Annette meets British student Nigel who takes photos of her.

In the meantime, Tiffany informs her daughter that Cecile is to be her new best friend since she wants to ask Cecile's mother Bunny for a contribution to the school's new library. Tiffany also remarks to Sebastian that his dad spends all his time on the yacht. When Sebastian goes to the yacht, he discovers his dad handcuffed to the bed and a woman named Lilly in the closet. He warns his dad not to screw up his life. When Tiffany has Cecile and her mother over for tea, Sebastian's dad comes back home still in handcuffs. Kathryn instructs her stepdad to take her mother out for dinner and gives him a set of keys to unlock the handcuffs. Kathryn tells Sebastian that he is the first family member she knows who is capable of an emotion other than hate. Sebastian thinks Annette is now interested in Nigel after he told Annette that both his mother and father are dead. Annette empathizes with him since her mother died two years ago. As Sebastian eavesdrops, Nigel cries while describing to Annette his mother's drowning death.

The headmaster has a ceremony for Tiffany about her fund raising efforts but announces the name of the library will be the "Bunny Caldwell Library" – not the "Tiffany Merteuil-Valmont Library." Sebastian explains to Annette that Nigel made up the story about the way his mother died. At school, Sebastian fences with Nigel in gym class. Nigel wins. However, then Sebastian and Nigel fist fight. Sebastian wins, but Annette feels sorry for Nigel. Kathryn tells Sebastian that she will take care of Nigel. She goes to Nigel's place. They kiss and reveal that they both know each other and that Kathryn gave Nigel permission to woe Annette.

Postscript: Although the series never aired, a direct-to-video movie, *Cruel Intentions II* was made from the TV episodes. The names of the characters portrayed by Sarah Thompson and Keri Lynn Pratt were changed in the film to Danielle Sherman and Cherie Claymon respectively. The movie ended with Sebastian finding that Danielle (Annette) was actually working with Kathryn in a secret plan to fool him into loving her. Sebastian says "if you can't beat them, join them," leading to a threesome. Sebastian then joins with Danielle and Kathryn to manipulate and dominate others. Sebastian's car runs over Cherie's bicycle. He offers to give her a ride and has sex with her. Kathryn and Danielle are in the front seat of the car pleased with what Sebastian is doing.

Fling – Investigating Marital Issues

Supposed to premiere on Fox sometime during the 2000-01 TV season but never aired.

Premise: This dramady dealt with the investigations of two private detectives working for a firm that specialized in cases involving marital disputes.

Cast of Characters:

> Elizabeth Gillcrest (Brooke Langton) – a young divorcee who becomes a private detective;
> Gene Rivers (Josh Hopkins) – a detective for Metropolitan Security Services;
> Maggie McClintock (Mary Louise Wilson) – the boss of the detective agency.

Background: In 1985, writer/producer Glenn Gordon Caron created a detective dramedy for ABC titled *Moonlighting*. Fashion model Maddie Hayes (Cybil Shepherd) discovers that her manager has cheated her out of the money she made. She has only one major asset left – the Blue Moon Detective Agency which she is about to sell until its one employee David Addison (Bruce Willis) convinces her not to and that she should become involved in the business. The series ran for four and a half seasons on ABC. Flash forward about eleven years, and Glenn Gordon Caron came up with a similar concept for a detective drama initially titled *What I What to Be When I Grow Up* which was shortened to *When I Grow Up* and then titled *Fling*. The series was produced by Caron's Picturemaker Productions in association with Paramount Network Television.

The Pilot:
The first draft pilot script dated November 1, 2000 titled "The Ending" opens with young Elizabeth Gillcrest leaving her sleeping older, wealthy husband Lloyd (Sydney Pollack) in the middle of the night to have an affair with a tennis pro at a local hotel in South Beach. She has second thoughts

about the tryst and leaves the tennis pro without having sex with him. However, when she returns home, her husband is waiting for her demanding a divorce and not believing her story that nothing happened. He gives her five minutes to leave the house. Having signed a prenuptial agreement, she is left with only a few possessions.

Elizabeth seeks to find the tennis pro so that he can explain to her husband that they really didn't have an affair. She tracks him down in New York City working for Metropolitan Security Services which Elizabeth thinks sells securities. Elizabeth discovers that he is not a tennis pro or an investment advisor but is a private detective named Gene Rivers who was hired by her husband to have an affair with her so he could free himself from the marriage because he had found someone else. After her initial disgust at what Gene does, she suggests to him and his boss Maggie McClintock that she join the firm as the female equivalent to Gene to "test" young men who want to marry older women.

Postscript: According to the *Los Angeles Times*, Fox sought to reduce its original commitment from thirteen episodes to eight because of differences over the series creative direction as well as Caron's reluctance to accept input from the network.[85] Paramount had invested about $10 million in the production.

In addition to the pilot, at least two other episodes were filmed titled "In Genes We Trust" and "At the End of the Day." After viewing the pilot and these two other episodes, Fox pulled the plug on the series.

Still Life – A Death in the Family
Supposed to premiere on Fox midseason 2003-04 but never aired.

Premise: This family drama dealt with the Morgan family attempting to reconcile to the death of their son Jake, a police officer who was killed on his first day on the job. What made the series unusual was that each episode was narrated by the dead son describing how his parents and siblings were leading their lives one year after his death.

Cast of Characters:

    Jake Morgan (Bryce Johnson) – the deceased son of the Morgan family who is only heard but not seen;
    Charlotte Morgan (Susanna Thompson) – Jake's mother in her forties who is married to Ben (David Keith), a police detective;

The Cast of *Still Life* – From the top of the staircase – Susanna Thompson, David Keith, Audrey Marie Anderson, Jeanette Brox, and Jensen Ackles.

Max (Jensen Ackles) – Jakes' twenty-one-year-old brother who has just returned from Paris with Jake's ashes;

Emily (Audrey Marie Anderson) – Jake's nineteen-year-old sister who quit college after his death and works in a strip club called Marlowe's;

Daisy (Jeanette Brox) – Jake's sixteen-year-old sister who still writes letters to him and feels his presence;

Maggie Jones (Morena Baccarin) – twenty-two-year old who was Jake's girlfriend and, before that, Max's girlfriend.

The Pilot:
Jake's mother Charlotte decides to run for mayor with the grudging support of her husband and encouraged by her father, Owen Foster, who is helping to manage her campaign. Max has just returned home after a year in Paris having taken Jake's ashes with him before the funeral a year earlier. Max feels that he should have been the brother who died and not Jake since Max always considered himself to be the black sheep of the family. Jake's oldest sister Emily works as a waitress in a strip club. She has just broken up with her boyfriend Ryan and is sexually attracted to a stripper at the club. Jake's youngest sister, Daisy, has an on again, off again relationship with a football player at school named Joe Hipps who pressures her to have sex with him, but she resists. Jake's killer, twenty-one year-old Eddie Marble, with no prior criminal record, is out on bail awaiting trial.

Other Episodes:

"Evidence"

Emily and Max question an entry in Jake's journal relating to "37 Channel, scored." They want to know if it is related to his death. Among Jake's effects left with Maggie, Max finds a map showing Channel Road in Oakland that was circled by Jake. He and Maggie go there on Jake's motorcycle and find that the house is occupied by Darien, a prostitute. Maggie thinks Jake was seeing the prostitute, but Darien denies ever meeting Jake. Later, Max returns to the house himself. Hiding behind a concrete support across the street from the house, he sees Eddie Marble, Jake's killer, go inside. He tells his dad that Jake was there to shadow Eddie while Eddie was the one visiting the prostitute. Meanwhile, Emily is dating Gideon, a friend from college. She quits her job at Marlowe's and asks the chef there whose nickname is "Stack" for tips on cooking spinach gnocchi. She has invited Gideon for dinner with her parents. On the night of the dinner, Stack shows up along with Gideon. Emily's dad seems to get along better with Stack than he does with Gideon. Gideon leaves before desert. Later, Emily goes to his apartment to find it ransacked and Gideon missing.

"Disappearances"
Emily and Stack go into the catering business together. Their first job is catering a fund raiser for Emily's mother. Max begins looking for work.

"Gravity"
Emily and Stack officially start their new business. Maggie and Max each begin seeing other people. Daisy is concerned that her mother may be having an affair with her assistant campaign manager. She informs her dad who begins spending more time with his wife.

"Not Fade Away"
At a press conference, a customer from Marlowe's recognizes Emily as a girl from the strip club. She finally reveals to her family where she has been working. Charlotte contemplates dropping out of the mayor's race because of its effect on her family, but she changes her mind after Emily delivers a speech supporting her.

"Caught"
Eddie appears at a convenience store where Max is, but he doesn't recognize Max. Max obtains a job at the machine shop where Eddie works and surreptitiously photographs Eddie with a co-worker named Lucas, a former convict. Max, Lucas, and Eddie go out for drinks after work. When Maggie comes to the bar, Eddie recognizes her. Max goes ballistic and questions Eddie about Jake's murder. Lucas is questioned by the police and tells them Eddie accidentally killed Jake. He is formally arrested for the murder.

Postscript: Fox initially picked up *Still Life* as a midseason replacement for the 2003-04 season, but never aired it presumably because the network felt the subject matter was too depressing.

12 Miles of Bad Road – Rich White Trash
Was to Premiere on HBO in 2007 but never aired.

Premise: The problems faced by a Texas family as a result of their tremendous wealth and powerful real estate business were the focus of this dramady.

Cast of Characters:

Amelia Shakespeare (Lily Tomlin) – the head of the family and CEO of its real estate company;

C.Z. (Mary Kay Place) – Amelia's younger sister;

Jerry Shakespeare (Gary Cole) – Amelia's son Jerry who is married to Jonelle (Kim Dickens);

Juliet Shakespeare (Katherine La Nasa) – Jerry's sister who is divorcing her husband Saxby Hall (David Andrews). Hall's girlfriend is Montserrat (Ivana Milicevic);

Gaylor Shakespeare (Eliza Coupe) – another Shakespeare sibling in her mid-thirties;

Kenny Kingman (Leslie Jordan) – Amelia's gay brother.

Background: Known for *Designing Women* among other works, Harry Thomason and Linda Bloodworth-Thomason created *12 Miles of Bad Road*. Two aspects of the series created controversy among critics who previewed it – the Leslie Jordan character liked to bed male hustlers and the inclusion of Amelia's mentally-challenged teen granddaughter whose disability was sometimes played for laughs.

The Pilot:

The pilot, written by Bloodworth-Thomason and Allen Crowe and directed by Michael Engler, introduces the extended Shakespeare family. Amelia's daughter Juliet is still living with her husband despite the divorce proceedings. Also, living in the house is her husband's girlfriend, Montserrat. Juliet had two daughters – Quinn and McKenna and a son who is opening a restaurant. McKenna, who is eighteen and mentally disabled, is trying to become a debutante, with the help of Aunt C.Z.

Amelia's other daughter, Gaylor, is trying, non-too-successfully, to stay sober. She lives in a bus on her brother Jerry's property and has squandered her inheritance financing her former boyfriend's singing career.

Ameila's son Jerry and his wife have three kids – a sixteen-year-old son Cameron, fourteen-year-old Brooke who is "engaged" to Jesus, and little Ashley. They also have a sixteen-year-old foreign exchange student living with them who is attracted to Gaylor. Jerry is having an affair with Marilyn Hartsong (Leigh Allyn Baker), his former receptionist, who now works in a mattress store. Marilyn, married to Lyle (Sean Bridgers), is undergoing chemotherapy for cancer and has a fifteen-year-old daughter Evian.

Other Episodes:

The story lines of the following episodes are unavailable: "The Dirty White Girl," "Tremors," "Collateral Verbiage," "Texas Stadium," and "Moonshadow."

Postscript: HBO originally ordered ten episodes of *12 Miles of Bad Road* but only six were produced. Production was shut down during a writer's strike and never resumed after the strike was settled. After a change in management at HBO, the cable service decided that the show's creative vision was not right for it.

Endnotes

1. Stacey Abbott, editor, *The Cult TV Book: From Star Trek to Dexter, New Approaches to TV Outside the Box*, New York: Soft Skull Press, 2010, 7.
2. Tracie Hotchner, Private communication with author, June 22, 2015.
3. Ibid.
4. Robert Lovenheim, Private communication with author, May 27, 2014.
5. Christopher Knopf, Private communication with author, February 13, 2015.
6. Ken Sanzel, Private communication with author, July 16, 2014.
7. Alex Strachan, "Shows Fight to Survive," *The Gazette*, November 13, 2004.
8. Tim Ryan, "Passion Soothes the Soul: Isles Inspire 'Wind on Water' Pilot," *Star-Bulletin*, April 17, 1998.
9. Ibid.
10. Charles Rosin, Private communication with author, February 19, 2015.
11. Larry Mollin, Private communication with author, March 10, 2015.
12. Robin Pogrebin, "Romeo and Juliet in a World of Politics and Pornography," *The New York Times*, October 19, 2003.
13. Jim Leonard, "Skin Series Bible: Exodus," October 7, 2003.
14. Noah Hawley, "Note from 'My Generation' Producer Noah Hawley," October 13, 2010, retrieved June 29, 2015.
15. Ibid.
16. Stan Rogow, Private communication with author, June 4, 2014.
17. Robert Strauss, "In the Dawn of 'Sunset's' Demise: Television" *Los Angeles Times*, November 13, 1993.
18. Angel Dean-Lopez, Private communication with author, September 17, 2014.

19 John Byrum, Private communication with author, May 31, 2014.
20 Sadie Gennis, "How *Wicked City* Hopes to Avoid Being Violence Porn," TVGuide.com, October 26, 2015, retrieved November 30, 2015.
21 William Blinn, Private communication with author, June 6, 2014.
22 Ibid.
23 John Stanley, "Return of the Doctors – Hunter vs the System," *The San Francisco Examiner*, September 9, 1979.
24 David Sheff, "'The Lazarus Syndrome' May Be Shelved, but, Bet on It, Lou Gossett Jr. Will Rise Again," *People Magazine,* October 22, 1979.
25 Blinn, June 6, 2014.
26 Marco Pennette, Private communication with author, September 2, 2014.
27 Ibid.
28 James L. Longworth, Jr., *TV Creators: Conversations with America's Top Producers of Television Drama*, Volume Two, Syracuse, NY: Syracuse University Press, 2002, 246.
29 Quoted in Daniel M. Kimmel, *The Fourth Network: How Fox Broke the Rules and Reinvented Television*, Chicago: Ivan R. Dee Publisher, 2004, 206.
30 Ibid.
31 John Showalter, Private communication with author, September 6, 2015.
32 Ibid.
33 "Planning the 'Heist,'" creativeplanetnetwork com, March 27, 2012, retrieved November 16, 2013.
34 David Kronke, "It's in the Bag 'Heist's' Major Players Plotting to Steal Off with a Midseason Hit," The Free Library.com, 2006, retrieved February 1, 2015.
35 Bill Keveney, "On Television, It's Harder to Tell Good from Bad," *The Desert Sun*, August 18, 2006.
36 Rob Owen, "Tuned In," *Pittsburgh Post-Gazette*, August 3, 2010.
37 Denise Martin, "The Playboy Club Boss on the Difference Between Bunnies and Playmates," TV Guide.com, September 18, 2011, retrieved October 29, 2015.
38 Lesley Goldberg, "Chad Hodge Talks 'Playboy Club' Lessons and His Wild Development Season," *The Hollywood Reporter*, January 28, 2013, retrieved October 29, 2015.

39 John Meredyth Lucas, *Eighty Odd Years in Hollywood: Memoir of a Career in Film and Television*, Jefferson, North Carolina: McFarland & Company, Inc., 2004, 196.
40 Frank Garcia and Mark Phillips, *Science Fiction Television Series, 1990-2004*, Jefferson, North Carolina: McFarland & Company, 2009, 255-57.
41 Quoted in Frank Garcia and Mark Phillips, *Science Fiction Television Series*, 253.
42 Trey Callaway, Private communication with author, September 10, 2014.
43 Garcia and Phillips, *Science Fiction*, 152.
44 Andy Meisler, "Do Aliens or Humans Inspire More Fear?," *The New York Times*, March 7, 1999.
45 Quoted in Frank Garcia and Mark Phillips, *Science Fiction Television Series*, 325.
46 Ed Zuckerman, Private communication with author, August 30, 2014.
47 Dusty Kay, Private communication with author, October 8, 2014.
48 Lee Margulies, "'Once a Hero' Is New TV Season's First Casualty," *The Los Angeles Times*, October 8, 1987.
49 Ibid.
50 Dusty Kay, Private communication with author.
51 Quoted in Nancy McAlister, "New Shows Go Back to the Future," *Jacksonville Times-Union*, September 27, 2002.
52 Judith S. Gillies, "'Wonderfalls:' Taking Orders from Animals," *Quad-City Times*, March 21, 2004.
53 "New Series Produced by Cannell," *Victoria Advocate*, June 27, 1982.
54 "Simply Put Blog: The Quest," March 8, 2016, retrieved August 21, 2020.
55 Description provided by Harv Zimmel, September 20, 2014.
56 Diane Haithman, "The Environment: TV Comes Down to Earth," *The Los Angeles Times*, February 10, 1990.
57 Bryce Zabel, Private communication with author, September 25, 2014.
58 John Herzfeld, Private communication with author, March 17, 2015.
59 Ibid., June 9, 2015.
60 Gerri Miller, "Inside 'Drive,'" HowStuffWorks, retrieved January 31, 2015.

61 Ibid.
62 Ben Queen, Private communication with author, February 20, 2015.
63 "What Would've Happened on the Canceled Series," tvseriesfinale.com, July 11, 2007, retrieved April 30, 2014.
64 Gerri Miller, "Inside 'Drive.'"
65 Jeffrey Lewis, Private communication with author, February 11, 2015.
66 Ibid.
67 Mark B. Perry, "Perfect for the Part . . .," markbperry.wordpress.com, May 15, 2014, retrieved November 14, 2014.
68 Ibid.
69 Mark B. Perry, Private communication with author, January 20, 2015.
70 "Q & A with Love Monkey Creator Michael Rauch," Unified Theory of Nothing Much blogspot.com, January 29, 2006, retrieved July 10, 2015.
71 Ibid.
72 "Ugliest Girl in Town Turns Out to Be a Boy," *The Ogden Standard-Examiner,* July 14, 1968.
73 Ron Powers, "Bob & Carol & Ted & Alice Won't Fit Movie Image," *The Akron Beacon Journal,* July 8, 1973.
74 "Bob & Carol & Ted & Alice," Television Review, *Variety,* September 26, 1973.
75 "The Texas Wheelers," Television Reviews, *Variety,* September 18, 1974.
76 Cecil Smith, "Wheelers Getting a Fast Shuffle?," *The Los Angeles Times,* October 4, 1974.
77 John Lester, "Radio and Television," *The Gazette and Daily* (York, PA), August 13, 1952.
78 E.B. Radcliffe, "E.B. Radcliffe's Theater," *The Cincinnati Enquirer,* June 28, 1950.
79 Peter Bonerz, Private communication with author, November 13, 2020.
80 Matt Schimkowitz, "Time Travel, Bazookas, and Robot Dinosaurs: A Look Back at the Weird, Wild Misstep of 'Steel Justice,'" February 19, 2013, retrieved September 23, 2020.
81 Boris Karloff, "Inside TV: Boris Karloff Star of Bizarre Series," *Statesman Journal,* November 24, 1958.

82 Episode descriptions based on Scott Palmer, *The Veil: The Series*, New York: Cypress Hill Press, 2020.
83 Scott D. Pierce, "Network TV Doesn't Get a Whole Lot 'Hollyweird'-er Than This," *Deseret News*, August 24, 1998.
84 Ibid.
85 Brian Lowry, "Fox Pulls Order for Paramount's 'When I Grow Up,'" *The Los Angeles Times*, May 10, 2001.

Index

A
Ackles, Jensen: 212, 213
Adams, Amy: 206, 207
Alonso, Daniella: 26
Anders, Laurie: 193
Anderson, Kevin: 19
Angel Street: 33-36

B
Bairstow, Scott: 109, 110
Baker, Simon: 74
Bay City Blues: 163-166
Becker, Tony: 186, 188
Berg, Peter: 51
Beyond Westworld: 87-91
Big Shamus, Little Shamus: 9, 10, 11
Blinn, William: 47, 50
Bloodworth-Thomason, Linda: 215
Bob & Carol & Ted & Alice: 182-185
Bochco, Steven: 163
Brooks, Mehcad: 25
Bulliard, James: 134
Busey, Gary: 186, 188
Byrum, John: 38, 42

C
Cake, Jonathan: 54, 55
Callaway, Trey: 96, 100
Cannell, Stephen: 63, 67, 123, 125, 129
Caron, Glenn Gordon: 210
Carter, Chris: 111
Cavanaugh, Tom: 171
Century City: 116-122
Cibrian, Eddie: 82
Coburn, James: 149
Cotrona, D. J.: 19

D
Davis, Viola: 117
Densham, Pen: 92, 95
Derek, Bo: 16
Dhavernas, Caroline: 139
Drive: 155-161
Dunne, Robin: 206, 207

E
E.A.R.T.H. Force: 145-149
Elam, Jack: 186
Elfman, Bodhi: 203, 204
Elizondo, Hector: 117

F
Fling: 210-211
Flippo, Fab: 203, 204
Fifth Corner, The: 149-155
Fillion, Nathan 155
Frey, Glenn: 36, 37, 38, 41, 42
Fuller, Bryan: 139

G
Garner, Kelli: 25
George, Melissa: 203, 204
Gerard, Gil: 145
Gidley, Pamela: 19, 33
Givens, Robin: 33
Gossett, Louis: 47, 50
Gross, Brian: 16, 19
Guinee, Tim: 101

H
Hamill, Mark: 186, 188
Ham-Let: 194
Harmon, Angie: 54, 55
Harsh Realm: 109-116
Hawley, Noah: 27, 31
Hefner, Hugh: 81, 82, 83
Heist: 71-74
Herzfeld, John: 151, 153, 154, 155
Hodge, Chad: 82, 85
Holland, Todd: 12, 13, 139
Hollyweird: 203-206
Hopkins, Josh: 210
Hunt, Linda: 91, 95

I-J
Inconceivable: 54-60
Jackman, Hugh: 68

K
Kaake, Jeff: 91
Karloff, Boris: 199
Kastner, Peter: 177, 178

Kay, Dusty: 129, 133, 134
Keith, David: 78, 211, 212
King, Jaime: 26
King, Perry: 123, 124, 129
King, Zalman: 15, 16

L
Langton, Brooke: 210
Lawless: 11, 12
Lazarus Syndrome: 47-50
Lee, William Gregory: 14, 16
Lester, Jeff: 129, 130
Levine, Ted: 50
Lewis, Jeffrey: 163
Liotta, Ray: 74
Little People: 189
Lone Star: 78-81
Love Monkey: 171-174
Luna, Gabriel: 42

M
Manchester Prep: 206-210
Marshall's Daughter: 193-194
Martin, Barney: 195, 196
McArthur, Alex: 149, 150
McGurk: A Dog's Life: 195-196
McRaven, Dale: 186
Mercy Point: 95-100
Miller, Jonny Lee: 74
Minear, Tim: 139, 156, 157, 161
Morris, Julian: 26
My Generation: 25-31

N-O
Nouri, Michael: 164
Oboler, Arch: 175, 176
Oboler Comedy Theatre: 175-176
O'Donnell, Keir: 26
Once a Hero: 129-134
Ormond, Ron: 189, 190, 191
Owen, Lloyd: 68

P
Pasdar, Adrian: 61, 62
Pennette, Marco: 54, 59
Perry, Mark B.: 168, 169, 171
Pests: 196-197
Playboy Club: 81-85
Portraits of Terror: 192
Profit: 61-67
Push: 166-171

Q-R
Quest, The: 123-129
Rogow, Stan: 38, 42

S
Sabu: 190-191
Scott, Dougray: 71
Silver, Ron: 19
Sisto, Jeremy: 42
Skin: 19-25
Smith: 74-78
Son, Anne: 26
South of Sunset: 36-42
Sozzi, Sebastian: 26
Space Rangers: 91-95
Spano, Joe: 95
Spears, Aries: 36, 37, 38, 41
Stahl-David, Michael: 26
Steel Justice: 197-198
Still Life: 211-214
Strange World: 101-109

T
Texas Wheelers, The: 185-188
That Was Then: 134-138
Thomason, Harry: 215
Ticotin, Rachel: 19
Tomlin, Lily: 215
Trese, Adam: 166, 167
12 Miles of Bad Road: 214-216

U-V
Ugliest Girl in Town: 176-182
Urich, Robert: 182
Veil, The: 199-203
Viva Laughlin: 68-71

W
Wainwright, James: 87
Wells, John: 33, 34, 75
Westwick, Ed: 42
Wicked City: 42-46
Wilde, Olivia: 19
Wind on Water: 15-18
Wolk, James: 78
Wonderfalls: 12, 139-144
Wonderland: 50-54
Wood, Ed: 12, 191, 192

X-Z
X-Files, The: 101, 111, 116
Zuckerman, Ed: 117, 122

www.ingramcontent.com/pod-product-compliance
Lightning Source LLC
Chambersburg PA
CBHW051910160426
43198CB00012B/1833